CHINA:

AN UNCENSORED LOOK

by

JULIAN SCHUMAN

1979

Second Chance Press

Sagaponack, NY

First published in 1956 by Whittier Books, Inc.
under the title: *Assignment China*

Copyright © 1956 by Julian Schuman

Library of Congress Catalogue Card Number 79-63789
International Standard Book Numbers:
Clothbound 0-933256-01-9
Paperbound 0-933256-04-3

SECOND CHANCE PRESS, INC.
Sagaponack, NY 11962

PREFACE

Twenty-four years have passed since this book was written. Originally titled ASSIGNMENT CHINA, it portrayed life there as Mao's new revolutionary government came to power. My observations were made as a working reporter.

When I returned to the United States in 1953 after spending six years in China, the atmosphere here was far different from that of today. McCarthyism still stalked the land. A partnership existed between agents of Chiang Kai-shek's regime and prestigious Americans who shared the belief that Chiang, after fleeing to Taiwan, should be fully supported. This China Lobby exerted strong political pressure and influence.

Since one of the goals of the Lobby was the destruction of the new government in Peking, "Red China" was considered anathema and anyone who had something positive to say about what was going on in China was suspected of being a subversive. This was the category I was to fall into. It was the same fate suffered by many of our government's China specialists during the late 1940's and 1950's, when the witch hunts eliminated many decent men from the State Department simply because they saw—and said clearly—that Chiang's regime had no popular support and was destined to be defeated by the communists.

Arriving in San Francisco in December after leaving Shanghai, I was greeted aboard ship by two F.B.I. agents who, along with the customs inspector, made it clear that I was suspect simply for staying on in China as long as I did. This same F.B.I. duo took no

1

pains to hide dogging my footsteps during the two weeks I spent in the Bay area.

I was shortly to discover that the papers I had written in 1948 and 1949 and the radio network I had done news broadcasts for from Shanghai were no longer interested in what I had to say. In Chicago, when I suggested that, as the only American journalist who had been in China during the first four years of the new government, I do a series of articles, the foreign editor of the *Sun-Times* assured me that nobody in that city "is interested in Red China." In New York, there was the same blank wall. ABC made it clear that they wanted nothing to do with me. The Wall Street Journal was not interested in an article on the possibilities of U.S.-China trade. Even the editor I saw at the Reporter, an ostensibly liberal magazine, said in no uncertain terms that if I tried to write something, he didn't want "an apologia for Mao."

Clearly and ironically a "Party Line" existed in *this* country at that point in history. And that "Line," fueled by the China Lobby, was that 1) some domestic traitors in our State Department had "lost" or "sold out" China and that 2) Mao Tse-tung's regime was barbaric, repressive, and unGodly. Since many observant people who challenged this thesis were disgraced, investigated, or found themselves out of work, it was little wonder that the major media would not readily greet my observations with open arms.

I began working on this book while holding down a job at a small publishing house in New York. By 1955 I had it well enough under way to look for a publisher. Thanks to the efforts of Angus Cameron, an early cold war casualty at Little Brown, I found a literary agent at Harold Ober Associates, Ivan Von Auw. After reading my outline and the completed manuscript, Van Auw agreed to represent me, warning me that while such a book would be hard to sell to a publisher, he believed that it should be in print.

Some half a dozen large houses turned the book down. The rejection letter from Simon & Schuster spelled out the reason quite clearly, saying that while it was a book that ought to be published, "the subject of Red China has to be handled with asbestos gloves."

Like the few other Americans who had returned home after being in China during the early years of the Peking government, I was called before the Senate Internal Security Committee headed by Senator Jenner in 1955; this occurring while I was completing my manuscript. By early 1956, a virtually unknown publisher, Whittier Books, agreed to bring the book out. Published at the end of that year it was met, with the exception of a rare review, with silence. That same year, along with John W. Powell and his wife Sylvia, I was indicted for sedition by a grand jury. Talk of timely co-incidences. Needless to say the first printing of 3,000 copies never sold out.

The indictment was ostensibly based upon what had been written about China and the war in Korea in *The China Monthly Review*, published in Shanghai by the Powells and of which I had been an associate editor from 1950 to 1953. The three of us went on trial in San Francisco in January, 1959. After a week, the judge ruled a mistrial. Two years later the government announced that it had dropped the case.

Much has happened over the years since this book was written, but the events of the period dealt with remain the same. And a proper understanding of that period is essential right now if we are to build our new relationship with China upon the solid ground of reality instead of the myths we were sold so long ago. Of late, vast changes have taken place in China which the makers of public opinion have not failed to note. But even here they do not refrain from sensationalism and distortion, some of which often stems from abysmal ignorance of China. This is particularly clear to me since I returned to live and work in Peking between the years 1963-1977.

"Modernization," for instance, is the big theme today. The picture presented in our press and on television is that this has all come about virtually overnight; since Mao's death in 1976. Actually, for several years before the late chairman died, China made it clear that high technology to be purchased from Japan and Western Europe was at the top of its shopping list abroad. Mao himself is on record decades ago as to the need China had to learn from the advanced industrial nations.

Many so called experts and commentators, who have either ignored Mao's writing or have never bothered to read them, still doggedly hue the line that the Chinese leader was "xenophobic," believed solely in "ideology," and ignored the Chinese people's economic well being. Conveniently brushed aside by such "authorities" is that the lot of the Chinese people improved vastly during the years Mao was in office, and that the opening of China to the United States, through the visit of the U.S. table tennis team in April, 1971, came when Mao was very much alive. Indeed, as far back as the war against Japan, in early 1945, the "xenophobic" Mao and Chou En-lai had sent a message to President Roosevelt offering to go to Washington to discuss current and future U.S.-China relations. Twenty-five years later, in December, 1970, it was Mao who told the American writer-journalist Edgar Snow that an American president, Richard Nixon, was welcome in China as head of state or as a tourist. China's Foreign Ministry, said Mao, was studying the matter of admitting Americans of all political stripes—left, right and center—to visit China. Life magazine carried the Mao-Snow talk in its April 30, 1971 issue.

The U.S.-China connection today is presented to the American public as something that the present "pragmatic" leaders in Peking have come up with as opposed to Mao's "revolutionary romanticism." Perhaps that is the way that those who've shaped our foreign policy throughout these many years could save face; could rationalize to the American public why we can now seek an accommodation with China. In truth, those of us who visited or worked in China during the days of non-recognition can testify that two of the hallmarks of the People's Republic, from its inception, were pragmatism and reasonableness. The reporter from *Time* magazine who wrote, during the recent visit here of Vice Premier Teng Hsiao-ping, that the visit "is the stunning climax of the Great Leap Outward that Teng conceived, planned and executed for China after xenophobic isolation," knows not whereof he speaks.

The fact is that China's better relations with Japan and Western Europe—political and economic—developed when Mao was alert and in power. Indeed, by the 1970's, the United States, which had set out to isolate the People's Republic from its inception, was the only major power which was isolated from China.

The world we live in today is far different than the one which existed when this book was written, and the new state of Sino-American relations is no small factor in this new age. These relations should continue to grow, not because Coca Cola is going to be available in China or because that nation wants to buy the technology that the United States excels in, but because the global interests of both countries far outweigh the real differences that exist between them. Living in a safe and secure world is of primary importance for both nations. And safety and security are only possible when each country can give a sympathetic understanding to the reality of the other.

It is my hope that CHINA: AN UNCENSORED LOOK can play some part in clearing up certain misconceptions so that Americans can begin to appreciate China as it truly exists.

J.S.

SAN FRANCISCO, 1979

China:

An Uncensored Look

Julian Schuman

CONTENTS

Around all of our cities
there are soldiers, and
the clash of arms;

       so does one feel
       how grand it would be
       could we but forge
       our weapons into tools
       for farmers to use;

so that every inch of land could
be ploughed with oxen; then, with ploughing done
silkworms be gathered;

       no need for soldiers to weep
       such pools of tears
       for dead heroes;
       rather
       from the men harvesting
       from the women spinning
       would there come back to us
       songs of happiness.

—Tu Fu (712–770 A.D.)

1

STRICTLY PERSONAL

The SS *Lisholt*, a diminutive Norwegian freighter, edged away from her pier in the early December dusk and headed across Hongkong harbor toward the Pacific. Standing at the aft rail, I gazed back across the choppy water for my last view of the Asia mainland.

To my left lay the imposing row of office buildings and warehouses that make up Hongkong's dockside business district. Behind them the scattered lights of the residential area traced a pattern up to the fashionable Peak. To my right stretched the blocks of low-roofed houses studded with new apartment buildings on suburban Kowloon peninsula. Just beyond was the frontier of China, from behind which I had emerged a few days before.

I was homeward bound—home from six years in China, including the first four and a half years of the new Chinese People's Republic.

In those six years an epoch of Chinese history had taken place, virtually under my eyes. I had seen the death throes of Chiang Kai-shek's China, had witnessed the passing of an old order rooted in four thousand years of tradition. I had lived both in the old and with the new. I had eaten, drunk and passed the time of day with British taipans and American diplomats, with Chiang officials, Mao Tse-tung revolutionaries, impartial political grafters, students on the right and students on the left, impoverished peasants and black-market billionaires. I had seen fantastic prosperity and unimaginable poverty, often side by side. I had seen pilferage and starvation, panic, street fighting, air bombings and sidewalk executions. And I had witnessed the birth of a new political regime.

9

Among the many Western journalists who had been present to record the fall of the Nationalists, I was one of the handful who had stayed to witness the evolution of the new China from the old. I was the last of all to leave. I was glad to have been there, to have seen it all and done it all. And now, in this December of 1953, I was glad to be going home.

This is a working journalist's report of what has happened in China. It is a report mainly of things seen with my own eyes, heard with my own ears. I sought both before and after the change in regime, through daily living among the people and daily contact with all classes, speaking their own language and listening to their views, to spell out the meaning of events behind the exterior facade of "news."

Why did the Communists win China? What are they doing with their victory? How firm a hold have they on the allegiance of the 600,-000,000 Chinese people? What are the future probabilities regarding their attitude toward the West? Toward Soviet Russia? How much of a threat, and of precisely what kind, do they hold for the United States? What are the possibilities of their overthrow from within? Or from without?

Confident answers to these questions are vouchsafed us from a variety of sources. Most of them, unfortunately, are based on the mental arithmetic of political speculation from such vantage points as New York or Washington. Some are offered by experts at Far East "listening posts" outside China, where little of what is listened to bears any resemblance to what goes on inside. Still others emanate from the supercharged vocal cords of politicians whose estimate of realities is often more the product of fervid wishes than of information.

I do not believe there are any easy answers. There can, however, be informed estimates of realities based on direct observation, combined with a knowledge of historical backgrounds. The importance of such estimates as a guide to action in place of guesswork, wishful thinking or patriotic slogans must surely be obvious. Whether in troubled peace or on the lethal "brink" of war, the United States cannot effectively deal with a nation of more than half a billion people newly allied to communism without knowing her true condition of affairs. It is one thing to speculate on the kind of China we would prefer; but it would be safer to know her as she really is.

It is for the purpose of contributing toward such knowledge that this book, based on an extended view of the China scene, is written.

2

THE WAY OF AN ARMY WITH A MAN

In the spring of 1943, when the Army Specialized Training Program was launched, I was fighting the war from behind my spectacles at Fort Hamilton in Brooklyn, consigned to limited service as a "record specialist" (uniformed file clerk). Except for the cocktail circuit ridden hard by public relations officers in New York and Washington, an assignment to Fort Hamilton was the softest touch a soldier could hope for in World War II.

My fellow inmates therefore expressed concern for my sanity when I volunteered to leave it for ASTP.

Not that I was likely to encounter any worse danger than exposure to an inferior grade of ice cream wherever the Training Program might lead me. But it was basic to the credo of all enlisted men that Fort Hamilton was the place to aspire to and, once attained, to cling to at all costs. Nevertheless, I was sick of the grinding boredom of my job and yearned for a change.

ASTP wanted young enlisted men who had studied foreign languages to enroll in a nine-months intensive course in the spoken language they had studied. Five years of French—three in high school and two in college—qualified me to apply.

I hadn't reckoned, however, on the bureaucratic gifts of my First Sergeant, named Gaffney, who suddenly discovered that I was indispensable to him. Three months of nagging and heckling, plus the intervention of the colonel, were needed to get me clear. When I at last

11

arrived at the testing center at City College in nearby Manhattan, I learned that limited service men had just been eliminated from the language-study portion of ASTP.

Back I journeyed into the vengeful arms of Sergeant Gaffney.

"So you wanna go to school, huh?" he snarled. "Okay, you're going."

A few days later I was on a train bound for Mississippi, assigned to an eight weeks' course in an Army clerk school. It was now the beginning of July. Less than a week after plunging into the mysteries of army clerking, I learned of a new order cancelling the cancellation of limited service men from the language program.

I sweated out my eight weeks in Mississippi, returned to Fort Hamilton, and immediately renewed my application for ASTP. This brought jeers from the ranks and fresh ingenuity on the part of Sergeant Gaffney. I found myself tending shoe stores in the bowels of a depot warehouse.

I juggled shoes, bucked for my assignment, and waited while September and October went by. By this time I was virtually obsessed with the idea of getting into that language program, although the army grapevine now reported an overabundance of linguists.

One brisk November day the order came. This time the embittered Gaffney, like a rejected parent, sent me away with a dire warning:

"You better make it this time! Because if you do or if you don't, you're out of Hamilton for keeps!"

He was right. Soon after my return to City College I was tossed into an assembly line of language aspirants and underwent a ten-day series of general aptitude tests, language aptitude tests, written and oral French exams. After the inevitable waiting period I was informed that I had been accepted and would be assigned to a college class for intensive training.

Heady with success, I renewed old visions of touring France and Europe in a staff car in the wake of the coming invasion, serving as interpreter to a four-star general and drinking in the glories of ancient cultures.

The momentous day came, and with 150 other linguists I was put on a train at Grand Central, heading north. No destination was announced. For some inscrutable reason we were supposed to be traveling "under sealed orders." But long before we approached Boston the word was out. Our objective was Harvard.

Again the ritual of waiting. Quartered in McKinlock Hall, in dormitory rooms, we speculated on the enchantments of Paris. In between we took perfunctory drills and marches. After a week we were herded into a hall to receive the word.

A slight feeling of uneasiness came over me as I watched a wiry little man mount the platform. He blinked pleasantly at us from behind bright spectacles. His teeth were large and very white. He was not an American; and he looked anything but French.

"Gentlemen," he said, "I have the honor to inform you that you have been assigned to the study of the Chinese language!"

Say what you like about Army efficiency, I can testify that the language portion of the Training Program was operated like a modern high-speed machine. And it achieved quite astonishing results.

After the first shock had worn off, and we had become used to the idea that Chinese could be spoken at all—let alone learned—our little band of former French scholars settled down to its task. Within a few days most of us were reconciled to our weird fate. By the end of a month many were intensely interested. As for me, I found it one of the most fascinating experiences of my life.

The group of 151 men was broken down into small units of seven to ten, each with its own instructor. All of these were well-educated Chinese, most of them students at Harvard. They were pleasant fellows, but rigorous taskmasters. Nearly all of the first month was devoted to drilling us in the fundamental sounds of the language and the vocal tones that make the Chinese tongue so different from those of the West. From there on the instructors insisted on carrying on their classes in Chinese.

Thus, with escape into English cut off, and with Chinese words, phrases and sentences dinned into our ears several hours each day by instructors and instruction records, we gradually came to feel at home in the language. Long before the nine-month course was over we were not only speaking it to our instructors and to each other, but were actually understanding a good deal of what was said. Nobody was expected to become fluent, and nobody did. But by the end of nine months most of the students had acquired a solid foundation in spoken Chinese which, once we arrived in China, could be rapidly expanded.

Along with the language study, courses were given by members of the Harvard faculty in Chinese history, economy, geography, art and society. It was made explicit to us, in that busy winter of 1943-4, that we were being prepared for service in China. And, as with many others in the group, that suited me fine. Long before the course ended I had forgotten my preoccupation with things French and had begun falling under the spell that China has exerted over so many Westerners.

Until that time China had been to me, as to millions of other Americans, a shapeless entity lying somewhere in the dimness that began just west of California. Now, in addition to my prescribed reading, I began devouring everything I could get my hands on about China. I went through the novels of Pearl Buck, then gobbled up the personal-experience books of writers like John Gunther, Vincent Sheehan, Edgar Snow, Emily Hahn and the rest. By the time my study courses and my readings were over, China was thoroughly in my blood. With many of my fellow ASTP students, I was eager for the day when we would ship out.

At last, in September, 1944, the course was finished. We were put on a train under special orders, destination secret. Excitement ran high. Embarkation port next stop? When the journey ended we were a little dashed to find ourselves at a camp in Virginia, just outside Washington. But we found that students of Chinese from other universities had been converging here; this gave hope that a big China mission was building.

Soon we were ordered to fall in and hear the time of day from a top sergeant whose encounters with any language, including English, could scarcely have been more than haphazard.

"Okay," he barked. "From here on out you guys can forget all about your Chinese!"

We were to embark on a new course of training, it appeared, as cryptanalyists deciphering code messages—in English only. The where-fores of it were never explained. Nobody even bothered to ask.

Some of us tried to get transferred to OSS, which we knew was sending men into China. It didn't work. After undergoing a security investigation and receiving clearance we were transformed into crypt-analysts in twelve weeks, and thus remained for the rest of our Army careers.

Finally we were shipped overseas—to Hawaii. Then later to the Philippines. After V-J Day I was sent briefly to Japan. But never to China.

In March, 1946, I was home again, one of the millions hovering between wartime service and the resumption of a normal life. At the time of my induction I had been a college student. I felt no great desire to go back to it. Nor had I any compelling notions about a particular kind of job. My special field of study—history and sociology —had prepared me for nothing in particular except the ultimate prospect of teaching, in which I now had little interest. I didn't quite know what I wanted to do, but I knew where I wanted to do it—in China.

My first step was to resume my Chinese studies. Under the G.I. Bill I enrolled in a course at Yale in the written language, including newspaper reading. Along with it I studied Chinese classical literature under Professor George Kennedy and took some advanced speech courses. I tarried at Yale until the summer of 1947, and then decided that it was time to get going. What I would live on when I got to China was far from clear in my mind. But my reading of Theodore White, Brooks Atkinson, Richard Watts, Jr., Robert Payne, and other war-time writers and China correspondents had given me some ideas.

Full of enthusiasm for the life of a roving journalist, but short on experience, I started beating the pavements of New York in the hope of finding a press connection. I hounded the foreign editors of United Press, International News Service, and Time magazine; they tactfully explained that a fellow must have experience. I went on to Joseph Barnes, then for ditor of the New York Herald-Tribune, and Ted Church of a Broadcasting System. They couldn't take me on, an them.

d to remain open. One was to wangle a e on a newspaper and spend years, per- to become a Far East correspondent. see what might happen. I chose the

ions were quick and simple. I turned all my asset bought minimum railroad passage and a steamer reserva the cost of air travel. I lingered on a few days, from old habit catch the Yankee-Dodger world series of 1947. Meanwhile I sought some last-minute briefing on China from two recently returned old hands—Theodore White, who had just written Thunder Out of China, and Harold Isaacs of Newsweek. Neither held out any rosy prospects, but both hazarded that in one way or another I would probably make out.

I saw the Dodgers go down into the dust, bought a handbook on journalism, said goodbye to my family in Brooklyn, and in the last week of October boarded a train for San Francisco, taking with me two suitcases, a portable typewriter, a camera, $150 in traveler's checks, and $33.75 in cash. Eight days later I boarded the SS *Iran Victory*, a beat-up service vessel turned freighter, now bound for Shanghai.

3

SHANGHAI'S LAST FLING

As an American soldier in Hawaii and the Philippines, and as a student of Chinese in the States, I had met a number of Chinese people of high and low degree. Hu Wen-show was the first Chinese I encountered in China. I spent no more than thirty minutes with him, but he lingers pleasantly in my memory.

It was a grey, bitterly cold morning in early December when the *Iran Victory*, completing her four-week wobble across the Pacific, dropped anchor off the North China port of Tientsin to unload freight and a few passengers. I found Mr. Hu, a slender, grave-looking gentleman, sipping tea at a small table in the ship's dining room.

I approached and saluted him in my best Mandarin. He smiled graciously, invited me to sit down, and complimented me on my proficiency in the language. (I was to learn before long that most Chinese, pleased and flattered that a foreigner has taken the trouble to learn their language, will praise his use of it whether actually it be good, bad or just awful.) Mr. Hu informed me that he was an official of the government. Not a big official; he was in fact about as minor as a government official can get, in China or elsewhere. Mr. Hu was a customs inspector.

Over my cup of coffee and his second round of tea we launched on a brisk conversation. Mr. Hu had a little English, but was happy to go along deciphering my Chinese, and I was glad of the chance to practice it. After beating about the bush for several minutes, in the

17

manner prescribed by Chinese etiquette, I asked him what part of the
country he hailed from.

"I was born here in Tientsin," said Hu Wen-show, "and have lived
nowhere else."

"And you have been long in the government service?"

He picked his nose delicately to indicate his judicious consideration
of my question, then answered, "Eleven, perhaps twelve years."

Mr. Hu went on to inform me that he was married and had four
children. He added that his salary amounted to the American equivalent of seven dollars a month.

"Then how do you manage?" I inquired. He answered with a shrug
and the familiar phrase, "*Mei yeou banfa!*" ("There is no way.") A
little later in the conversation, however, I discovered that there was a
way, and that it doubtless was the way of most government servants in
China. Mr. Hu suggested that the best procedure for bringing my
dutiable typewriter and camera into Shanghai would be to "reward"
the customs inspector there. A few minutes later he shook hands,
bowed, invited me to look him up if I ever returned to Tientsin, and
left to examine the luggage of disembarking passengers and doubtless
collect his own "rewards."

I liked Mr. Hu, his courtesy, his solemn dignity, and his noncha-
lant frankness. Though I was later to return to Tientsin, I never saw
him again.

The *Iran Victory* rumbled on to Shanghai, where we docked on
the eighth of December. Since I was traveling light and held an
American passport, I had little difficulty in getting ashore. The customs
inspector, true to Hu Wen-show's hinted prediction, was kind enough
to suggest that I might avoid the inconveniences of red tape by paying
directly to him the duty on my typewriter and second-hand camera.
Else, he explained regretfully, it might take weeks for them to get
through. He named the nice round sum of ten American dollars. I
paid.

On the advice of some of the old hands with whom I had talked
in New York, I had written ahead to engage a room at the American
Club. This turned out to be a happy idea, since Shanghai was suffering an acute coal shortage during that particularly chilly and clammy
winter, and most Chinese-owned buildings were unheated. My steam-
heated room at the American Club stood me seventy-five American

dollars a month—a fabulous price in terms of Chinese currency, but moderate compared to the rates of ten to twenty dollars a day that prevailed at the big foreign-style hotels.

With the security afforded by my couple of hundred dollars in United States cash I felt no immediate urgency about getting launched on my hoped-for newspaper career. I spent my first week or two scouting the town and its people.

Shanghai at the close of 1947 was a roaring, teeming jumble of garish sights, jangling noises, emphatic smells, swarming crowds and frenzied motion. The irritated honking of jammed traffic filled the air of the downtown section along Nanking Road, the Bund, and the streets that cross these two main thoroughfares. The big Western-style hotels, the tall buildings along the Bund housing the Hongkong-Shanghai Bank and the Glen Line and a host of other foreign firms, the swirl of jostling, shoving crowds, all contributed to the impression of a big foreign metropolis. Yet side by side with all this were many signs of a city indelibly Chinese. Millions of native folk had scarcely ever seen a foreigner and had nothing at all in common with him or with the veneer of Western civilization that overlay this community of some six million souls.

There were in fact not one but many Shanghais. There was the Shanghai of lower Nanking Road, the main business artery just off the Bund, with its department stores and speciality shops where tourists and well-heeled residents could acquire luxury goods from New York, Paris and London. In these broad streets cars, trucks, pedicabs and rickshaws were jammed together in a perpetual traffic snarl.

There was the Shanghai of night club society, where high government dignitaries and black-market billionaires entertained their friends, relatives and concubines at feasts that would have rivalled Nero's, to the accompaniment of American jive and dancing by "hostesses." Gambling joints large and small were the nightly gathering place of the heavy-spending set. An opium pipe was always available even in the best hotels.

There was the Shanghai of the waterfront, with its dingy wharves and "godowns" (warehouses) and its grubby seamen's bars, squatting beside lofty skyscrapers and slick modern industrial buildings.

There was the Shanghai of Frenchtown, which the French in palmier days had carved out as their Concession, complete with homes and shops, a French-owned bus line, trolley line and power plant; and within it the colony of some 20,000 White Russians knit together in a homogeneous community, speaking several tongues, running their own small shops and cafes.

There was the Shanghai of the American and British residential quarters in the Hoongjao district, home of the Western overseers, where the big taipans had their own lavish estates complete with gardens and orchards, kennels and stables, playing-fields and servants' quarters.

There was the Shanghai of Nanking and Tibet Roads, the red-light district where palaces of sport of all degrees from squalid to splendiferous held open house, and where no male from eight to eighty could walk more than a few steps without feeling a feminine hand tugging at his elbow. There was the Shanghai of the side streets and alleys where the un-Westernized "natives" lived—families of Chinese existing in one-room hovels under conditions of poverty, superstition and degradation impossible to imagine. And there was, too, the Shanghai of the professional beggars who slept in the streets and, in that inclement winter, froze to death by the hundreds.

I spent most of my first two weeks traversing the city on foot, in trolleys, buses and taxis, and finally, when I got used to the idea, in pedicabs. Like many other newcomers, it took me a long time before I could mount a rickshaw to be hauled along by another human being. Oldtimers pointed out that this involved less physical exertion than pedalling one or two people on a bicycle, which is what the pedicab driver's job entailed.

Prowling about the streets, I soon became aware that even in this foreign-influenced city the sight of a *na gwo ning* (Shanghai dialect for "foreigner") could elicit stares and comments. Now and then a group of children or a pair of bumpkins in from the country would turn to gape at me. One afternoon, while I stood on a corner waiting for the trolley to Frenchtown, an old grandfather came along carrying a small child in his arms. He paused beside me, shoved the infant close to my face, and bade it look at the foreigner and his *gau byi tzy* (high nose).

The Shanghailander's appetite for public spectacle is probably no different from that of people the world over. In Shanghai it seldom went unsatisfied very long. Street brawls were an accepted part of the city's life, had their own rhythm and ceremony, and never failed to attract an enchanted audience.

A great deal of shouted bluster and insult, some of it fairly ingenious, featured these poor man's sporting events. But rarely was a blow struck. The conventional wind-up was an appeal to the gallery for adjudication, which was willingly rendered and usually abided by. But often when a rickshaw or a pedicab man was involved, a policeman would break it up by dealing the fellow an accurately-placed kick for blocking traffic, or a pummeling on general principles. This was the solution often employed by Westerners, too.

But it was the life in the narrow lanes and alleyways, where no automobiles ventured and foreigners were rarely seen, that afforded the most intriguing of my Shanghai discoveries. Here one came across little Chinese drug shops offering everything from medicinal herbs to tiger bones which, when boiled, were prized for their alleged invigorating qualities. Open-air barber shops fronted the streets, where an ear-cleaning went along with a haircut. Food vendors roved about carrying portable kitchens on bamboo poles slung over their shoulders, offering sizzling bean curd and onion pancakes cooked to order. And everywhere were tiny restaurants where the stove occupied more space than the five or six little tables; and corner noodle stands where the passerby could fill his stomach for a few cents. Throughout the city, in open streets back of tall office buildings and modern department stores, professional letter writers and fortune tellers held court for the illiterate and the superstitious.

A little later, as a reporter and city editor on a Shanghai daily, I was to gain some acquaintance with the city's bizarre underworld life. But even in those first days its fringe manifestations were evident enough, in two Shanghai institutions: the beggars by day and the street girls by night. Both professions had their free-lance practitioners, but in the main both operated in a highly organized way.

The beggars were everywhere, particularly where foreigners were to be found. They could size you up in an instant, guess accurately where you had come from and how long you had been in Shanghai. The newer and greener you looked, the more rewarding a prospect they naturally considered you. When I was freshly arrived they beset me in droves, often converging on me from several directions. After I had been around for a while and had begun to master the proper unseeing stare they usually passed me by.

Most of the beggars were organized into gangs run by underworld gentry who knew how to hold a tight rein on them. In my neophyte days I would occasionally bestow an inflated Chinese note upon an outstretched palm and then follow my beneficiary as he scurried around the corner and delivered it to his boss. If he didn't he risked a memorable beating. To insure the perpetuation of their beggardom, the beggars received only a small cut of their take. The police usually let them alone. They had bigger problems, and besides there was always the possibility of a cut-in arrangement.

As to the streetwalkers, their annals were no doubt the same as in many another seaport, with perhaps one difference. Many were literally the personal property of wholesale procurers who had bought them for cash from their parents. Agents for Shanghai "vice rings" took periodic trips into the countryside to make such purchases from peasants who had no other solution to their perpetual hard times caused by bad crops, floods and inability to meet taxes. It was all quite legal.

The streetwalkers infested not only the red light district of upper Nanking Road, but appeared by the hundreds in other areas of the city after dark. Usually the girl was accompanied by an elderly woman whom she referred to as her *Mama*. (Even in Chinese the word is pretty much the same.) Medical supervision of these prostitutes was lax, so that the harm they spread was more than solely moral. Nevertheless they were an established Shanghai institution. The money they brought in to procurers, gangsters, operators and crooked officials gave them immunity from interference, if from nothing else. And they played their part in the wild, chaotic pattern that was Shanghai.

A popular illusion about China that the Western visitor soon loses is that all Chinese look more or less alike. In the melting pot of Shanghai I lost it very fast. I was soon able to distinguish more varied types than among the white-skinned foreigners who came from all over the globe.

Numerous among the laborers who jammed the trolleys and buses were short, wiry, thin-faced men and women from the south. The typical policeman was a tall, oval-faced, raw-boned ex-peasant, easily identifiable as a native of Shantung province. In many restaurants run by North Chinese I found waiters and cooks with the plump, sometimes pot-bellied contours characteristic of their part of the country. Most barbers hailed from nearby north Kiangsu province across the

Yangtze River. They were of medium height, often with round eyes and sharp features. Heavy-bearded, burly Manchurians who spoke Russian were to be found in the Russian-style restaurants in Frenchtown.

And there were the native Shanghai compradores, Chinese contact men for foreign firms, smooth-skinned and well-fed looking; and big operators with two-inch little-finger nails, whose speech was almost as rapid-fire as some of the deals they brought off.

The importance of "face," or status, to the Chinese has to be seen to be appreciated. It goes beyond the childish pride or vanity to which many people attribute it. It has more to do with the instinct for dignity and formality that is deep-rooted in the Chinese character. Face is vital to every Chinese, but its importance rises with the individual's station in life.

One of the earliest friends I made in Shanghai was Yu Ling, junior partner in a family import-export firm downtown on Szechuan Road, and a nephew of one of my Chinese instructors in America during the war. Yu was a smiling, amiable man of about thirty-five, the father of three children. He was interested in my story of how I came to China and my ambition to know it better. I got into the habit of dropping in at his office or his home. One day I commented on the, to me, curious Chinese phenomenon of "face."

Yu had a sense of humor. Moreover, it was a sense of humor tinged with some understanding of Western attitudes, for as a boy he had spent several years with his uncle in the United States. He offered to take me to a place where Chinese emphasis on face was practiced to the ultimate degree.

Accordingly, that evening, we went to a famous restaurant called Hoong Chang Shing, meaning "a flood of lengthy prosperity." It is an inconspicuous place tucked away in a side street known as Flower Street opposite the Race Course. The proprietor was a Mohammedan Chinese from Peking, and so were all his fifty or more employes, virtually all named Mr. Ma—roughly the equivalent of "Jones" among Chinese Mohammedans.

Hoong Chang Shing was a two-story restaurant. The lower floor catered to the poor, offering meals for as little as the equivalent of fifteen cents. The upper floor was for the middle to extreme upper classes. A fairly good dinner could be had for seventy-five cents, a sumptuous one for twenty dollars. My friend Yu Ling led me to a table on the upper floor; we were, after all, engaged in sociological research.

I don't remember now just what my dinner consisted of; it may have been the house specialty, *shuai yang row* (sliced mutton with vegetables, a galaxy of sauces and a delicious soup all boiled in a kind of chafing dish on the table), or it may have been different dishes of chicken, fish, mixed vegetables, Moslem hamburger and a pungent sour and peppery soup. Such delicacies were still new enough to command my wide-eyed attention; but right now I was even more interested in the promised demonstration of reliance on face.

After we had been eating and chatting for a while, Yu gave me a gentle kick under the table and muttered, "Look discreetly to your left!" I jerked my head around and focused my eyes on a table a short distance away where half a dozen resplendently gowned Chinese gentlemen had finished their dinner. Four were seated with eyes half closed, picking their teeth with languor and distinction; the other two were on their feet, engaged in a noisy shouting match.

"What's the matter?" I asked Yu. "Big argument?"

He chuckled. "In a way, yes. But in another way, no. They are arguing for the privilege of paying the bill."

"Very noble," I commented. "But I should think they'd have had an understanding about it before they sat down."

"I am quite certain that everything was completely understood beforehand, and that everything is understood now. If I am not mistaken, it is the taller gentleman's turn to pay."

"Then what's the other one yelling about? Why doesn't he let him?"

"He will," Yu predicted. "But elementary dignity requires him to put up a desperate battle first. However, I think he has by now about discharged his obligation, so watch what happens."

The shorter gentleman suddenly shot out his right hand and firmly gripped his adversary's left arm, keeping up the verbal argument all the while. The fellow with the imprisoned left arm made a triumphant gesture with his right, though a somewhat perfunctory one it seemed to me, then plunged his right hand into his trouser pocket and drew out a roll of bank notes. His friend then released his left arm, and he used it to take the check from the center of the table. As if at a signal, their four companions stowed away their ornamented toothpicks and got to their feet.

"The little fellow gave in at last, eh?" I said.

"No, no," said Yu Ling. "Not at all. It is merely that his right hand was occupied in clutching his companion's left arm, so that he could not produce the funds. His friend, on the other hand, had his right arm free, and he took advantage of the situation to claim the bill and bring forth the means of hospitality. A very unfair advantage, you must agree."

"Cruelly unfair," I agreed. "The little fellow, who wasn't supposed to pay in the first place, can keep his thirty-five bucks and gets credit for a college try at being the host. So that's face among the elite?"

"Wait and listen," said Yu imperturbably. "You have seen, as you would put it, nothing yet. There they go to the stairs."

I looked over at the sextet as they reached the head of the winding wooden stairway. The waiter still lingered at their table. At the precise moment when they were about to start down the steep stairs, the waiter squared his shoulders and in clear Peking dialect bellowed loud enough for the whole establishment to hear:

"The bill—four million eight hundred thousand! The tip—five hundred thousand!"

The host of the party smiled his acknowledgment of this public recognition and then disappeared down the stairs, followed by his contented guests.

"Have you gained now," inquired Yu, "an insight into what can be the meaning of face?"

"I sure have," I acknowledged. "But here comes the waiter with our check."

"Ah," said Yu, "you must permit me to be your host, since I suggested the occasion."

"Yu, old friend," I answered, "you may consider my right arm completely immobilized, and yours entirely free."

"You are a pacific man, Tze Jang," he smiled as he paid the bill. "And when we next dine together I shall endeavor to follow your self-sacrificing example."

One morning toward the end of my second week in Shanghai I was strolling along Avenue Edward VII, thinking about my dwindling bankroll. I came upon a moderate-sized office building I had not noticed before. Over the entrance was a sign: "China Press—Offices Third Floor."

I stopped, considered a moment, and started climbing the stairs. By now I had some idea of what Shanghai was like. It was time to settle down and get a job if I could. I had sampled the *China Press* along with every other English-language newspaper I could find in Shanghai. It was owned by David Kung, son of H. H. Kung—the head of one of China's Big Four Families, a man highly placed in Chiang Kai-shek's government and reputedly one of the richest men in all China.

On the third floor I found a large office that looked like a scaled-down version of the city rooms I had seen during my hunt for a news-paper job in New York. Half a dozen youthful-looking Chinese were seated at desks, pecking at rather dilapidated typewriters. A copy boy, aged about fifty, ambled around the room, stopping now and then at a small horse-shoe shaped copy desk, which at the moment was unoc-cupied. The atmosphere was quiet, the floor unlittered, the tempo relaxed as befitted modern practice in daily journalism.

I found K. S. Chang, the managing editor, in a small private office off the reporters' bull pen. He was a strapping fellow of about fifty, and looked slightly under forty.

"What papers have you worked on?" came the inevitable question.

I told him I had worked on none; that my only knowledge of the craft was from books and a smattering derived from lectures on journal-ism in a college English course.

"And you've only been here two weeks," said Chang. "Know any Chinese?"

I gave him a brief demonstration. He took my spoken Chinese in his stride; but my ability to read impressed him, possibly because few Americans or Britishers who had come out to China, whether briefly or for a long sojourn, ever got around to investigating even the rudi-ments of the written language.

"We're pretty well staffed," he said. I put on my hat. "But we could use a rewrite man." I kept my hat on. So far I wasn't even a reporter.

"See those fellows out there?" he continued, pointing through the open door to the Chinese lads struggling with their typewriters. "They're nice boys, pretty good reporters. Some of them went to Harvard or Stanford or some place like that, and the English they

write is horrible. Do you think you could edit their copy and make
it fit to read?"

I said I thought I could. Mr. Chang decided to try me out, starting the next day. We agreed on a salary of slightly more than eleven
million Chinese dollars, equal to around a hundred American dollars
a month.

"We'd better break you in as a reporter for awhile," said Chang
as I thanked him and started to leave. "You can do some rewriting in
the evening when you come back from your beat." I agreed.

"By the way," he added as I reached the doorway, "we need somebody to cover local film openings. You might as well handle that too."
I said that would be fine.

"And, oh," said Chang when I was halfway through the door,
"Grace Liu who handles the society column needs some hard reading
on her copy. You might keep a special eye out for that."

I thanked him hurriedly and left. Unlimited vistas of newspaper
experience spread before me, perhaps a little more than I had counted
on. But eleven million dollars a month is, after all, a lot of money.

4

TWELVE MILLION TO ONE

Not to be altogether facetious about it, eleven million Chinese dollars—or CNC (Chinese National Currency) 11,000,000, as it was commonly expressed—did have some value in that third week of December, 1947. It was worth, as I have said, about a hundred dollars in American money. But the disease of inflation then gripping China was still in a comparatively mild stage. The time was approaching when CNC 11,000,000 would be literally small change—much less than a dollar.

This condition was one of the basic facts of Chinese life in that period—as important in some ways to the country's future as the advance of the Communist armies in the north. It was chiefly responsible for the atmosphere of chaos that pervaded Shanghai life beginning early in 1948.

The official exchange rate toward the end of 1947 was 12,000 Chinese to one American dollar—a purely nominal, meaningless figure. The black-market rate, which governed all commercial and private transactions, was 150,000 to one. Two months later it had climbed to 200,000. By March 20, 1948, it was 500,000, and going higher day by day.

The ordinary Chinese, who had no access to foreign specie, was caught like a squirrel in a whirling cage. The prices of his necessities rose automatically with the rising money rate; the amount of depreciated money he took in could never catch up. If he was a businessman the value of the, say, fifty million Chinese dollars, for which he

28

had sold his goods, might be one-third less when he collected it a month later. If he was a workingman earning the equivalent of ten American dollars in a given month, this wage might be worth only three to six dollars the following month if he hung on to his money. Whether or not his wages were "adjusted" by his employer, and how much, necessarily depended on the employer—who might be the same businessman staggering under the same depreciation when collecting his bills.

The "adjustment" of prices eventually took place on an hourly basis. A housewife would enter a crowded rice shop to bargain for a picul of rationed rice valued at, say, CNC 500,000. During the hour consumed in awaiting her turn and driving the traditional bargain, the rice dealer might reasonably assume that the currency rate had advanced, and add another CNC 100,000 to the price.

The rice riots of this period were occasioned not by a scarcity of the food but by the dealers' frequent practice of closing their shops in the middle of the day to await the next day's inevitable higher prices on rice they already had on hand. Incensed housewives, often reinforced by their menfolk, stormed the shops and battled the hastily summoned police.

As for myself, an American armed with a few of Uncle Sam's dollars, I was little affected personally by all this. Like other foreigners and "better-type" Chinese, I simply turned my dollars into Chinese currency at the black-market rate from day to day in sufficient quantity to meet my daily needs. But even at the American Club, an island of comparative stability amid the general chaos, where patrons' accounts were backed by U. S. dollars, the inflation made itself felt. The point was ultimately reached where the English manager, a Mr. Clark, was forced to place room rent and meals on a weekly and, in some cases, even a daily pay-as-you-go basis.

By spring of 1948 government officials were nervously announcing that money was approaching a point where it literally wasn't worth the paper it was printed on. The cost of printing a Chinese 10,000-dollar note, for example, was 7,000 dollars. The government's answer was simple: It printed money in larger denominations, and 50,000-dollar notes took the place of small change.

It was no uncommon sight on the streets of Shanghai to see messengers on their way to banks carrying huge bundles of money tied up with cord. Often, for an ordinary cash business transaction, a rickshaw or a pedicab was hired to transport the funds with the "chit boy" perched on top of bundles of CNC "dollars."

Of course, if you knew the right people and were able to turn your Chinese currency into American greenbacks or gold bars somewhere along the line, your inflation troubles were nil. This was the common practice among the professional speculators, the black-market dealers, and the affluent set generally. At the *China Press* I quickly learned that on pay day the business manager, James Lee, would convert our rolls of CNC for U. S. dollars at a slight discount for his trouble. But for the average Chinese, restricted to money that was deteriorating faster than a sand castle in a flash flood, his best bet was to turn his vanishing funds as quickly as he could into whatever staples—such as rice, coal, cooking oil or cloth—he could lay his hands on. Which is exactly what everyone was doing by the summer of 1948.

August, 1948 saw the Kuomintang, or Nationalist Party, come up with its ill-fated attempt at currency reform—the straw that finally broke the back of the urban middle-class. With much fanfare and many public assurances that the Nanking government was making a sincere effort at reform, the new currency, called Gold Yuan, replaced the now utterly worthless CNC. Along with the announcement of this reform came the order to turn in all foreign currency, gold and silver, and precious objects because the new Gold Yuan, later known as GY, was going to be stable. The brand new GY bills, printed in the United States, had an official value of four to one American dollar.

Extreme efforts were made—for a brief time—to keep the new currency stable. Chiang Ching-kuo, the Generalissimo's son, was made economic czar of Shanghai, the nation's financial center. Some none too prominent businessmen were arrested for speculating and a few black-market dealers were executed, and it seemed that the government meant business. But the skeptics, of whom there were more than a few, were sure that the currency could not hold.

What happened is history now—the history of one more, and final, milking of its own people by the Chiang Kai-shek government.

In three months' time the loudly proclaimed currency reform had proved a failure. Valued at four to one on August 19, the GY was being sold on the black market at the rate of fifty to one by the beginning of November. Many Chinese newspapers at the outset had called the GY "Chiang's last trump." China's urban middle-class, the small businessmen, storekeepers, professional men and office workers, had looked to it to save their country's inflation-ridden economy. These groups, who at one time were among Chiang's strongest supporters, obeyed the order to convert private holdings of foreign currency, gold and silver into the new money. But, having converted chiefly during August and September when the official value was maintained, they were soon left high and dry with stacks of a much devaluated money. Early in November the government officially recognized the black-market rate of fifty to one, set a new nominal rate of twenty to one, and abandoned all restrictions on the possession of gold, silver and foreign currency.

In November 1948, in a dispatch to *The Nation*, I reported the GY crack-up in these terms:

> As the black market rate climbed, the people swarmed into the shops to exchange their fast depreciating money for goods. Goods, however, were scarce, and prices were pegged far above the black-market rate. There was not much the holders of the GY could do but watch the value drop. The foreign currency, gold and silver turned in amounted to about $190,000,000 [in American money], according to official Kuomintang figures. Wealthy Chinese are not believed to have contributed very much. It is no secret that they have sent most of their property abroad.
>
> It is not too difficult to see what is eating the little man here, the man who had faith in his government and put his small holdings into the new money. Not only is his investment losing its value, but his money is not accepted when he tries to buy something. The rice dealer and the butcher have no desire to part with their vital commodities for 'Chiang's last trump.'

By the time the Communist armies arrived in Shanghai in May of the following year, Chiang's GY had gone the same way as had the preceding currency. From the original four to one, the rate had gone by mid-May to more than 12,000,000 to one, and people were not using it; they preferred bartering goods on the streets. The incompetence of his government along with the cold-blooded shakedown of the very people who made up his chief support in the large cities, left them with a bitter taste for Chiang Kai-shek. It may be hard for Americans to believe, but by the time the forces of Communist General Chen Yi were closing in on Shanghai, people who had been anti-Communist were shrugging their shoulders with a "Nothing-could-be-worse-than-what-we've-had!" They were not so much taken over by the Communists as catapulted into their arms by the Kuomintang.

5

COVERING THE DEBACLE

K. S. Chang of the *China Press* had hired me as a rewrite man and factotum scribe, but he evidently had even loftier plans for me. What he really needed, and badly, was a city editor. The most recent incumbent, one Bill Chang (no relation), had gone to Hawaii on a holiday and sent word that he had decided to make it permanent.

Since then K. S. himself had been doubling as managing editor and city editor, but he was not at ease in his dual job. Just why he settled upon me ' relieve him of half of it I don't know. But the *Press* was an English-language paper, and I suspect that Chang's main concern was to install a willing soul who was native to that tongue.

Whatever his reasoning, he immediately assigned me to sit opposite him at the desk where he slumped several hours each day in his role as city editor, to learn how to read copy (i.e., check and correct it) and how to write headlines. With his sleeves rolled back, a cigar butt clamped between his teeth, and slightly dated American slang spouting from behind it, the lanky K. S. gave a reasonable imitation of an American movie-style city editor as he slaved over my tutelage, plainly hoping that I would soon catch on to the trade and allow him to return, as soon as possible, to his preferred desk—the big one in the private office marked Managing Editor.

The *China Press*, Mr. Chang gave me to understand, had a glamorous past if a somewhat ramshackle present. Smoking his interminable cigars, he would reminisce about the great days in the Thirties

32

when he had been sports editor and the paper had boasted a staff of American and English writers, some of whom, like Tillman Durdin and Mark Gayn, had become well-known correspondents for American papers. When he had momentarily exhausted this subject he would hold forth on his domestic troubles, all of which sprang from the problem of feeding, clothing and schooling his five children. As it happened, they were all girls; and if this is a source of discontent in Western countries, it is considered bleak disaster among the Chinese. Chang's lamentations on the subject rivaled those of Eddie Cantor, but he lacked the consolation of getting paid for them.

Since the *Press* was a morning paper (complete with Stateside comics and crossword puzzles) my working day started at three in the afternoon and ended at midnight. Like every one else on the staff I worked a six-day week; and on my day off, which sometimes fell on Sunday and sometimes on a weekday, K. S. usually saw to it that I had a pass to review Shanghai's latest Hollywood import. Among the *Press* staff of twenty or so there were two other Westerners besides myself. One was a young White Russian who served as foreign editor. He also read copy on K. S. Chang's editorials. The other was an elderly German newspaperman, a refugee from Hitler in 1938, who was our financial editor. In his spare time, he served as correspondent for the *Financial Times* of London.

The Chinese staff members, aside from the aging shipping news editor who came to work costumed in a long Chinese gown, were mainly young fellows. They would turn up from their assignments at five or six in the evening, make a couple of telephone calls, bang out their copy, and be off by eight or nine. My favorite among this crew was a lad who liked to be called "Scoop" Liu. He rebuked me bitterly the first time I changed one of his stories, assuring me that his news copy was always written in the strictest *Time* magazine style.

As I gradually took over from Chang the duties of headline writing and makeup on the city page, and the paper remained in business, he began to turn over the job of drawing up and following through the reporters' daily assignment sheets. With this activity more or less firmly in hand, two months after joining the *China Press*, I was officially installed as city editor with a salary of sixty million a month.

At about this time I seized an opportunity to trim my personal budget and incidentally to live in true Chinese style by sharing an apartment with a Shanghai couple of my acquaintance, forsaking my comparatively expensive room at the American Club. A New Yorker named Sidney Shapiro, with whom I had become friendly during my Army days, had preceded me to China in 1947. In May, 1948, he married Feng-tze, a Shanghai writer and actress, who bequeathed me her apartment on condition that I share it with her cousin, Yao Ping, and his wife.

The apartment, situated in a Japanese-style apartment house in the Yangtzepoo district, was poor by foreign standards, but luxurious by the standards of most Chinese. It consisted of one large room, a bathroom with only cold water, and a cubbyhole too small to be described even as half a room. The arrangement was rendered feasible by the fact that Yao Ping's wife, a music teacher, and their little daughter lived six days a week at the elementary school where the wife taught. During the week Yao and I shared the main room, and on Saturday nights I slept on a straw mat in the cubbyhole.

The Yaos spoke no English, and their Mandarin was heavily flavored with a Shanghai accent, but we got along fine for six months, when a change in my circumstances led me to take up private quarters at a hotel.

Nothwithstanding my rocket-like rise on the *Press*, I had in the meantime been corresponding with Irving Pflaum, foreign editor of the *Chicago Sun-Times*. He now encouraged me to try my hand at dispatches on the Shanghai scene. From the vantage point of my desk on the *China Press*, and with more than half the daytime hours free for my own pursuits, I was able to round up five stories and sent them along. The *Sun-Times* bought two and asked to see more. Thus I was launched as a "stringer," or special correspondent who writes for one or more newspapers on a freelance basis.

During the next several months I continued sending dispatches to the *Chicago Sun-Times*, which sometimes used one or two a week and more when the news front waxed hot. There was plenty to write about in those increasingly febrile days. I covered the American view of the heightening civil war as evinced by our Shanghai businessmen and diplomats; the impact of the swirling inflation; the fear and uncertainty more and more evident in Nationalist circles; the rapid shifts and changes in the Kuomintang government as the Communist forces steadily advanced.

The armies of Mao Tse-tung had now assumed the offensive

throughout the north and were beginning the drive which in six months was to win them all Manchuria and bring them to the banks of the Yangtze River, dividing line between North and South China. In this spring offensive the Communist armies for the first time seized the initiative and were to hold it thenceforth until they had driven the Nationalist forces from the mainland.

By the middle of 1948, with the pattern of events plainly moving toward some sort of climax, the routine concerns of Shanghai city journalism seemed increasingly dull and pointless. Feeling more or less secure in my part-time tenure as *Sun-Times* correspondent, and wishing to enhance my status as a journalist on the international scene, I left the *China Press* and took a temporary job that was open on the *China Weekly Review*.

The *Review*, founded in 1917 by the American correspondent and publicist J. B. Powell, had gained a world-wide reputation as one of the most reliable English-language organs of information about China and the Far East. During the period of the Japanese invasion, Powell through his periodical was a vital force in rallying both Chinese and American resistance. When the Japanese took Shanghai he was seized and interned. He emerged from the privations of a Japanese prison with both feet frozen. After his repatriation to the States they were amputated. He died soon after, lauded throughout the American press as well as by the China hands who had known him.

His son, John William Powell, took over the publication and editorship of the *Review*. Bill Powell, a serious-minded and energetic youth, born in Shanghai and educated at the University of Missouri, dedicated himself to carrying on the high standards set by his honored father, printing the facts about Chinese and Far Eastern affairs fully and without prejudice. The magazine, largely supported by the advertising of American business firms—oil, banking, insurance and shipping—covered the China scene in all its aspects. In general it reflected the opinion of American business in China at that time, especially with regard to the deteriorating morale and business-hampering practices of the Kuomintang. When the civil war was resumed in earnest, Bill Powell covered it impartially, frequently criticizing both sides, but pointing out that the growing corruption of the Nationalist government was dooming old China.

The *Review*, most of whose contributors were Chinese journalists and scholars, also devoted a great deal of attention to Chinese literature, art and history. Among its regular features was a page quoting current opinions of American newspapers and magazines on events in and out of China.

Perhaps the chief contribution of the Review at this crucial point in Chinese history was its reflection of the growing intellectual opposition of the Chinese themselves to Chiang Kai-shek's government. Since it was an English-language periodical, the Chinese who contributed to it and those who read it were necessarily those who had studied English and in some way had come in contact with Western education and ideas. As the Nationalist clampdown on the press grew harsher, the Review became the sole avenue through which Chinese under Kuomintang rule could voice their opinions about the rapidly worsening conditions under which they lived.

"Intellectual opposition to the government," wrote the American correspondent Jack Belden of this period in his book, *China Shakes The World*, "came daily more into the open. From all over China letters poured into the offices of the *China Weekly Review*, one of the few public opinion outlets available to the oppressed Chinese people. 'Can such things happen in a democratic country?' inquires a student from North China College. The question more than contains its own answer. The acme of disillusion, however, is expressed by a student writing from Wuhu in Anhwei Province: 'A half a year ago I had interest in reading criticisms of the government. . . . Now they seem to me, just as does the government, meaningless. If there are men who still believe in the Kuomintang, they are idiotic.' "

As Belden added: "The letter columns of the *China Weekly Review* became a kind of wailing wall where the people howled out their anguish."

When the assistant editor whose place I had taken returned to the Review at the end of 1948 I retired from the staff. But I was to renew my connection in 1950, and remained as associate editor until the summer of 1953. Then, its income having dwindled because of diminishing circulation and an American postal embargo which cut off circulation in the States, the magazine was forced to cease publication.

While working on the Review in 1948 I had continued corresponding for the *Chicago Sun-Times*, sending both mail and cable dispatches. By early fall I had also begun contributing regular Sunday feature articles to the *Denver Post*. Then, one December morning, a cablegram came from John Madigan, news director of the American Broadcasting

Company, inquiring whether I would take on the assignment as their China correspondent.

I lost no time cabling my acceptance and blithely plunged into this mysterious new field. I had never been closer to a microphone than a seat in the audience at a Fred Allen show; but with coaching in Shanghai mike technique by Pepper Martin, then China correspondent for the Columbia Broadcasting System, and by his attractive wife Lee, I managed to get through my first broadcast. The fact that it was done from a little booth in downtown Shanghai, at a safe ten-thousand miles distance from my audience, probably had something to do with my finding the courage to attempt it.

As 1948 ended, correspondence for two newspapers and frequent broadcasts kept me fairly busy. With the military collapse of the Nationalists in North China and Manchuria and the continued sweep of the Communist armies down to the Yangtze River, 1949 promised to be lively.

Reporting the China scene at this stage of the civil war, it seemed obvious to me that the end of Chiang Kai-shek's rule on the mainland was simply a matter of time. In response to a request from the Sunday editor of the *Denver Post* for an article on American opinion in Shanghai regarding Chiang's chances of survival, I had sent this estimate, which appeared in the issue of November 28, 1948:

> Imminent collapse of Chiang Kai-shek's Nationalist government in China is foreseen by Americans in China. . . . Opinion prevalent among Americans in official capacities here about prospects for Chiang and his government was best described as 'running the gamut of pessimism; from deep to ordinary pessimism.' Despite reports of government victories in the battle for vital Suchow, key to Nanking, there was little expectation of a change in the ultimate outcome. It was pointed out that at the time the government made statements about throwing back the Communists on this front, high officials and ministries were in the process of leaving for Canton. Daily flights of planes from Nanking with ministerial files and records were reported in Shanghai.

6

FINIS TO FORTY CENTURIES

As the fateful year 1949 dawned, and Mao Tse-tung's forces fronted the Yangtze ready to cross over and drive on to Shanghai, Pepper Martin and I decided to go up north across the river for a quick look at what was known as the liberated area.

A seven-hour journey, covering 120 miles by train, boat and rickshaw, brought us to the city of Taichow in North Kiangsu province, a good-sized market town of over 200,000 population. This was one of the northernmost outposts of Nationalist territory; less than fifteen miles farther on were the Communist front lines. Taichow expected to be taken any day, but was going about its business in a state of philosophic calm. The people we talked to confessed their war weariness and looked forward to the end of the struggle with more anticipation than dread. The merchants were quietly trading with towns in the enemy-held area, apparently with profit to both sides.

We found an American missionary couple named Richardson, who put us up for the night. Next morning after breakfast we bade them goodbye, hired rickshaws, and started northeast along a road that cut across the rich Kiangsu farmland. On our way we passed many farmers and merchants traveling in both directions, obviously plying between the two territories. Two miles out of Taichow the line of telephone poles ended, and we knew we had reached the extreme border of Nationalist territory and were entering a sort of quiescent no man's land.

We dismissed our rickshawmen and proceeded by foot for the remaining ten or twelve miles. Four and a half hours after leaving Taichow we entered the Communist-held town of Kiangyan.

Uniformed soldiers were about, but no sentry bothered us; it was an informal war, at least in that sector. Kiangyan is a typical countryside town of the Yangtze Valley, where the farmers bring their cotton, rice and grain and in return buy store goods. We wandered through the town, interviewing anybody who would talk to us. Most people were willing, although nobody spoke English and no foreigners had been seen there since before Pearl Harbor

We talked to the district magistrate, a Communist political worker, a Chinese Presbyterian minister, several shopkeepers, and people in the streets. The recurrent wish expressed was for peace. The merchants said they were doing business with people in both Nationalist and liberated territory, and liked it. The Chinese minister said he had been conducting services unhampered.

After a day in Kiangyan we retraced our steps to Taichow, still ignored by authorities, and returned to Shanghai.

In mid-January the forces led by Communist General Lin Piao, which for strategic reasons had by-passed the ancient capital city of Peking on their way down from Manchuria, turned back and took the two big cities of North China—Tientsin, a vital port just south of Peking, and Peking itself. (The negotiated surrender of Peking by Nationalist general Fu Tso-yi was a bitter blow to official American circles who had long advocated shipping arms directly to general Fu's armies because he was considered more "reliable" than any other Nationalist commander in putting them to use against the Communists.)

Following the fall of these two cities there began a lull in the fighting which was to last about three months, while the Red armies prepared for the eventual crossing of the Yangtze River.

Meanwhile from Nanking, his capital, Chiang Kai-shek sent a delegation by air to Peking to explore possibilities of a peace arrangement. No agreement was arrived at and a reduced Kuomintang delegation flew home. Several of the negotiators, including "elder statesman" Shao Li-tze, had prudently decided to throw in their lot with Mao Tse-tung's forces.

At the beginning of April, with the lull still on, I flew to Formosa and spent a week there with a number of other correspondents, watching the Nationalists begin preparations to turn the island into their final stronghold. Then, boarding an American Army plane, I proceeded south to Foochow and Canton to report on south China's reaction to the mounting Communist military threat.

From Canton I went by train to Hongkong to do a broadcast on Nationalist morale in south China. I was soon interrupted by a cable from Pepper Martin, with whom I had an understanding that he would notify me of any sudden break in the war situation. The break had come. The troops of Mao Tse-tung had crossed the Yangtze and were occupying Nanking. Their next major objective obviously was Shanghai.

I quickly boarded a plane (travel from Hongkong to Shanghai was now very sparse, though the planes going the other way were loaded to capacity). I was back in Shanghai on April 25, the day Nanking surrendered. The Communist forces were now within striking distance of Shanghai, and the network was cabling me excited instructions to stand by and cover the city's resistance or capture.

About three weeks were to pass before the final move was made to take Shanghai. The Communist command used the interval to bring up fresh troops, sound out Kuomintang officials on surrender possibilities, and shell ammunition dumps on the outskirts of the city. The shelling developed once or twice into a spectacular artillery duel which the correspondents watched from the roof of Broadway Mansions. I had moved into that hotel the previous winter after being elected to the Foreign Correspondents' Club. During one of these artillery exchanges the Shanghai overseas radio transmitter was blasted out of action, and I was forced to continue my radio reporting by means of cable dispatches to the San Francisco news room, which were read over the network.

By the middle of May it was plain that the fall of Shanghai was imminent. Most of the Kuomintang officials and high dignitaries had already left, taking with them their gold bars and their concubines. Yet a show of resistance, mainly verbal, was being made. On the afternoon of May 23, I found a message under the door of my hotel room:

> To: All foreign correspondents
> From: Chinese Government Information Office,
>   Shanghai Office, Broadway Mansions
>   You are cordially invited to an informal tea-party given by Mr. Fang Chih, Secretary-General of the Political Council of the Nanking-Shanghai-Hangchow Garrison Headquarters, at 11:00 hours tomorrow, May 24, 1949, at Apt. 40, 13th floor, Broadway Mansions.   R S V P

With a good many other members of the foreign press corps, I duly reported at Apartment 40 at 11 o'clock. Special correspondents and agency men from the United States, England, France, Australia and other countries filled the room. We were sipping our tea, served Western style, when Mr. Fang Chih arrived—one of the last of the Kuomintang high officials remaining in the city.

Through an interpreter Fang read a prepared speech:

> In order to deal the fatal blow at the Communist bandits, the Government made a decision to defend Shanghai to the last. Gen. Tang En-po [head of Shanghai's defenses], with the highest determination, the groundwork completed, with happy and strong defense works, huge manpower, endless reserves of wealth, and the highest morale yet seen, has determined to defend the land and the people. . . . Being thoroughly trained and well-balanced correpondents I would not doubt your duty to report this to the world. . . . Shanghai will be defended like Stalingrad. . . .

At five o'clock that afternoon Fang Chih, accompanied by General Tang En-po, the last-ditch defender of Shanghai, boarded an evacuation plane headed for the temporary safety of Nationalist-held Canton.

Shanghai went to bed that night with the knowledge that it might be its last under Nationalist rule. A curfew was in effect and was being rigidly enforced against everyone, including newspapermen, who had no direct government connections. The curfew hours at first had been from midnight to 6 A.M. nightly. But in the last few weeks, with the city's fall recognized as inevitable by the Kuomintang rulers, they had begun unloading the contents of their banks and shipping the bullion, securities and foreign currency out of the city. During this delicate operation they found it convenient to keep people off the streets.

Hence the curfew had been extended to a full twelve hours—from 6 P.M. to 6 A.M. I had taken the precaution, however, of arranging with a Chinese friend, one of the editors of a Chinese-language newspaper which had news sources in the government, to cover me on any important developments that might break during curfew hours.

At a few minutes after three in the morning I was awakened by the telephone in my room. Tommy Chen, my newspaper friend, was on the wire. The Nationalist troops were evacuating quietly and in good order—in fact, he thought it their most effective operation of the entire war. Advance units of the Communist troops, he added, were beginning to enter the city through Frenchtown. The fall of Shanghai was in progress—so far without the firing of a shot.

I called Pepper, who had a room just down the hall from mine, and we wrote our dispatches—he for the *New York Post*, I for the ABC network and the *Chicago Sun-Times*. The problem still remained whether we could get to the cable office through whatever troops might be in possession of the streets, and file our stories. The office was on the other side of Soochow Creek, about ten minutes' walk from Broadway Mansions. We decided to forget about the curfew, and set out.

We walked a few steps to the Garden Bridge in the awakening light of a fine May dawn, through empty streets. But on arriving at the creek we found a rearguard unit of Nationalist soldiers blocking the bridge while apparently waiting for the word to withdraw. A sentry came to meet us, growled an order to halt, and demanded to know our business.

"American newspapermen," said Pepper cheerfully, waving his press card.

"We have business in there," I added in Chinese, pointing to the American Consulate which stood on the other side of the bridge, a couple of blocks from the cable office.

At the suggestion that we might be American officials the soldier's attitude immediately changed. He stepped aside and muttered, "Go ahead." We crossed the bridge, went into the cable office, and sent our stories. No questions were asked; Nationalist censorship in Shanghai was already a thing of the past.

Emerging from the cable office, we hurried on downtown. A short distance ahead we could hear spasmodic machine gun fire. Some Nationalist units, having set up a few emplacements on the other side of Soochow Creek, were raking some of the side streets with intermittent bursts. No soldiers were nearby, however. By hopping across the street between bursts we were able to move along unimpeded.

The first columns of Communist troops were just beginning to appear, marching down Avenue Edward VII to the Bund. They looked desperately weary, but marched along looking neither to right nor left, as if this were just any march on any day of the war. When they came to street fortifications they deployed and took them over in a matter-of-fact way, as though the whole thing had been rehearsed. The streets were all theirs, Shanghai's customary traffic snarl having completely disappeared. But the people of Shanghai had started pouring out of their houses and thronging the sidewalks.

White flags were flying from the City Hall, the police station opposite, and the pill boxes and sandbag emplacements all over town. The fall of Shanghai was all but complete.

People began pulling down Nationalist street banners and slogans ("Communist Bandits Are Traitors," "Defend Shanghai to the Death"), and put up new ones recounting their recent hardships and welcoming the new army. Although a delaying action was being fought just north of Soochow Creek, as far as Shanghai itself was concerned the war was over. Peace had come, the first in many years. One could feel it that afternoon of May 25, 1949, in Shanghai's sunny streets.

The surface impressions of those first days of the changeover were something that everyone could share. Above everything else was a general feeling of relief at the absence of any disorder. That there had been real fear of looting and rioting was evident everywhere in the boarded-up homes, shops and office buildings. Shanghai's suburbs had suffered greatly from General Tang En-po's defense construction; houses and entire small villages had been razed, trees chopped down, fields torn up for the erection of pill boxes. Nationalist soldiers before withdrawing had looted a number of buildings where they had been stationed.

But the widespread looting feared by everyone during the interim between Nationalist retreat and Communist takeover had happily failed to materialize, for the simple reason that there was no interim period. The Kuomintang withdrawal had been quiet and speedy and the troops of Mao Tse-tung had come in hard on their heels.

As to the behavior of the People's Liberation Army, the name by which the victorious forces were officially known, their remarkable self-discipline and general good conduct were widely noted at the time. An Associated Press dispatch datelined May 26 from Shanghai, and printed in a number of American newspapers, said:

> Behavior of Communist troops here makes clear one reason why they are winning the war. . . . The Communists have made a good first impression on Shanghai.
> An anti-Communist merchant related how he saw a Communist soldier eating a bowl of dry rice. A coolie offered the soldier a glass of boiling water, which is a poor man's substitute for tea.

The soldier declined the water and lectured the coolie and crowd that gathered on how the People's Liberation Army never take anything from the public.

Still other Communist soldiers declined the use of beds, preferring the sidewalk. They said that they did not wish to impose on the public.

This sort of behavior was repeatedly contrasted in the dispatch with the looting and general brutality to which the people had become accustomed from Chiang Kai-shek's troops. The pattern of Communist military behavior already had been officially acknowledged months earlier and reported to the American State Department by Robert L. Smythe, our Consul-General in Tientsin. According to a Washington dispatch in the *New York Times* January 15, 1949, Smythe had described the conduct of the troops who had captured Tientsin as "exemplary."

For weeks after the entrance of the People's Liberation Army a holiday air pervaded the city, with daily parades, mass meetings, street dancing and singing. Roaming the streets and the surrounding countryside, I saw crowds everywhere listening to speeches, watching skits that told of the victories of the Red Army, and learning the new revolutionary songs from radio loudspeakers mounted out of doors. Solid rows of houses displayed red banners, apparently made over from old Kuomintang flags. New cartoons and posters hailed the new era. Some, addressed to foreigners, bore messages in English such as, "Foreigners in China Should Immediately Correct the Wrong Conception of Despising the Chinese People" and "Liberation Army Completely Protects Lives and Property of All Foreigners."

In a car with other correspondents, I rode past groups of students enthusiastically performing the hitherto forbidden *yangko*, a folk dance which originated in the northwest province of Shansi and which long since had been adopted in the old liberated areas as a sort of latter-day *carmagnole*. In the outskirts of the city we paused to inspect General Tang En-po's fabulous city-circling fortification system—a wooden fence! The only plausible explanation one heard for this prodigy was that the General had relatives in the lumber business.

Shanghai's victory celebrations, obviously enough, were inspired by the new authorities and led by the radical student movement in the city. But just as obviously the majority of the populace went happily

along. From the outside looking in this may seem strange; but for anyone who had lived among Shanghai's millions under the Kuomintang
regime it held little mystery.

The havoc visited upon Chinese life by Chiang Kai-shek and his
Kuomintang government has been described by innumerable journalists and historians. At least ninety percent of the Chinese people, including many antipathetic to communism, had come to hate him and
his clique more than they hated the Communists.

First appearing on the scene in the mid-Twenties as the promising
young leader of China's national revolution against the warlords and
foreign interests, heir of the great national hero Sun Yat-sen, Chiang
soon revealed himself as a cold and opportunistic dictator. The slaughter of many thousands of his countrymen on mere suspicion of dissent,
and the enslavement and despoliation of his people, are documented
facts of history. This was the man under whom Shanghai, and all that
still remained of Nationalist China, had been groaning and starving in
that spring of 1949.

This picture of Chiang Kai-shek, true enough, differs from the official image of him widely displayed in the United States. But until
1950, when the American government and press began building up
Chiang as a simon-pure symbol of democratic freedom, many Western observers, including Americans, plainly identified him for what he
was. These included many who were as implacably anti-communist as
Chiang himself. Among them was the veteran correspondent of the
New York Times, Tillman Durdin, who in a dispatch from Shanghai
as early as August, 1946, called the Chiang government "corrupt,
inefficient and heavy-handed."

In the American State Department's famous White Paper released
in August, 1949, documentary evidence is given to show that the
greater part of two billion dollars in American monetary aid to Chiang
since 1945 had been embezzled, and that another billion dollars' worth
of military supplies furnished to his generals had been sold and surrendered by them to the Communists.

As an example of Chiang's idea of democracy, the White Paper
reproduced this statement, contained in a report made to the Secretary
of State by Gen. Albert C. Wedemeyer, avowed enemy of all communists, concerning conditions in Formosa under Kuomintang rule
in 1947:

"They fear that the Central Government contemplates bleeding their island to support the tottering and corrupt Nanking [Chiang Kai-shek] machine and I think their fears well-founded."

Also these statements by Gen. Wedemeyer in a speech before high Nationalist functionaries on August 22, 1947:

"One hears reports on all sides concerning corruption among government officials, high and low and also throughout the economic life of the country. . . . Nepotism is rife and in my investigations I have found that sons, nephews and brothers of government officials have been put in positions within the government-sponsored firms, or in private firms to enable them to make huge profits at the expense of their government and their people. It would be interesting and revealing if you would conduct an investigation into various large banking organizations and other newly created business organizations, to ascertain how much money has been made by such organizations and to what individuals or groups of individuals the money has been paid."

And Gen. Wedemeyer added:

"I have had reported to me many instances of misdirection and abuse in meting out punishments to offenders, political or otherwise. . . . People disappear. Students are thrown into jail. No trials and no sentences. Actions of this nature do not win support for the government. Quite the contrary. Everyone lives with a feeling of fear and loses confidence in the government."

Even in the present day of American idealization of Chiang Kai-shek, Gen. Wedemeyer's unvarnished words, based on observation during a tour of duty in China as Chiang's Chief-of-Staff during the civil war, can scarcely be shrugged off, much less answered with the conventional cry of "pro-Communist." But his frank criticisms, needless to say, were lost on the Generalissimo and his associates. Their rule grew more corrupt and more brutal as their *Goetterdammerung* closed in on them.

In those last weeks before their retreat from Shanghai an old-fashioned reign of terror was visited upon the city. The people's lives and property were completely at the mercy of the military. Students were rounded up and shot, and political prisoners and suspects were executed wholesale. The shootings went on daily. On the last day before they evacuated the city Kuomintang troops executed more than three hundred political prisoners at Sung Park. Nine students imprisoned at the Foochow Road police station were shot on orders of Police Commissioner Mao Sen, and their bodies were removed virtually under the windows of the American Club next door.

One spectacle I witnessed, which I am not likely to forget, was the street execution of half a dozen captive students. Bound and kneeling, they had their brains blown out by Chiang's warriors before a great crowd of people in Yangtzepoo, a workers' residential district. This took place on the seventh of May, while shouting gendarmes beat back the crowd with long bamboo whips, their customary weapon. The overseas radio transmitter was still in operation and I described the incident in my broadcast to the ABC Network on the following day. The Chinese press also carried reports of it.

Following in the wake of the retreating Kuomintang, even a casual onlooker was able to gauge the vast scale on which American-supplied military equipment was being destroyed or lost by the Nationalists. On a trip to Woosung (the naval base guarding the river approach to Shanghai) with Walter Sullivan of the *New York Times* and Robert Doyle of *Time* magazine a few days after the takeover, we saw long lines of military vehicles loaded with army goods which had been wrecked and left standing in the road. At one point near the Woosung docks, loaded trucks had been driven onto wharves saturated with gasoline, and the wharves set afire.

In spite of this destruction, fabulous quantities of materiel were captured by the incoming army. It is difficult to reconcile this mass of equipment with the lamentations heard in America that we had "lost China" by failing to supply Chiang adequately. Having seen the fall of Shanghai and heard the accounts of American newsmen who had witnessed the surrender of Peking four months earlier, I was able to appreciate the meaning of the quip current in Shanghai to the effect that America had shipped Chiang Kai-shek enough to arm both sides!

Scant wonder that the great mass of Shanghai people welcomed the arrival of the Communists. Many were uncertain as to what they were going to get; but they knew what they had been rid of, and they considered that ample cause for rejoicing.

7

THE MORNING AFTER

Gradually the outward face of Shanghai began to change. The old picturesque but crippling traffic jam was permanently unsnarled. The haphazard postal service was reorganized and put on a rational schedule. Pavement holes and neglected sewer pipes, the cause of fetid street lakes for decades past, were repaired. The police, who formerly had kicked around the common folk pretty much at will, began behaving like servants of the people instead of their masters. And the soldiery, while still much in evidence, made themselves a friendly element in the community instead of a privileged class licensed to roister about or to rob and assault the citizens.

The need for all this had been obvious enough, and people of all social classes welcomed it. As the weeks went by and the wheels got rolling again, people noted the changes with outspoken satisfaction. When I asked city folk or those in the surrounding countryside how they were getting along, they would point to some improvement large or small and compare it with *jiow sheh huei*, "the old society."

To me, one of the most striking examples of the contrast between the old and the new appeared in the handling of Shanghai's fabled traffic problem. Formerly there were only sporadic attempts at control, and the busier thoroughfares had presented an impenetrable tangle of cars, trucks, rickshaws, pedicabs and dodging pedestrians. An attempt to get across the city was a major project. Occasionally a Traffic Observance Week was staged, which meant the stationing of a few hundred auxiliary policemen at busy crossings to beat up rickshaw, pedicab, or cart men who ignored traffic lanes or failed to stop behind the crosswalks. Those who earned the particular ire of the police were deprived of their seat cushions and could retrieve them only by bribing the officer or paying a fine at the station house.

Drivers of motor vehicles, however, were seldom bothered. After a few days the auxiliary policemen were withdrawn, and street traffic returned to its usual chaos.

In the first month after the takeover, People's Liberation Army forces, assisted by the regular police (only the high officers had fled) inaugurated a traffic-control campaign. Firmly, but without violence, offending drivers were stopped and instructed to stay in their proper lanes and to halt short of the crossings. No pedicab or rickshaw man lost his seat cushion. The beating or kicking around of these drivers—a custom taken for granted by most Westerners in China—was ended. For the first time operators of motorized vehicles were admonished or disciplined the same as rickshaw and pedicab drivers, and thus lost what had been in effect a privileged right of way. The new traffic control was made permanent, and gradually the street tangle became a thing of the past.

Such reform by organized persuasion instead of force was even more strikingly applied against street peddling of silver dollars. Pedlars had roamed the town exchanging their big coins for the newly instituted paper currency (*Jen Min Piao* or *JMP*). Offering higher than official rates, they were an inflationary force. Coupled with the effect of commodity shortages and war conditions, this could have served to defeat the new government's effort at currency stabilization.

Some silver-dollar pedlars were officially licensed with the understanding that they would adhere to the legal rate; but many were illegitimate operators suspected of having been left behind by the Kuomintang forces to sabotage the new government's economy. Another of their suspected functions was to spread rumors about the return of Chiang Kai-shek. Such rumors were common during the early days of the changeover, and there can be no doubt that they contributed to the spectacular price rises and inflation during the weeks before the new currency was stabilized.

No move was made, however, to suppress the silver-dollar hawkers by police action. Instead, a campaign of public education was undertaken to impress upon the people the harmful effect of the silver-dollar curb market and its economic consequences upon their own pocket-books.

Students paraded with banners denouncing the hawkers and those who patronized them. Soapbox lecturers demonstrated the practical economics of the matter. Street plays and skits drove the lesson home. Students remonstrated with the pedlars themselves. Thus Shanghai literally was talked out of its damaging silver-dollar trade. Soon only a stubborn core of diehards remained to ply it. These were rounded up by the police; but those who could prove that they were observing the legal rate of exchange were turned loose.

More than the cleaning up of the black-market in silver dollars was needed, of course, to secure the stability of the new currency. The fixed official rate of exchange was supplemented with new quotations issued daily to conform to the actual value of the currency. This practice, by making pointless any resort to the black market with its self-propelling tendencies toward inflation, in time caused it to wither away. Another successful measure was the inauguration of the Parity Unit system applying both to bank deposits and to wages, which has become a permanent feature of economic life in China. The value of money deposited or money earned is measured in terms of basic commodities. Thus, if a depositor wishes to withdraw his funds, settlement is made by Parity Units and he receives their current instead of their original cash value. This means that he cannot suffer from the effects of inflation. This also applies to wages earned.

But, above all, public confidence is necessary before a currency can become stable. The fact that the new JMP currency did soon become stable is perhaps the best evidence of the Chinese people's attitude toward the new government and its program.

On June 25, 1949, with civil war still being waged in the south and southwest and a huge rehabilitation job to be done, a Military Control Commission was instituted in Shanghai. Gen. Chen Yi was its director and Gen. Su Yu his deputy. Chen Yi, who enjoys a wide reputation in China as a poet and a chess champion, spent some of his early years in France as a college student majoring in chemistry, working his way by operating a lathe in a Paris machine shop.

One of the first acts of the Commission was to organize a Financial and Economic Takeover Committee to operate banks and industrial firms owned by the Nationalist government or its more powerful members, especially those of the Big Four Families—Chiang, Kung, Soong and Chen. This Committee also was charged with operating the Shanghai City Government, the Railway Administration, the Post Office, the Bureau of Navigation, the Telecommunications Administration, and other public agencies which had been government-operated under the Kuomintang. Privately-owned business enterprises, unless they had Kuomintang affiliations, were left in their owners' hands.

The absence of corruption on the part of the new officials in these vast operations is one of the outstanding facts of the changeover. The unbridled graft on the part of the Nationalist government and armies had contributed more than anything else to their downfall. It was evident that the new government had no intention of committing the same error, and even its most violent critics have never alleged corruption. In Shanghai itself, a city whose name had stood almost as a synonym for official corruption, there was not even a rumor of graft. Would-be grafters were quickly run down, called to account and forced to return any goods or money bribes they had taken.

The only drawback incident to this rule of personal austerity was that it sometimes slowed up the process of takeover. Some of the new officials, inexperienced in the ways of business management and finance, had to have each step in their new jobs painstakingly explained to them, and it took some time before they got the hang of things. Or they were suspicious of the people who had to do the explaining.

Running the city of Shanghai was considered by old hands to be just about the most onerous job in the world. Nevertheless Shanghailanders of all classes were more than glad to swap the old system of nepotism, squeeze and general corruption for the honest if at times slow-starting government that took over. Even cynical Old China Hands found themselves obliged to admit that it was working out.

Among the chief problems confronting the government were the feeding of the city's six million people, putting the factories back into operation, and providing work for the unemployed. Chiang Kai-shek's officials had been frankly dependent on outside help for supplies, and America's Economic Cooperation Administration (ECA) had been furnishing some fifty percent of the city's rice requirements, as well as thousands of bales of raw cotton and yarn to keep Shanghai's textile industry going. Not only was ECA aid now withdrawn, but large shipments of ECA supplies scheduled for Shanghai had been diverted. Thus, when the People's Liberation Army arrived, the city was down to rock bottom in its most essential supplies.

The Military Control Commission promptly started moving in vital supplies of rice, flour, coal and cooking oils from other parts of the country. By the second week in June more than 20,000,000 catties of rice (a catty equals one and one-third pounds) had been moved into the city. Another 60,000,000 catties had arrived by the end of the month. Supplies of other necessities were shipped in with equal dispatch, and a threatened crisis was averted.

More difficult and complex was the task of reviving Shanghai industry. After years of civil war, inflation and systematic robbery by its political bosses, Shanghai like most of Nationalist-held China was near collapse. Factories were closed; more than half the labor force was unemployed; business and industry had all but ceased to function.

Particularly desperate were the laborers, who had no resources but their wages. Even for those who still had jobs, the money they received was worthless. Many lacked even the illusion of wages, for their bankrupt employers were operating on "deferred" payrolls.

When Shanghai changed hands many destitute workers expected instant prosperity. The Communists, they reasoned, were the party of the workers and must immediately provide for them. The jobless descended upon their union headquarters, or on the offices of the new government's labor bureau, and demanded jobs at once. Others who had jobs came to demand a raise. Still others, who had been laid off unpaid, turned up at their old places of employment shouting for their back pay.

It did little good for the employers to explain to them that, under any kind of government, factories could not be reopened without capital or operated without raw materials. And the heads of the labor bureau had scarcely better success in convincing them that, although they had been promised work and wages under the new regime, these things could not be materialized overnight. All that summer the Shanghai industrial scene, or what remained of it, was in constant turmoil. In some cases, aggrieved workers took over shops and factories only to find them impossible to operate until raw materials could be brought in.

In point of fact the government, while promising labor a solution to its problems, had also pledged cooperation to industry in getting the economy back on its feet. The labor policy of the government was put forth in these general terms:

(1) Workers should not ask wage increases beyond what management was able to pay.

(2) Management, however, must not pay less than it formerly had paid.

(3) Management must do all within its power to improve the working conditions as well as the general welfare of the workers, while the People's Government would do all it could to help management obtain operating capital, raw materials and markets.

These precepts were in line with Mao Tse-tung's principle of "New Democracy," which I will have occasion to describe farther on in this chapter. The government's effort to alleviate the distress of both labor and capital, with a fair shake to each as far as possible, was the major factor in overcoming Shanghai's industrial depression during that first summer.

For the most part workers swallowed their disappointment at the postponement of immediate redress of all their grievances and went back to their jobs on the best terms available, but with new hope for a better deal when conditions improved. Many voted voluntary wage cuts when it was proved to them that their employers were operating at a loss. Others set themselves increased production quotas and launched campaigns to cut down waste. In the No. 4 Worsted Mill of the China Textile Industries, a state combine operating the country's largest group of textile mills, the dyeing and finishing workers gave up thirty minutes of their lunch hour to increase their output.

But where the labor bureau found factory owners falsely pleading poverty in order to keep down wages, it backed up and enforced the workers' demands. When employes in a match factory demanded a hundred percent wage increase and proved that they were grossly underpaid, the bureau after investigation ordered management to comply. When the company still pleaded inability to pay, the bureau, having formed its own conclusions on the subject, took over the plant, compensated the owners, and granted the pay increase.

Meanwhile the government, in order to get production going, provided loans to plant owners who were willing to reconstitute their businesses. As shipments of raw materials began rolling into Shanghai from the hinterland, and the new currency was stabilized through the measures already described, the industrial scene gradually changed. Factories

produced goods in increasing quantities and employed workers in greater numbers.

The depression hit its low point by the end of June, after which
a general upturn was in progress. By August most plants were operating three days and three nights a week. By September the average
work week had increased to four days and four nights, and further
increases were recorded by mid-October. An index to the general improvement is provided by the overall performance of Shanghai's match
industry, which produced 5,400 cases in June, 8,100 in July, and 10,100
in August.

The Chinese Communist policy with relation to industry—the policy of encouraging private enterprise and aiding it with loans where
necessary—was no improvisation to meet emergencies. Neither was it
a cynical departure from principle for the sake of ready results. It was
part of a comprehensive plan for the organization of Chinese society,
worked out years before and methodically put into practice wherever
the forces of the People's Liberation Army had taken over new territory. That plan, as described by Mao Tse-tung, was called "New
Democracy."

Its underlying theory was that China, with her unique form of
social organization and her unique history, must seek her own path to
socialism. "Colonialism and feudalism," with the effects which their
long history had produced on Chinese society, were the main conditions, according to Mao, that had to be overcome before the nation
could set out on the road to full socialism. In this she was unlike
Russia at the time of her revolution.

For Russia had already experienced a considerable capitalist development; whereas China's modern industry—what little there was of
it—was mainly light industry, foreign-owned or foreign-controlled. And
while Russia in 1917 still had some feudal elements in her social structure, China's had been predominantly feudal. About eighty-five percent
of China's population were peasants the majority of whom owned no
land. Modern industry was almost non-existent outside a few of the
largest cities. And eighty percent of the people were illiterate.

In his writings Mao Tse-tung had declared that a thoroughly developed capitalism was an indispensable way station on the path to
socialism for China. In *New Democracy*, written in 1940, he stated:

"The Chinese revolution must proceed in two steps. The first step is new democracy and the second step is toward socialism. The first takes a relatively long time. We are not idle dreamers. We cannot shut our eyes to the present actual conditions."

Five years later, in *Coalition Government*, Mao wrote:

"Some people fail to understand why the Chinese Communists do not fear capitalism. Instead, the Chinese Communists advocate developing capitalism. . . . Basing our analysis on the Marxist interpretation of the law governing the development of society, we Communists understand perfectly well that under a new democratic state it is essential to offer broad facilities for the development of private enterprise apart from the state-operated enterprises and the cooperative economy. This is good for the government and the people. . . ."

The Chinese Communists are of course openly dedicated to a goal of socialism and eventual communism in China. But their planning projects it as a necessarily future achievement that may take decades. Their first objective was to lay the foundations of a socialist industry while permitting private enterprise to develop alongside. As this system has worked out in China, private profits have been limited, but they have also been guaranteed through the investment of state funds.

This differs from free enterprise as we know it in the United States. But it has had its advantages, especially for the small or medium Chinese entrepeneur.

For example, the owner of a Shanghai canning factory, whose son I knew as a clerk in the United States Information Service office, wanted to reopen his plant after the May, 1949, changeover. He needed capital to modernize his machinery and to buy raw materials. Under the old Nationalist regime he would have had to apply to one of the banks owned—as all of them were directly or indirectly—by one of the Big Four Families; give a mortgage on his plant; and pay interest at somewhere between seven and twenty-five percent *per month*, depending on how good were his Kuomintang connections. He would, in addition, have been subject to an elaborate complex of government licensing regulations, operating restrictions, "squeezes" (bribes), demands by racketeer labor bosses, and the dumping of American canned goods.

Under the new government this manufacturer had to apply to a bank, now usually state-owned. The requested funds would be forthcoming, he was told, on his aceptance of one of three choices: continuing to operate privately and repaying the loan at a low rate of interest;

operating the plant with the state as an equal partner; or selling out to the government and remaining as factory manager on a salary.

He chose the partnership deal, and at the time I left Shanghai was running the plant and receiving half the profits. His personal property, including his good-sized house in the Hoongjao suburb, remained untouched. Since he was sure of government orders for canned foods to the limit of his plant capacity, getting business was no problem.

In the case of factories that were operating when the new government took over, those in noncritical industries were permitted to remain fully in private hands at the option of the owners. But the government reserved the right to fix prices and limit profits. On the other hand, the government saw to it that such privately-owned plants were bailed out of any serious difficulties through the infusion of fresh capital, the relaxation of taxes, or the placing of government orders. It is to the national interest that production be kept up unhampered.

Thousands of Chinese businessmen, and a few foreigners, have operated under one or another of these arrangements. When I left China at the end of 1953, thirty-eight percent of all industry was still in private hands and nine percent either privately owned with state support or on a cooperative basis. In wholesaling and retailing the proportions were considerably higher. Most of the privately-owned factories were in consumer-goods industries, but these included many sizeable plants employing hundreds of workers.

The factories in primary industry such as steel forging and machine-tool making, and in heavy manufacturing such as locomotives, were wholly operated by the government. But there was plenty of opportunity for individual entrepreneurs in industry generally, and the government encouraged their activity. Known as "national capitalists," they still occupy a respected place in the new social organization. The government needs their experience and enterprise, and they need the government's resources and its vast consumers' market. As far as I was able to see, it works.

Some time was still to elapse before the city's aged and creaky industrial plant could be rehabilitated to approach maximum output. But the improvement went on steadily, and by 1950 employment, production, and total wages earned had passed the point considered normal under Kuomintang rule.

Similar recovery was going on throughout China; and it proved to be just a beginning. By the end of 1952, according to a United Nations survey, China's industrial output was twenty-six percent higher than the highest previous year in its history, and more than double the 1949 figure.* The proportion of capital goods produced had increased from one-third the total production in 1949 to 43.8 percent, but consumer's goods had also increased along with a rise in the nation's purchasing power.

Shanghai's light industry, in fact, doubled its turnover between 1950 and 1952. By the end of the latter year it was producing most of the consumer products which before 1949 had been imported.

That there was nothing temporary about this trend my later observations were to show, and further United Nations production reports issued since I left China have confirmed. Even the Western press, which periodically publishes fanciful reports of agricultural setbacks, famines and assorted disasters in China, does not question her industrial progress.

---

*UN, *World Economic Report 1951-52*, p. 52

❧ 8 ☙

NEW BROOMS—THE COMMON PROGRAM

September, 1949. The red-walled assembly hall of the Imperial Palace in Peking was gay with banners and brightly-colored slogans. Its corridors and its many chambers, the latter now turned into committee rooms, buzzed with excitement.

The first all-national parliamentary body of new China, called the People's Political Consultative Conference, had convened for the purpose of founding a new Republic. On its agenda were the election of a new government, the adoption of a new flag, the choice of a new capital, the formal institution of the Gregorian, or Western, calendar. And, most important of all, the adoption of a new body of laws.

Six hundred and sixty delegates were there, representing all regions of the country and all strata of its society. Some had been chosen in regional elections; others had been named as representatives of the various political parties. Still others had been sent by trade union federations, youth groups, students', women's, peasants', or educational associations. Some represented army groups.

Side by side with smooth-faced students sat grey-haired army generals. Peasants from the Northwest and tribesmen from the remote Southwest rubbed elbows with factory workers and merchants from the Eastern cities. There were authors, teachers, manufacturers, social science workers, and—yes—religious leaders. Seventy of the delegates were women.

On the ornate platform, under a banner that read, "Practicability is the essence," Mao Tse-tung, as chairman, arose to welcome the delegates. "We have a feeling in common that our work will be written down in the history of mankind. It will be said, 'the Chinese people, one quarter of humanity, from this time forth stood up. . . .' "

For four weeks the delegates to the Political Consultative Conference met—alternately in groups and in committee of the whole—to thrash out a set of laws and a blueprint for action (called the Common Program) to guide the new nation until the adoption of a permanent Constitution. This all took place in September, 1949, when the Nationalist armies had been substantially driven from the mainland and economic rehabilitation was starting to show results. The move had been planned, however, since May, 1948, when the Communist Party proposed the formation of a coalition government and met with a favorable response from other anti-Kuomintang parties in the field.

The Common Program finally adopted was based on a preliminary draft drawn up by a preparatory committee and submitted to the delegates. Taking the name of their body literally, the members of the Consultative Conference took this initial draft, broke up into small groups to consult over its provisions one by one, then reassembled and revised the overall document on the basis of their deliberations. This process was repeated seven times, with a newly revised draft resulting each time. Finally, when all the suggestions acceptable to the body as a whole had been incorporated, the Common Program was adopted.

Since the composition of the assemblage was broad, embracing many diverse elements in the nation, it omitted from this national program anything on which all could not agree. "Practicability is the essence." Adherence to the Marxian dialectic was rejected because some of the delegates disagreed. Also rejected was a detailed welfare program which some considered unrealistic. On land reform, however, the proposed measures won common consent.

A glance at the constituency of the Political Consultative Conference might cause a revision of some notions as to its "monolithic" character. Fourteen political parties were represented. While all of them accepted the leadership of the Communist Party because it was the only one that had been able to come forward with a comprehensive and workable plan, they nevertheless reflected many diverse viewpoints held by people outside the Communist ranks.

These parties included the Democratic League of China, the Revolutionary (anti-Chiang) Committee of the Kuomintang, the Peasants' and Workers' Democratic Party, the Democratic National Reconstruction Association, the Tze Kung Party, the Chiu San Association, and others. All had been in existence under the Nationalists, but the Revolutionary Committee of the Kuomintang and the Democratic League had been outlawed. The Democratic League was, and remains, a non-Communist party exerting considerable influence among intellectuals. Organizations other than political parties included the All-China Democratic Women's Federation, the All-China Federation of Labor, the Shanghai Association of Civic Bodies, the All-China Association of Literary and Artistic Workers, peasant associations from the old liberated areas, businessmen's and professional workers' groups, ethnic minorities, and religious organizations.

The Common Program as finally adopted was a broad charter—the first—of new China's aims and policies both domestic and foreign. Its seven chapters codified the new way of life for which the revolution had been fought, and presented a set of rules which later, with minor changes, were to be made permanent in the 1954 Constitution. This means of course that they removed a good deal that was old and instituted much that was new.

Chapter One laid down general principles, founded on the theory of New Democracy. The feudal system of land ownership was abolished and a policy of peasant land-ownership proclaimed; "prerogatives of imperialist countries in China" were repudiated; "bureaucratic capital" (i.e. capital owned or controlled by top Kuomintang leaders) was to be confiscated; but private property and all legitimate private investments were protected. . . . "Steadily transforming China from an agrarian into an industrial economy" was the stated objective.

Chapter Two dealt with the projected election of an All-China People's Congress through universal suffrage. Pending the carrying-out of this goal, the People's Political Consultative Conference was to exercise the functions and powers of the proposed body. (The Congress was elected and held its first session in 1954.)

Chapter Three called for the maintenance of a modern army, navy and air force, and for work contribution by their personnel in peacetime, for which they would be paid.

Chapter Four laid down an economic policy based on land reform and industrialization. "Agrarian reform is the essential condition for the development of the productive forces and the industrialization of the country."

Chapter Five dealt with an educational and cultural policy, including the encouragement of literature and the arts, popularization of scientific knowledge, and promotion of sports.

Chapter Six provided regional autonomy for national minorities, with full representation in the government and "the freedom to develop their dialects and languages, to preserve or reform their customs, habits and religious beliefs."

Chapter Seven, on foreign policy, declared friendship and alliance "first of all with the Soviet Union," but avowed the desire to enter into diplomatic and trade relations with all countries "on the basis of equality, mutual benefit and mutual respect for territory and sovereignty."

The Political Consultative Conference, having adopted this program, elected national officers of the new government with Mao Tse-tung as Chairman or head of state. Mme. Sun Yat-sen (Soong Ching-ling), widow of the founder of China's first republic and a representative of the Revolutionary Committee of the Kuomintang, was elected a member of the Central People's Government Council, the nation's highest administrative body, pending the formation of a permanent government. Among other representatives of non-Communist parties elected to this Council were:

Li Chi-sen, a colleague of Sun Yat-sen's and former comrade-in-arms of Chiang Kai-shek, who like Mme. Sun was a member of the Revolutionary Committee of the Kuomintang.

Chang Lan, leader of the Democratic League, whose political career goes back to the Manchu Dynasty in the early part of the twentieth century.

Fu Tso-yi, formerly one of Chiang Kai-shek's top generals, who left him in disgust and joined the People's Government. He has been Minister of Water Conservancy since 1949.

Shi Liang, a prominent woman lawyer and long a well-known middle-of-the-road political figure, who has held the post of Minister of Justice.

On October first the founding of the People's Republic of China was announced. The day was proclaimed a national holiday and was celebrated throughout the land. In Shanghai a million people paraded.

Millions more filled the streets cheering, capering and dancing the *yangko*. At night fireworks banged and blazed, boat whistles sang on the Whangpoo River, and the roistering went on until dawn. I stood about the streets watching it; and from where I stood, the people seemed to like what they had acquired.

9

NEW CHINA FROM A RINGSIDE SEAT

During the late spring and summer following the May, 1949, take-over of Shanghai there was plenty for the foreign correspondents to write home about.

Newscasting to the States had ended for me with the destruction of the transmitter in the battle outside Shanghai. But I continued to send dispatches as a "stringer" to the *Chicago Sun-Times* and the *Denver Post*, and furnished a special article to the *San Francisco Chronicle* on "The New Look in Old Shanghai."

Correspondents for the *New York Times*, *Time* magazine, the *New York Post*, several London papers, the American press syndicates and other British and French news services as well as *Le Monde* of Paris, similarly kept on the job. With the civil war still continuing in the south and southwest, and frequent Nationalist air raids on Shanghai, military censorship had been imposed. But the transmission of non-military news was unhampered.

The changing pattern of life in Shanghai affected foreigners in various ways. The Old China Hands had lived under the Kuomintang regime for years as a superior class representing foreign industrial control. The city had been dependent on Britain and America even for its rice and cotton. At first they found it impossible to believe that the good old days of privilege and luxury were coming to an end. "After all, you know, these new people are just Chinese! They'll have to come to us!" So ran the talk at the club bars and on the golf course. "They talk about industrializing China—well, with what?"

But the Old Hands were to learn before long that the heyday of the taipan in China was over. They were still welcome to stay and do business, but on the same terms as Chinese businessmen. Officials no longer bowed and scraped before them; it was no longer possible to dodge taxes, bribe the nearest public servant, grab a concession at a fraction of its value, to turn a fast black-market profit in foreign currency or gold bullion. The "new people" were indeed Chinese, and proudly conscious of their national heritage. Chinese instead of English became the language of official business, to the discomfiture of foreigners who had spent as much as twenty years in the country without bothering to learn its speech. A "native" was now the equal of a Westerner. Even the humblest coolie could no longer be kicked out of the way.

Still, business could be done in China, even though the tightening-up of regulations now made it difficult to turn a profit of more than twenty-five percent. Also, a new tariff system was applied, on a familiar Western pattern, for the protection of home industries. Imports of luxury goods, and of ersatz merchandise which foreign importers had considered good enough for the Chinese at regular prices, were banned. On top of that came the Nationalist blockade against all foreign shipping, whose exclusion of merchandise crippled the import-exporter and whose American backing did not endear the foreigner to the Chinese.

American and British business men began striking their tents and going home. With them went a number of missionaries who had been recalled, or whose efforts to convert Chinese souls had struck the new government as extending noticeably beyond the realm of the spirit. With them, too, went William Olive, the American vice-consul, whose scuffle with and jailing by Shanghai police over an alleged traffic violation did nothing to improve the general atmosphere.

The arrest and alleged rough handling of Olive by Shanghai police was one of a number of like incidents which occurred in those early days. It is possible, though far from certain, that these events had an important bearing on the direction of American policy toward the "new people" and toward the new national government they later established.

It is undoubtedly true that some readiness was apparent in the State Department for a reorientation of its China policy toward a move to disentangle itself from Chiang Kai-shek. The fact that Ambassador Leighton Stuart, like most of the other foreign ambassadors, remained in Nanking when it fell to the conquering army in April, 1949, was regarded as a sign that he would be ready to talk to the new government authorities. But they ignored him, along with the other members of the diplomatic corps who had stayed. Moreover, a brief flurry of excited feeling arose, with prominent headlines in the American press, when some People's Liberation Army men blundered into Stuart's home one night and entered his bedroom. No harm was done anyone, and the affair was soon forgotten.

Nevertheless, the strict Chinese policy of avoiding both social and diplomatic relations with any representatives of the Western countries, during this period prior to the setting up of a new national government, doubtless irked Dr. Stuart. When he was head of Yenching University he had known as students a number of the people who now assumed official posts in Nanking, and who held themselves rigidly aloof.

As the Communist-led armies crossed the Yangtze and then swept down through south China, Chiang's prestige hit bottom. But all was not yet lost. He had faithful friends in the United States, and they began exerting their evidently very powerful influence to cause the American government to stand by him. These efforts were described in vast detail nearly three years later in The Reporter Magazine, in a remarkable pair of articles featured in its issue of April 15 and April 29, 1952.

These articles, entitled "The China Lobby," cited massive evidence including names, places, dates and amounts of money spent, to show the operation of that loosely formed but highly effective pro-Chiang pressure group in the United States during the period of Chiang's final defeat and subsequently. The Reporter, a liberal anti-Communist periodical, traced step by step the manner in which the China Lobbyists, led by representatives of Nationalist China's Big Four families armed with apparently limitless funds, established social, economic and political ties in high Washington circles, influenced state and Congressional elections, and gained access to the White House.*

During Chiang's last days on the mainland it was the function of this Lobby, working through its friends in the United States Government, in Congress, in the press and elsewhere, to make difficult any

---

*The Reporter articles also discussed, among many other political curiosa, the remarkable prescience on the part of Senator Joseph R. McCarthy and a group of his friends, undisguised in their pro-Nationalist sympathies, who made a financial killing through speculation in Chinese soyabeans in 1950, a few days before the outbreak of fighting in Korea made that commodity a scarce item on the world market.

change in America's China policy by attacking as "soft on communism" and "friendly to the Chinese Reds" anyone who countenanced
the idea of such a change. They did their work well. According to *The
Reporter*, when the Chinese formally established their new People's
Republic in October, 1949, and invited Ambassador Stuart to Peking for
talks, the State Department was still in favor of his going; but the
avalanche of propaganda put forth by the China Lobby in the meantime caused President Truman to hold back. In any event, he vetoed
the idea.

It was *The Reporter's* opinion that the early "intransigeant" attitude of the Chinese toward Stuart, plus a number of incidents like the
one involving William Olive in Shanghai, made possible the success
of the China Lobby campaign (by no means its only successful campaign in this country). This opinion is still held by some China
thinkers today. Perhaps that is so. Yet, as world events continued to
develop, it seems to me doubtful that the pro-Nationalist forces in this
country, deeply entrenched and heavily financed in a period when the
cold-war atmosphere was rising toward its peak of frenzy, would have
permitted any kind of understanding between the United States and
the new Chinese government to remain intact, even if it could have
been established at the time.

By September, 1949, relations between the United States and China
had deteriorated to such a degree that some American newspapers summoned their correspondents home. They had their opportunity to
leave at the end of the month when the American liner *General Gordon*, by the grace of Chiang Kai-shek and the U. S. State Department,
was permitted to put into Shanghai.

I remember vividly the scene at the Hongkew dock when I went
aboard the *General Gordon* to bid goodbye to some of my colleagues
who were sailing. The event had been publicized abroad as the rescue
of imperiled American refugees from the Chinese "red terror." But of
the 1,500 to 2,000 Americans still living in the Shanghai area, only
about 350 felt sufficiently imperiled to want to leave.

The atmosphere was one of gaiety rather than of crisis or danger.
Laughing and chatting people of a dozen nationalities crowded the
decks to see friends or relatives off. Henry Lieberman of the *Times* ordered drinks of whatever seemly beverage a *Times* man orders, and
we drank a farewell toast. He was particularly glad to see me in the
somewhat intemperate checked suit he had sold me a few days before,

throwing in with it five one-pound cans of Blue Boar pipe-tobacco. As we shook hands he repeated the advice he had given me a few days before: "Stick around here as long as you can, kid; there are going to be big things doing, and very few newspapermen on the spot to see them." I have always felt that he was quite right, and sometimes have regretted that he did not take his own advice to heart.

I looked for Pepper Martin, who had engaged passage as far as Japan, but he was nowhere to be seen. As the ship's whistle gave a warning toot and I made for the gangway, there was a yell from shore and Pepper came pounding aboard.

"Almost didn't get away from that farewell party," shouted Pepper, grasping my hand as I went by. "See you in New York!"

I successfully made the pier; the gangway was hauled in; the *General Gordon* bellowed again. Then she cast off, and the tug began nudging her out into the stream. People on deck and people ashore were screaming goodbyes, laughing, waving, shouting. Seldom can there have been so many carefree "refugees" or so many happy-go-lucky left-behinds.

A few days later, as a byproduct of the American State Department's disapproval of new China for her inconsiderate treatment of Chiang Kai-shek, I suddenly found myself unemployed. The hoped-for diplomatic recognition having failed to materialize, the Chinese government issued an order forbidding foreign correspondents to work for publications of countries with which it had no diplomatic relations. It was saying, in effect: "When our newspapers can be represented in your countries, then yours can be represented here."

One hope sustained me, however, and at the moment it seemed a promising one. Among the newspapermen who had sailed on the *General Gordon* was Harrison Forman, the veteran China correspondent who lately had been working for the London *Daily Telegraph*. He had recommended me as his replacement, and I had been negotiating with the newspaper toward that end. By now the deal was virtually completed, and since it was common knowledge that Britain was about to extend recognition, my problem seemed solved. I made inquiries and was assured that a correspondent's nationality was not considered relevant so long as he represented a publication in a country with which China had diplomatic relations.

I therefore sat down to wait hopefully for British recognition. On the sixth of January, 1950, it came. But it did nothing to solve my employment problem. The Chinese, incensed at a British statement that their recognition implied neither approval of the Chinese government nor any break with the Nationalists on Formosa, refused to recognize the British in return. This meant only one-way recognition; still no British newspaper representation in China; and no *Daily Telegraph* job for me.

By now all but two of the remaining American correspondents besides myself had left. The two were Walter Sullivan of the *New York Times* and Amos Landman of the National Broadcasting Company. We were all still hoping for a change in the situation that would permit us to function. If I could stick it out there was a good chance of my becoming eventually the dean—and sole member—of the American press corps in China.

I counted my inconsiderable savings, took a hitch in my belt, and decided to stay. I had already moved from my comparatively expensive room at Broadway Mansions and was now inhabiting a one-room unheated flat (hot water twice a day) in a large office-apartment house in the center of the downtown district. The rent was equivalent to thirty American dollars a month; and since living costs generally were relatively cheap, $100 a month was quite enough to support a bachelor existence.

In the early spring both Sullivan and Landman took off. My determination increased to stay as long as I could, remember and record everything I saw and heard, and eventually report it in a book. But my capital was dwindling, and I felt the need of some occupation besides the keeping of a diary. I sought out Bill Powell and asked him for another job on the *China Weekly Review*.

"Ask me again come April," said Bill. "We're full up now, but Alun Falconer is talking about leaving in April."

In April Falconer went off to his native New Zealand, and I moved in as news editor. In September, when the *Review* changed from a weekly to a monthly, I became associate editor.

Shanghai, an international crossroads, had always been a rumor factory. When I arrived, more than a year before the armies of Mao Tsetung came down from the north and took over, the rumors had been concerned with such things as price changes, the black market, business opportunities, Nationalist government shakeups, and what trillionaire had paid how much for what other trillionaire's daughter in marriage.

After May, 1949, and the departure of the Kuomintang, the rumors buzzed as thickly as ever, but they modulated to a different key. Much of the talk now had to do with the alleged shakiness of the new government and the certainty of Chiang Kai-shek's return. It would be foolish to go along with these Communists, said the whispers. They knew nothing about how to govern; their new money was even more worthless than the old; their land reform and reconstruction plans were insane; they were only robbers of the people. And besides, when Chiang came back to power, it would be held against all who cooperated with these impostors.

The new government knew the source of these rumors, and occasionally issued warnings to the Kuomintang agents who had been left behind to sow them. But the spreading of rumors continued, along with attempts at industrial sabotage, physical assaults and assassinations, and other standard counter-revolutionary practices. One class of rumors, however, soon turned out to be quite accurate: namely, that Chiang Kai-shek would send bombers over Shanghai to take revenge for his expulsion.

The raids began during the middle of 1949 and continued intermittently for several months. At that time the army had neither fighters, nor anti-aircraft in sufficient strength to meet a bombing raid. The Kuomintang planes came over leisurely and unloaded their bombs at will, with nothing worse to contend with than machinegun fire from the rooftops. As far as any military value was concerned the raids were senseless. The civil war was over and everyone knew it. Chiang, holed up on his island more than a hundred miles offshore, lacked the military forces needed to attempt an invasion. Even if he had had the requisite air power to flatten the entire country—which he did not— he still could have done nothing about retaking the mainland.

These air raids, it was obvious to everyone, were carried out solely from motives of spite and revenge. It was equally well known that the planes, ammunition and fuel had largely been furnished to Chiang by the United States. American statesmen and political savants who at the time were wondering loudly why we "lost China" could have found the answer in the faces of the people of Shanghai as they huddled in doorways and watched the American-made B-24s overhead, choosing their targets and letting go their bombs.

During two weeks in February, 1950, civilian casualties ran in the hundreds, families were left homeless, and a number of factories on which jobs and the necessities of life depended were destroyed or damaged. These factories, and the dockyards and rail centers which also were hit, might have been considered "military targets" had a military situation existed. As it was, their destruction merely amounted to war against the civil population.

In one of the worst of these February raids the big American-owned power plant was hit and the power system disrupted for several days. A few days later the B-24's come over again at about 11:30 in the morning. I was walking with an American friend, Frank Miles, and two of his Quaker colleagues on our way to lunch at the Hwei Bing Low, a well-known Peking-style restaurant, when we heard the first bomb detonations in the southern part of the city.

We all ducked into a shop doorway on Hopei Road, not far from our destination. A number of other pedestrians, all Chinese, joined us. We stood peering out at the sky as two of the bombers sailed directly overhead. Someone emitted an eloquent oath and added, "If we just knocked down one of old Chiang's planes they'd never come back!"

After about an hour of bombing the planes flew off, sped on their way by the angry but futile rattling of rooftop machine guns. We finished our walk to the restaurant. Sitting at the table waiting for our Peking duck, we were conscious of the curious stares of Chinese people all around us who a few minutes before had been dodging Chiang's explosives. As usual, the looks they cast at the "high-nosed" foreigners, in whose land the planes and bombs had been built, were puzzled yet friendly.

"You know," said Frank, looking around him, "I can't help wondering what would have happened if things were reversed and a bombing like this had taken place over New York!"

In some of its facets the Shanghai scene changed rapidly during that first KMT-less summer; in others it seemed to go on just about the same as before.

One of the holdovers from the old days was the exclusive American-owned Columbia Country Club, a prime example of the Shanghai tycoon's "pleasure dome" situated on the way to the Hoongjao suburb. The Columbia Country Club, naturally, had always pursued a "whites only" policy, excluding even the wealthiest Chinese, who could have bought out the entire Western membership without feeling any pinch.

For a time the new government ignored this establishment, racist policies and all, save for insistence on the payment of taxes. In the past its tax bills had been filed away and forgotten. The necessity of footing these bills, and the loss of dues income caused by the departure from Shanghai of members who disapproved of recent events, ultimately brought the club to a financial impasse. As a handy solution to the problem, one already adopted by the American Club downtown and later imitated by the British Country Club and the Italian Club, the Columbia Country Club rented its buildings and grounds to Chinese organizations at what was generally conceded to be a handsome fee.

During its flourishing period the Columbia Country Club was a pleasant playground for the more or less hardworking members of the foreign press corps. Besides an outdoor swimming pool, a library and a bar and dining room, it afforded a full-sized baseball diamond, bowling alleys, and a row of tennis courts circled by a running track. For some American newsmen the baseball field was a favorite attraction second only to the bar. Those of us who were addicted to the game found places on one of the six teams that formed the club's intramural "league." We played side by side with importers, bank and oil company employes, consulate officials and an occasional infiltrating British trader.

In the more real world of an everyday struggle to consolidate a new society and make it work, constant changes in the general scene were going on in Shanghai. One of the most noticeable changes was in the demeanor of the plain people in the streets, the shops, the places where they worked, and in their homes. I have said, in describing the aftermath of the taking of Shanghai, that a new feeling of hopefulness appeared—a feeling so palpable that one could almost reach out and grasp it. This proved to be more than a temporary holiday atmosphere.

The poor people, the common laborers, the pedicab drivers, even the beggars in the streets had a feeling that at last somebody was interested in them. This alone, even if it had brought no material change in their condition, would have been cause enough for a new air of purpose in their movements and a new animation in their talk. As some of the more flagrant abuses under which they had suffered most of their lives were removed—the brutality and crookedness of officials, the uncertainty of employment, the worthlessness of money, the miserable condition of public facilities—it was little wonder that the working people began to feel that they had a goal in life and at least a chance to achieve it.

This change in spirit began to manifest itself in many practical ways. Everybody wanted to help what was going on—or if not everybody, at least great numbers of people where nobody had cared before. The Shanghai trolley conductors got together through their union and decided that the time had come to abolish their ancient custom of pinching fares; they were being paid a little better now, and although the trolley lines remained so far under private British and French ownership they felt a greater sense of responsibility in their jobs. The motormen, whose long-standing habit had been to whiz past stops and leave passengers waiting on street corners, while they congregated at the terminal for gossip or tea, voted to forego this pleasant tradition and give better service.

The steel workers, called into consultation by the government labor officials to give their views on how Shanghai's broken-down steel industry could best be revived, responded to this unwonted show of respect by pitching in on their jobs in a way they had never felt any reason for doing before. This played its part in the quick restoration of the city's steel mills, which had been close to bankruptcy.

The destitute families of marine workers whom the Nationalist army had "shanghaied" to man their Formosa-bound evacuation boats, were encouraged to form a work cooperative and support themselves, instead of becoming permanent public charges. Sewing, caring for children, domestic jobs, cigarette rolling and other simple work were found for the destitute women by the cooperative. Small loans from local banks and some aid from the new Bureau of Navigation were granted them.

The postal workers, whose fidelity to their jobs had been notable in Kuomintang days despite the civil war, frequent disruption of communications and harassment by KMT secret police, now rehabilitated their dormant union and reorganized their services. They set about checking and classifying the postal department's ancient archives and taking the first thorough inventory, in many years, of its physical property and supplies. Duncan C. Lee, an educated, English-speaking postal clerk whom I had met when he contributed an article to the

Review in 1948, described to me the new spirit that pervaded the department.

"Before the liberation an atmosphere of oppression hung over the entire outfit. But after the entry of the PLA the place began stirring. Choruses, drama and Peking opera groups, and bands have been formed. Everybody hums and sings now, even while working. Another change we like is that all instructions, accounts and correspondence, except that which is going abroad, must now be written in Chinese."

As the working people found their new place in Shanghai's reconstituted society some of the city's more violent external contrasts between extreme private wealth and total poverty began to be modified. The foreign settlements in particular had been marked by splendiferous mansions, some with grounds covering an entire city block. One big real estate and stock market operator had dubbed his resplendent home "Marble Hall," and equipped it with a ballroom big enough for six hundred people. A wealthy American lawyer had built himself a near replica of Mount Vernon. Shanghai had hundreds of such residences where Chinese and foreign magnates lived in splendor, while the Chinese poor for miles around crowded into half-room tenements or huddled in huts or straw hovels.

The changeover in Shanghai and other cities did not bring about the confiscation of private dwellings, however grandiose. But those abandoned in flight by Kuomintang officials or military officers were taken over and put to the common use. Many badly-needed nurseries and schools were established where formerly one family had lived in showy luxury.

An early example of private magnificence converted to public usefulness was the new home of the Educational Workers' Union. Set on a huge plot of ground along Bubbling Well Road, this mansion, once inhabited by an elderly bachelor, had three garages, quarters for thirty servants, and stables accommodating sixteen horses. It was turned into a meeting and recreation hall for Shanghai's teachers and school workers.

A still more elaborate building, a seven-story hotel in the downtown area which the Shanghai General Trade Union bought and renovated, was opened on October 1, 1950, as a recreational and social center for all the city's workers. Called the Shanghai Workers' Cultural Palace, it is open alike to factory hands, office workers and teachers. A gym, a sewing room, an auditorium equipped for movie and stage presentations, two libraries, music rooms, classes in sculpturing and in dancing, a dental clinic, and a surgical clinic and hospital are among the services it offers. Having lived in the old Shanghai for a year and a half, and seen the brutal indifference which its government exhibited toward the common people's needs, I had little trouble understanding the new spirit abroad in China as I wandered through this building.

Such were the changes in the foreground of China's biggest city, while on the national canvas such sweeping developments as land reform, the emancipation of women, local self-government in politics, and industrialization were under way. China was changing in appearance and in her ways—some of them the ways of countless centuries—before one's eyes.

For the vast majority who had nothing to cast off but old burdens and old wretchedness it was an easy change. For a smaller yet considerable number, those of the middle class who had not been in want but whose common sense and humanity showed them the need for change, it was a little harder to rid themselves of the ideas of an old society under which they had lived well—the only one they knew, even though they could see its faults. But most of these learned to accept a change which offered the prospect of a decent life for all in exchange for riches and power for an exclusive few.

One of those who proved unable to learn it, as I discovered one day, was my old boss on the *China Press*, the melancholy Chang. I hadn't seen K. S. since before the fall of Shanghai. But I knew that the paper, owned by the Kungs, had been taken over by the new government along with all the other Big Four Family properties. I ran into K. S. in November, 1949, as he was coming out of the Sun Sun Department Store on Nanking Road, and I was a little startled to see him wearing the civil service uniform.

"So you're working for the government, K. S.?" I remarked after greeting him.

"Well, I'm training for it," he sighed. "I didn't know what to do after they shut down the paper, and they offered us this indoctrination course, learning how to become reporters or editors for the English-language section of *Hsinhua* [New China News Agency]. So most of us enrolled."

"What are you living on in the meantime?" I inquired, remembering his five daughters.

"Oh, they're paying us our salaries—same as we made before. But I don't know. The course will be over in another month, and I don't think I'm going to make the grade."

"What about the other fellows?"

K. S. leaned forward and ducked his head to one side, his manner of assuming a confidential air.

"You know, it's a funny thing. Most of those guys don't seem to mind it—in fact, it seems they actually believe in the stuff! James Lee turned out to be real hot on the New Democracy business, and your friend Scoop Liu came along so fast they've already sent him up to Peking to start work."

"Well, that's nice for Scoop. But what about you, K. S.?"

He shook his head. "Guess I'm too old a dog to learn new tricks. Peasants and workers leading the nation toward a new collective society—all that stuff! What does it mean to an old newspaperman who's spent almost his whole life in Shanghai covering sports? I've really tried—but I couldn't care less about what the peasant associations in Fukien are doing, and that's the way it is!"

"Then—?"

"I don't know. I've been told I might be able to get a loan and open a little retail shop if this doesn't work out. But I've got other ideas."

We were walking along Kiangsi Road, and had reached the corner of Avenue Edward VII, now renamed Yenan Road. K. S. stopped suddenly and held out his hand. "I'm going up here. So long."

A few weeks later I heard that he had departed for Hongkong, leaving his wife and five daughters to manage as best they could.

At about the same time I witnessed a different kind of adjustment —and a happier one—made by a long-time employe of an old-established Shanghai institution. This was the fat little waiter, named Chen, who usually served me at Jimmy's Kitchen on Nanking Road. Jimmy's, which specialized in American food, was a popular eating place with Westerners and Chinese businessmen both before and after the changeover. It was my habit to drop in there nearly every morning for breakfast.

At this time, a month or so after National Day—The October 1 proclamation at Peking of the new Chinese People's Republic—the hoopla of celebrations and street parades was still almost unabated in Shanghai. Trade unions, shopkeepers, organizations, and youth clubs paraded almost daily to hail the new era. Here and there, however, thoughtful people had begun to raise a questioning eyebrow at the time lost from normal working hours in these celebrations.

On this particular morning I had entered Jimmy's Kitchen prepared for poor service because a parade of the restaurant workers' union had been announced. But I found waiter Chen at his post as usual.

"What about the parade?" I asked him.

Chen looked unhappy. "It was cancelled. Today there is nothing but to work."

"You'd rather march than work, Chen? Either way you're on your feet."

"Yes. But in here do I breathe any fresh air? Do girls admire me from the windows? Can I wear my white suit and hat that become me so well?"

"No," I countered. "But in a parade can you serve food to hungry people?"

"*Ai-yo*, that's the trouble! Suddenly everyone is beginning to remember that parades and work do not go together. Soon the fun will be over, except on May Day and National Day." He started away toward the kitchen, but turned back.

"I will tell you this, *Toong-tze*," said Chen. "It is still a good thing to have something to celebrate, even if we do not celebrate it every day. In the old days we did not march, but for a good reason. We did not have anything to march about."

He trotted off to fetch my eggs.

❧ **10** ❧

WOMEN RAISE THEIR HEADS

The Marriage Law of 1950, a sweeping bill of rights for Chinese women, occasioned a popular joke which quickly went the rounds in Shanghai. I first heard it from Fu Ma, my housekeeper, who had picked it up in the Tihwa Road marketplace on which she relied for most of her gossip. Roughly translated, it went like this:

"Land reform is good; the new money system is wonderful; but when they won't let a man beat his wife any more, that's going too far!"

This saying pleased Fu Ma, who chose to take it seriously. Her response to the new freedom idea for women matched that of many of the older generation, though it was scarcely typical of Chinese women as a whole.

A tiny but formidable dame of perhaps sixty who haled from Peking, she was illiterate like most women of her class. But she held plenty of strong opinions about life. When I began reading her the May, 1950, Marriage Law to assay her feelings about it, she stopped her ears and cried, "*Hu shuo bah dao!*"—"Crazy talk eight ways!" Women as "equal partners" with their husbands? The right to initiate divorce and to remarry? Abolition of child marriages, of marriage contracts without the consent of the bride? Fu Ma's seamy faced puckered with indignation and she repeated, "*hu shuo!*"

I pointed out that some of these measures were already in practice in the north. Fu Ma shrugged. "When the men were fighting or hiding

77

or running away, the women could take their places and become the
men. Now that they are back home again, what woman would dare
raise her voice above a whisper or try to tell her husband what is to
be done? If my husband were alive today, would he stay home and
cook for me and let me go gadding about with my bones unbroken,
just because a law has been passed in Peking? Or would I even want
him to?"

Fu Ma, in all truth, was not a likely candidate for the role of a
Chinese Amelia Bloomer. She had no grudges against the male of the
species. For a woman of peasant origin her lot had not been particularly hard. Her husband, a merchant from Tsinan who had taken a
fancy to her as a young girl, had paid her parents a good price for her
and had treated her well during his lifetime. Aside from the death of
five of her six children in infancy, her married life had by no means
been the saga of tragedy one heard so often about Chinese women.

To earn her keep after her husband's death (for the inheritance of
property by a widow was not customary) Fu Ma had gone into domestic work and spent several years in the service of a government official,
receiving her food and lodging but no cash salary. Early in 1950, needing an *amah* to do my cooking and cleaning and mending (I was now
living in a small apartment), and wanting one who spoke no English so that I would be forced to keep up on my Chinese, I had hired
her at a fairly comfortable wage by Shanghai standards.

Fu Ma, in short, considered herself well-off. Under the new government she had a chance to join the state-sponsored domestic workers' union. But this was not compulsory, and like many of the older
amahs she elected to stay out. She displayed her rugged individualism
in other ways, defying the anti-black-market regulations as long as she
could, ducking the inoculation campaign, and so on. At the same
time she was keen about her rights, and eventually threatened to hale
me into a police court when we had a difference of opinion about her
dismissal pay.

My *amah's* hostility toward the projected new freedom for women
was far from typical, except in some of the more remote rural areas. In
the big cities the government campaign found enthusiastic support.
Even before the new marriage law was instituted, a nationwide Wom-
en's Federation was formed with branches in thousands of cities and
towns, and with government backing. The more adventurous women,

sometimes literally taking their lives in their hands, began enrolling in trade unions and night schools.

Some housewives, defying their husbands' outraged threats and invoking the protection of the government, took part-time jobs to gain a measure of financial independence. Others availed themselves of the public nurseries, kindergartens, cooperative kitchens and mess halls which the Women's Federation had begun to set up in various towns to lighten the domestic burdens of mothers.

In parts of the countryside the campaign started off less promisingly, and in some areas the women's rights movement encountered great difficulties. Many women on farms and in small villages, who had known nothing but vassalage in a feudal society centuries old, were afraid to step forward and grasp the new fruit. In some remote provinces—Shensi in the northwest and Fukien in the southeast, for example—the campaign of education had to be halted. But in 1953 the government, encouraged by widespread success in the more advanced parts of the country and aided by experience, renewed its drive. By the time this intensive campaign was over, the women in at least eighty percent of China had taken some step to assert their freedom or at least had become thoroughly aware of their right to do so.

The method of persuasion used here by the People's Government was similar to that used in other points of its program. As with land reform, the abolition of black-marketing, and the public health drive undertaken at about the same time, methods of education and *shuo fu*, which means "to convince by talking to," were employed.

In the summer of 1950, after the passage of the Marriage Law, volunteer teams of educational workers went out to the provinces to announce and explain the law. Women's meetings were held, and they were exhorted to attend classes in literacy and hygiene, to resist the sale of their daughters into forced marriage, to demand the share in their husbands' property guaranteed them by the new law, and so on. The women were also advised of their right to humane treatment, and their right to seek a divorce and a property settlement if their husbands abused them.

This represented a profound social revolution, the overturn of traditions unquestioned from time immemorial. Small wonder that when the movement first began it ran into a certain amount of opposition. In less developed regions particularly, not only the men but sometimes the womenfolk wanted nothing to do with the intruding emissaries of new freedom, and in some cases drove them off the land.

Not only by custom but by law, women in China, as everywhere in Asia, had generally occupied the status of slaves. They had no legal rights, least of all in marriage. The courts upheld the right of men to treat them as chattels. They could be—and many were—bought and sold in marriage, concubinage, prostitution, or slavery. They received no protection from the law.

The sale of girls into marriage or concubinage was one of the best-known aspects of Chinese life before the revolution. Not only the daughters of the poor, but also those of the intellectual and moneyed classes, were subject to the practice. These marriages were commonly arranged by professional brokers while the child was still in her infancy —sometimes before birth. During 1948 and early 1949, in the last year or so of the civil war, when I made frequent trips into the countryside, such deals were common topics of conversation in the village wine-shops or wayside inns. Nobody was secretive about it.

The girl of course had nothing to say about the arrangements. Often she never laid eyes on her husband until the wedding. A girl in her teens could be, and often was, married to a middle-aged, or elderly man who had divorced—i.e., kicked out—his wife or killed her with toil and mistreatment. The man might be personable or he might be repulsive; he might be humane or he might be brutal. It made no difference. For disobedience was barely dreamed of.

The wife of one of the "floor boys" at Broadway Mansions, where I lived during late 1948 and 1949, told me of her experience as a teen-age girl forced into marriage. Tsu Hsin was a silent, bedraggled, limping woman with greyish hair and many missing teeth. Her lost teeth had resulted in a misshapen mouth, but a marked symmetry of her general features hinted that she might once have been unusually attractive.

I would often come back to my room at eight or nine in the morning to catch up on sleep after having done a seven o'clock broadcast to the States. (At seven in the morning in Shanghai it is six o'clock of the evening before in New York.) On these occasions I would usually find Tsu Hsin in the room, cleaning up. My first casual attempts at conversation brought little response from her beyond the matutinal greeting, *tzao*. But with the passage of months we gradually progressed to a friendly chatting basis. One morning, hearing her curse the hardship of stooping with her bad limb to sweep under the bed, I asked her what had caused her deformity. She hesitated; then with the frankness of the reticent who have finally decided to talk, she told me her story.

Tsu Hsin had grown up on a sizeable farm outside Chungking. Her father, Tsu Li-yueh, had been a middle peasant, which meant that he owned his own farm. But hard luck had beset him in the form of a succession of daughters, interrupted by only one son. He had worked the land as best he could with the aid of his single son, but the boy went off to Chungking when he was eighteen. A year or two later the father fell ill and took to his bed. His six daughters, of whom Tsu Hsin was the youngest, did what they could, but their efforts were of little avail.

Soon Tsu Li-yueh was deeply in debt for food and animal hire to his landlord-neighbor, Ho Shen. Ho pressed him for payment, but he had no money and little grain. Ho, a hale man in his sixties, had started out as a middle peasant but had acquired many farms and tenants by lending money to his neighbors and taking over their land piece by piece when they proved unable to pay him back. This was a common procedure and quite in accordance with the law.

Ho had a wife of about his own age, and had not yet got around to acquiring a concubine. He looked at Tsu's daughters and decided that the time had come. He offered to cancel the entire debt and even advance Tsu some seed for the spring planting in return for Tsu Hsin, then turning fifteen.

Tsu Li-yueh refused. He loved his children, and he knew that concubinage could mean a life of misery for his daughter, as a private whore and even as a beast of burden. Ho, a patient man, let the matter drop for a time. But a few weeks later he returned, announced that he had divorced his wife, and proposed to take Tsu Hsin in marriage on the same terms as before.

This generous offer Tsu found harder to decline. It was in fact, by all prevailing standards, a stroke of good fortune. He could wipe out his debt and at the same time gain much face by marrying his daughter to the rich landlord. True, he saw that the girl was revolted almost to illness at the thought of becoming the bedfellow of the old man; and this gave Tsu much unhappiness. But the debt was there, and *mei yeou banfa*—there was no way out. Law, custom and public opinion

not only sanctioned what he was about to do, but virtually demanded it.

And Tsu Hsin knew that it would be useless for her to resist.

So the wedding took place. Her brother, who now had a little shop
in Chungking, came home for the festivities; but her father was too
ill to leave his bed. Tsu Hsin went through the ceremony without joy
but without protest. When the feast was over and the guests had
gone, she followed her bridegroom dutifully into his chamber. But
when he extinguished the light and approached her, she broke into
loud sobs and begged him to let her alone.

Ho Shen was outraged; he protested angrily. He approached her
again; this time she pushed him away, wailing with terror. Then Ho
Shen lost control. In a shouting rage he wrenched a leg from a stool
and beat her. Then, having exhausted himself, he left the room. Tsu
Hsin, her left side and leg numb where he had flailed her, crept into a
corner and wept.

But Ho Shen had counted on a wedding night, and he meant to
have it. An hour or so later he returned to the room and found Tsu
Hsin still crouching in her corner, moaning with the pain that now
throbbed in her leg. Without preliminaries he seized her where she lay
and, heedless of her injury, exacted his marriage right.

When Ho had fallen asleep on his bed Tsu Hsin crept out of the
room, dragging her injured leg. Silently, she stole from the house and
crawled across the fields to her father's home. Daylight was beginning
to glow in the east. She found her brother, who had spent the night
at the farm house, already about, hitching up his cart for the journey
back to Chungking. Tsu Hsin crept to his side and begged to be taken
with him. Her brother knew that this was wrong, and was horrified,
but at last gave in to compassion. He lifted her into the cart, drove her
to Chungking, and gave her shelter in his little rooms behind the shop.

Tsu Hsin's brother took care of her for the better part of a year,
telling no one where she was. He did what he could for her shattered
leg, but it healed very slowly; or rather, it did not heal at all. The
bone grew together after a fashion, but a crooked fashion. The limb
was a good inch shorter than its mate. Here the woman sat down on
the edge of my bed and thrust out her two legs, exhibiting the difference.

After Tsu Hsin was able to limp about, her brother tried to find
something for her to do, for he was about to marry and would not be

able to support her. One of his wealthier customers gave her a job as a domestic. From then on, a cripple for life, she had supported herself by working in one home after another, first in Chungking, then in Nanking, then in Shanghai. After V-J Day, without bothering to confirm a rumor of her elderly husband's death at the hands of the Japanese, she had married a middle-aged "floor boy" at Broadway Mansions.

Such histories, many of them far more tragic, were commonplace throughout China. In few cases did the wretched victim of forced marriage or concubinage have any place to which she could escape; usually she lived out her life in drudgery, abuse and starvation.

Yet, regardless of regimes old or new, it would be a mistake to draw from this fact any sweeping generalizations about Chinese character. Custom has always been a more potent factor than inherent moral sense in shaping the social behavior of people. From the days of the ancient sage Lao-tze the Chinese have been known for their peacefulness, kindliness, politeness and general good will. Having lived among them for six years, under both the old regime and the new, I too can testify to this.

How, then, could such a people condone and practice the virtual enslavement of their womenfolk? It is quite true that a Chinese, pausing during his day's concerns to perform some act of kindness to a total stranger at great inconvenience to himself, might then go home and maltreat his own wife. In the old days I used to raise the question with intellectuals and students I knew in Shanghai and Peking. They were apt to point out in reply that it was, after all, less than a century since the institution of slavery had ended in America.

"I have read," so the argument would go, "that the most cultivated, the most nobly born, the most Christian people in your South would treat their Negroes like animals and sell them like merchandise. . . . Nobody considered that the people who did this were any the less noble or less Christian."

Huantze, a young Peking actress who was a graduate of Beida University in Peking and who tutored me in Chinese literature for a while, once put it this way: "Yes, we have this custom, and no doubt it is barbaric. But in the many thousands of years since civilization began, the difference of a couple of centuries or so is small. Only two or three hundred years ago it was considered highly moral among you Westerners to torture and horribly mutilate your wrongdoers. Nor was this a practice confined to harsh rulers and abhorred by the people. On the contrary we know that such events made gay holidays for the common folk, who would throng with their children to see some miserable fellow have his ears or tongue cut off, or be burned at the stake or publicly disemboweled. Yet we don't say that your ancestors were an evil race; it was the custom of the times, and eventually it was outgrown."

In many respects the Marriage Law of 1950 parallels the body of common and statute law which forms the legal marriage relationship in the United States. In some ways it goes farther. In divorce, for example, mutual consent is all that is required, but it is possible to secure a divorce for cause where the other party contests the action. "The exaction of money or gifts in connection with marriage" is prohibited—a rule that has spelled the end of marriages arranged as commercial transactions. Illegitimate children under the new Chinese law are given "the same rights as children born in lawful wedlock," which means the equalization of their socal status and the right to paternal support.

The Marriage Law as a whole sweeps away all social inequalities between the sexes. Article 1, a general preamble, states that "the arbitrary and compulsory feudal marriage system, which is based on the superiority of man over woman and which ignores the children's interests, shall be abolished." Article 2 proceeds to ban "bigamy, concubinage, child betrothal, and interference with the remarriage of widows." But, under a supplementary regulation, those who had concubines are permitted to keep them if the concubine agrees. Minimum marriage ages of twenty years for men and eighteen years for women are set. "Neither party shall use compulsion and no third party shall be allowed to interfere."

Another section, headed "Rights and Duties of Husband and Wife," establishes "equal status in the home, equal rights in the possession and management of family property," and the right to "free choice of occupation and free participation in work or in social activities" for both parties.

Equality, however, is extended to the male sex as well. Article 25 provides that "after divorce, if one party has not remarried and has difficulties in maintenance, the other party shall render assistance." No distinction is made between the parties: a divorced husband who finds the financial going tough can look to his ex-wife for support. This is one provision that might find considerable favor with beleaguered alimony payers in the West.

Nevertheless the 1950 Marriage Law was undeniably a thoroughgoing Magna Charta of women's rights. One of its immediately noticeable effects was a quick rise in the number of divorce suits, the great majority instituted by women. Even in Shanghai, where the subordination of women was less extreme than elsewhere, I noted that the number of divorce cases had nearly doubled within a few weeks after the proclamation of the law. Many were contested, and some were dismissed. But in general where the woman could produce witnesses to show mistreatment or incompatibility, or where she was obviously much younger than her husband (a common result of the child-marriage custom), the divorce was likely to be granted. Frequent grounds offered in these divorce pleas by women were "cruel mistreatment by mother-in-law permitted by husband," and "no feeling of love between husband and wife." Where it could be shown that the marriage had been arranged by the woman's parents without her consent, the granting of a divorce was automatic.

Other cities, too, recorded a great increase in divorce proceedings, mostly brought by women. In North China, where similar regulations were already in effect, divorce cases comprised sixty-five percent of all civil actions, and more than eighty percent were instituted by women. In Peking sixty percent of divorce suits were announced as having been brought by the wife, and the figure went as high as ninety percent in Liaotung province in Northeast China (Manchuria).

Not all divorce suits resulted in a severance of the marriage bond. The People's Courts before which they were heard made strenuous efforts to reconcile the couples on the basis of a new, more equal relationship. They were in fact required to do this by provision of the law. In many cases the husband faced the fact that his days of male dominance were over, and won back his wife with a promise to abide by the new order. Where the differences were judged irreconcilable, a divorce was granted.

Many of the wives thus freed, especially the younger ones, soon took advantage of the newly granted right of divorced women to remarry. But for those who remained unmarried, either through choice or force of circumstances, other avenues of interest were opening up. They could get jobs in industry on an equal status with men. In

Shanghai, by the end of 1950, one could observe a sharp increase in the number of women married and unmarried, who were enrolling in technical schools and going on to jobs as skilled or semi-skilled industrial workers. A couple of years later, when I made a trip to the Northeast and to the Huai River, I saw large numbers of women working at jobs from shovel wielder on the Huai flood control project, to locomotive engineer on the Peking-Tientsin railroad. It was not uncommon for women to win election as "model workers" in competition with men.

Public affairs furnished another outlet for the energies of women released by their new unrestricted status. In the old liberated areas women were taking part in elections and were already numerous in local government and other public posts, some as mayors or commissioners in the towns and villages of North China. In some districts forty percent of elected officials were said to be women. Of the 660 delegates assembled in Peking in October, 1949, for the People's Political Consultative Conference, seventy were women. And when the People's Congress, elected by popular vote to choose a national government, met in 1954, fourteen percent of its members were women.

Ancient social attitudes do not vanish overnight. In the first few years the reform of women's status progressed unevenly, here and there with considerable difficulty. Administrators of the marriage law admitted serious reverses in 1949 and 1950. But the reform goes on, and even the least developed elements of the population are learning that the change is inevitable. The leaders of new China are patient. "Step by step," a phrase used constantly by Premier Chou En-lai in his reports, expresses the measure of their expectation as well as their progress.

The immense organized vice industry which had flourished throughout China for centuries presented one of the more lurid aspects of the sex-equality problem. Shanghai with its teeming brothels and gaudy bordello-hotels was the most vice-ridden city in China and probably the entire world; but prostitution was also a thriving industry throughout the country. The business operated on many levels, from petty retail to wholesale. But all of it was highly and intricately organized, and virtually every woman whose body was offered for sale was owned by a syndicate or its subsidiary.

The Kuomintang bosses of Shanghai, especially in their last stages, announced periodic "clean-up" drives which never went further than the publicity. Nobody took it seriously. It was common knowledge that Kuomintang chiefs were themselves in the racket.

Late in 1949, when the new government in Shanghai was a going concern, warnings were issued to brothel owners that their day was over and they had best close up shop quietly. During the ensuing year the warning was repeated frequently, while plans were made to implement it. In November, 1950, the warnings having had little effect, the police instituted wholesale raids, rounding up prostitutes, owners and procurers.

For the girls, excepting those too far gone in tuberculosis or venereal disease, a rehabilitation program was put into effect. After a period of political education designed to convince them that a better life was possible for them, they were placed in occupational training courses to fit them for productive work. Those who came from peasant families were given the choice of returning to the land.

Some liked it, others didn't. It would be romantic to suppose that every bordello inhabitant was a pure-souled prisoner who yearned only to escape from her life of shame. Some of the more attractive ones, who had earned high incomes and enjoyed privileges, resented this interruption of their careers. Others, who had grown up from childhood in the atmosphere of vice, luxury and easy money, doubtless had some difficulty in understanding why they had to be saved.

But the average prostitute in China was of quite another kind. Sold or kidnapped from a peasant home or city slum, or forced by economic desperation to sell herself, she was the uncontested property of the brothel boss, for the police would never interfere as long as the weekly graft payments came through. Some of these miserable girls were kept in mean little rooms from which they were never permitted to emerge. Others were forced to go out into the streets and solicit trade. If any showed resistance they were tortured into submission. When their usefulness had passed—and this generally happened well before the age of thirty—they would be kicked out into the street with nothing but the rags on their backs, or simply dispatched with a knife or bludgeon.

If this recital of brothel life in China sounds exaggerated, it is nevertheless substantiated by hundreds of first-hand accounts published long before the advent of the People's Government. Any one whose path led him even to the outskirts of the Shanghai underworld, as mine did during my days on the *China Press* in 1948, would have no difficulty in believing every detail of it.

The number of these luckless women throughout China probably approached a million. The task of rehabilitating them and refitting them into some useful pattern of life was an enormous undertaking, but it was vigorously pursued. Most of the girls were so glad to be released from their onerous bondage that they were ready to do whatever was required of them.

At one rehabilitation center in Peking a group of these former prostitutes, with the guidance of their instructors, wrote and enacted a play about their sufferings at the hands of their former masters, about conniving police officials and medical examiners, about efforts of some to escape and the rescue and reclamation of the survivors.

After playing before large audiences in Peking, this production was translated to film. I saw it in Shanghai. While most of the acting was below professional standards, the story had undeniable power and left its audiences thoroughly moved.

The peculiar status of women in China, both old and new, had so pervasive an effect on the nation's life that I was not altogether surprised to find it impinging on my own household indirectly through my amah.

For all her idiosyncrasies, Fu Ma was a model housekeeper. She had plenty of ideas about everything, including strong maternal convictions about what I should eat and wear, how late I ought to be out at night and what time it was proper for me to be up in the morning But she invariably kept her own counsel unless invited to sound off. Whenever I wanted to read, study, write or listen to the radio in my rooms she would become a silent ghost, postponing whatever fussing about she had to do and retiring to her own little room to sit and rock endlessly and wordlessly. But although accustomed to her silence, I began to notice that she had become moody and abstracted while at her work. I realized that something must be on her mind, but she said nothing, and politeness prevented me from asking questions.

I then noticed that once in awhile she would disappear from the apartment for a couple of hours on transparent pretexts. I couldn't imagine where she might be going, and she clearly considered that it was none of my business.

One evening I dined out with a White Russian friend who was

living in Shanghai after many years as a fur dealer in Manchuria and North China. We had planned to spend the evening at the Peking opera, but finding the theatre sold out we repaired to my apartment to listen to records. Arriving unexpectedly, we found Fu Ma taking leave of a visitor, a Chinese girl who might have been nineteen. Fu Ma's manners were usually adequate, but she made no move to introduce us, and the girl left without looking at us. Since this after all was my home, and my curiosity had grown too great to contain, I asked Fu Ma who it was.

"My granddaughter," she said simply, with a patient shrug as if indicating that she realized the time for secrecy was over.

"Your granddaughter? But you never spoke of a granddaughter."

"Until a few months ago," Fu Ma explained, "I did not know that she was alive. Shortly before he died my only son married her to a business man in Peking. She was then fourteen. She displeased her husband, and before a year had passed he divorced her. That was the last I heard of Shau Yen, my granddaughter."

"And now?"

"Now she is in Shanghai, and I have found out about her. Rather, she has found me, and now and then we see each other. After all she is my granddaughter, and she is happy to have a family-member in the world."

"But aren't you happy, too?"

Fu Ma seemed reluctant to answer. But she faced me and had it out. "Shau Yen has been a yau jier, a prostitute, for some years. She had to do it in order to live—there was no other way. But she had a bad time."

I said something about being sorry to hear it, and added, "But it's over now. Sooner or later she'll forget it."

"It is more than a question of forgetting. She is not well. In the place where she worked they did not treat her kindly. When diseased ones came to her, she was not allowed to refuse them. If she had they would send in another to help him deal with her, and both would take her. When she got sick they brought her no doctor and would not let her go out to see one. Often she did not even have enough to eat, and no warm clothes to wear. You could see that she has not been well."

There was nothing to do but mumble some consoling words. "Never mind. They can cure those diseases now, and then maybe she can get a useful job or even remarry."

The glimmer of a smile came into her wrinkled face. "Yes, that would be good. If my granddaughter could find a good husband, that would be good indeed." And she went off into her room and shut the door, doubtless to rock and dream of her putative great-grandchildren.

The red light districts and the roving streetwalkers are gone from Shanghai today, and from the other parts of new China I saw. The government claims that they have disappeared in every part of the country, and judging from the vigor of the onslaught this is not hard to believe. In the introduction to his famous book, *Devils, Drugs and Doctors*, Dr. H. W. Haggard wrote, "The condition of women in any civilization is an index of the advancement of that civilization." On this the leaders of the Chinese People's Republic may well rest their case.*

---

*Reg Leonard, Australian newspaperman discussing the effects of the Marriage Law in a Canton dispatch appearing in the *New York Times* August 25, 1956, wrote:

"Since then, women have gone ahead boldly in China. Today, they are independent, hard-working, apparently quite capable when they have the opportunities . . . China's women are generally happy in their new life of equality. In fact, they seem to prefer today's status to the restraints and inferiority that might come with restoration of the old order."

Mr. Leonard appeared troubled by what he described as the Chinese woman's indifference to "make-up," "high-necked gowns," and general glamor-consciousness, but left no doubt in the reader's mind that she is tremendously better off in matters of freedom, opportunity, and other vital concerns of daily living.

❧ 11 ❧

CURTAIN FALLS ON FEUDALISM

Mao Tse-tung, discussing the reform of China's ancient system of land ownership in the summer of 1950, estimated that the process would take "about three years or a little longer."

He erred on the side of conservatism. By the end of 1952 the realignment of land ownership was complete except in certain national minority regions of the Far West and the South, where reform was deliberately kept at a slower pace. Here too, however, it was completed by the end of 1953.

China's recovery and industrial expansion would have been impossible without a basic revision of the feudal land system which had existed without essential change for four thousand years. Land reform was needed for other reasons besides the rescue of most of China's peasantry from abject servitude. It was a sine qua non for the raising of agricultural productivity and the development of industry.

By the end of 1952 China, for the first time in history, was producing enough rice for all her needs and exporting some in exchange for other commodities. Her total grain crops were forty-five percent higher than in 1949, and her production of cotton nearly three times as much. In the following two years, despite the worst floods in half a century, production increased still further. (It might as well be noted here that the tremendous floods of the summer of 1954, in spite of hair-raising fictions circulated in the American press, produced no food shortages but were swiftly counteracted by the new flood-control apparatus and

91

by production surpluses in the nine-tenths of cultivated land not affected.) The 1955 grain production, 184 million metric tons, topped all previous records by twelve million metric tons.

It would require a hefty volume in itself to correct popular misapprehensions in the West about the meaning of Chinese land reform. I will touch on a few for the sake of admitting some of the light of reality into a subject often beclouded on this side of the Pacific.

1. The object of land reform was not to do away with private ownership of land, but to widen it. "Landlordism," a kind of medieval system of sharecropping under which the landless peasant belonged virtually body and soul to the big landlord, has been abolished. The peasants now own the land they till.

2. Under the new system the peasants do not "work for the state." They own their land, and its product is theirs. They pay a tax to the government, which averages about fifteen percent of their production —a small fraction of what they formerly paid their landlords.

3. Land reform is not synonymous with "collectivization," a system under which land is either owned in common by peasants who farm it cooperatively and share the product according to the work they contribute, or is owned by the state. During my stay in China collective farming remained pretty much in the experimental stage. But since 1955, as the peasants have turned increasingly to cooperative methods, the program for collectively owned and operated farms has gained rapid momentum, and at present it accounts for more than fifty percent of all farming.*

---

*Vice-Premier Teng Tzu-hui reported in June, 1956 that 56 percent of all Chinese peasant families are now in "higher-stage co-operatives," the term used for commonly-owned collective farms.

Such statistics issuing from official Chinese sources are, more often than not, greeted with skepticism or downright derision by many Western commentators. Under Kuomintang China such doubts were well merited; and when the new government came in I, in common with all China correspondents, took a cynical view of its official reports. I gradually learned, however, from seeing what was going on about me, that reports of progress, whether stated in percentages or in absolute figures, were apt to prove conservative in comparison with the observable facts. In other words, when the People's Government claimed that general wages in 1952 had risen a good deal above 1949, it was easy to believe this when I saw the improved living conditions of the people all about me. The same is true of reports on grain production, industrial output, etc. They were borne out by objective conditions discernible in the country.

Western writers who used to complain that Chinese officialdom made reports "only in percentages, not in actual quantities," now dismiss as "Communist figures" the quantitative reports which China started issuing more than a year ago. Nevertheless, when the time comes for getting down to serious appraisals of Chinese progress under the new regime, one notes a regular tendency on the part of the American

4. Contrary to the mythology dispensed to Western newspaper readers, there has been no famine in China since the institution of land reform.

5. Stories about "wholesale slaughter" of former landlords are no less mythical. The assertion by Assistant Secretary of State Walter S. Robertson, that "fifteen million landlords were liquidated" in China, is pure cold-war whimsy, bearing the marks of a State Department press agent's imagination.

Before land reform there were twenty million landlords in China. During the period of land distribution a few thousand lost their lives. That would be a few thousand too many if their deaths had been the result of vengeance or class hate. But the fact is, as it appears in the records of many a court trial, that most of them were guilty of crimes of violence punishable by death in any country.

The landlords of old China were governed by no law but their own will. They were accustomed for centuries to treating their tenants like subhuman slaves. Many allied themselves with the Japanese during the occupation, and did not hesitate to take part in crimes against their own people. Many who were proved guilty of murder, theft, rape, kidnapping and other major crimes got off with four or five-year jail sentences. I have seen records of some cases where the released peasantry, unable to contain their rage at what had been done to them during a lifetime of oppression, fell upon their landlords and did them in. But this was in spite of, not in pursuance of, the government's efforts.

It took more than the passage of the Agrarian Reform Law (in September, 1950) to rouse the feudally enslaved peasants in many parts of China from their fear and apathy, and induce them to cooperate actively in taking over the land. As with the institution of other reforms, a planned campaign of verbal persuasion was the government's chief instrument.

Groups of workers called Rural Service Corps, each numbering from five to ten, went out to the countryside to explain the law to the people and to encourage them to assert their new rights. Progress very often was slow, but patient effort was the deliberate policy of the Rural Service workers. They were prepared to stay in a village for days, weeks,

---

press to base its calculations, quite matter-of-factly, on Chinese official reports. This was notably true in a Reuters dispatch on land collectivization printed in the *Christian Science Monitor* (June 16, 1956), and in articles by Harry Schwartz on China's industrial progress which appeared in the *New York Times* in July, 1956.

or even months, talking to the illiterate peasants until they had convinced them of the safety of facing up to their old masters. When the peasants were at last convinced that the law was now on their side, they would form a Peasant Association and call a meeting to which the local landlord would be summoned. These gatherings, called *shuo ku*, or "Speak Bitterness" meetings, took place throughout China and marked a historic turning point in her emergence from age-old feudalism.

The "Speak Bitterness" meetings had been going on for years in the old liberated areas where land reform had been instituted as territory was taken over from Kuomintang rule. Shortly after the new government was set up in Shanghai, and before the passage of the Agrarian Reform Law, I sought out and interviewed a young official of the Rural Service Corps who had come down from the north to organize groups for field work in the newly liberated territory of the East and South. He was a former medical student, a slight, mild-mannered youth in his middle twenties, named Huang.

He described the incredulity of many peasants on hearing that they were now entitled to own the land they worked on; their fear of confronting their landlords; the resistance sometimes shown by the armed thugs whom many landlords maintained; the growing determination of the peasants when the idea finally sank in that now, at last, they could really be free. "When the moment of realization comes—the realization that it is within their own power to end the misery and terror that have ruled their lives—then they act swiftly to overthrow their oppressor and reapportion the land."

Some months later I was invited by my friend, Peter Tang, a one-time newspaperman turned shirt manufacturer, to meet a brother-in-law of whom he was rather proud. I had become friendly with Tang during my old days on the *China Press*, when he had been a reporter on the *Shin Min Bao* before borrowing a stake from relatives to go into the shirt business. He was indifferent about the change in regime, his policy being to run his little factory with government assistance, enjoy his new prestige and his income as a national capitalist, and let others worry about China's future.

But his brother-in-law, Wang Wen-ching, a graduate of the American-endowed St. John's University in Shanghai, had always had advanced political ideas. When land reform was launched in the southern provinces Wang had joined the Rural Service Corps and had soon become a group leader. Peter Tang liked the idea of having a relative in the government service and made a point of exhibiting him as a badge of respectability to his friends.

Wang Wen-ching, a serious-looking man of about thirty wearing the plain blue uniform of the government civil servant, launched at once into a discussion of his work, while Peter sat between us and darted bright glances from one to the other as if to show his alert appreciation of the subject.

I asked Wang what kind of life a landlord would be apt to lead after his land had been distributed among his tenants.

"It would depend on himself," Wang said. "In the first place, he would not be left destitute. He would receive an equal share of land —enough to live on if he is willing to work it. If he has a large family, he receives more land according to his needs. He will fare no better than the others, no worse."

"Then he would become one more peasant among the others?"

"Exactly so. Except that he is deprived of the rights of a citizen until he has proved his willingness to abide by the law. After five years he is eligible to have the right to vote and to make his voice heard in the village affairs. But not sooner."

"What about property that he owned in addition to the land? Buildings, or animals, or stores of grain?"

"Such property would not really be his, for it would have been produced for him by his tenants' sweat. Furthermore, it would be needed by them in order to work productively. Hence it would be taken from the landlord, the same as his land, and divided among the peasants."

I was about to ask another question, but he held up his hand and went on.

"It is important to remember also that many landlords, in addition to their land and farming equipment and so on, own shops or small factories. In no case, except where the man is an outright criminal, do we deprive him of such property or interfere with his business activities. For it is important that the production of goods continue, and the People's Government encourages it everywhere."

"The landlords who are accused by their tenants at these meetings," I said. "Can they all really be so bad?"

He frowned a little. "Can they all really be so bad? How bad would you have them be before justice overtakes them? True, many have done nothing not sanctioned by the unwritten law of the Kuomintang. But that was a law under which it was considered proper for a landlord to take as much as four-fifths of a peasant's crop for rent, and for local authorities to levy taxes of thirty percent on what remained. It was a law under which a landlord could send his gou tuei, 'dog's legs,' into a peasant's hut and steal whatever grain he had managed to store, or to take his ox if he was lucky enough to have one. And if the peasant objected, it was not considered wrong for the landlord to have him beaten into insensibility or to break his arms, his legs, his nose."

"The eh ba," grunted Peter Tang.

"Yes, the eh ba," Wang Wen-ching repeated. He regarded me speculatively. "You are a journalist. You say you have been here almost three years—you have traveled to Kuangtung province and to Taiwan and Peking and in the countryside. Surely you have heard of the eh ba?"

I nodded. Now and then while passing through the countryside I had stopped to inquire directions or to buy a meal at a village restaurant and had engaged the farmers in conversation. The home of the eh ba, the local strong-arm leader, often would be pointed out to me as one of the more substantial houses in the community. Sometimes, but not always, the eh ba was also the local big landowner. The peasants would say little about him, but I gathered that he was usually an important personage.

"One month ago," Wang went on, "I was sent to Fukien province with a group of Rural Service Corps workers. In our work we use no compulsion; we explain the Agrarian Reform Law to the peasants and encourage them to embrace its benefits. But the first thing that must be done in any area is to rid it of the terror of its eh ba. In the province of Fukien alone there are more than ten thousand of these eh ba, ruffians with armed men in their employ who knew no law but violence, and whom no law restrained. Sometimes the eh ba owns most of the land, more often he is the agent of the big landowner; many had connections of one kind or another with Chiang's bandit government.

"So terrorized are the peasants by these eh ba that it is all but impossible to induce them to face their persecutors with an accusation of their crimes. A lifetime of fear cannot be overcome in a day.

"Yet the eh ba, like their masters the landlords, must be dragged out into the light with all their crimes recounted, before the new life of a village can make a healthy start. It is for this purpose that we help the people organize their 'Speak Bitterness' meetings or Struggle Meetings which, after they have mastered their fear, they compel the *eh ba* and the landlords to attend.

"Then those who have suffered at their hands are invited to come forward and speak. It is only when they have brought forth their agonies for the whole village to hear, and confronted their oppressor with them, that the infection of dread can be cast out of the village life and the body become whole and clean for the future."

"And when the peasants have told their agonies," I said, "how goes it then with the landlord?"

"How goes it?" Wang Wen-ching's friendly manner turned cool. "It is plain what you are interested in, my foreign journalist friend," he said. "You would like to know about the stories they tell abroad that many landlords are put to death by their former victims. It does not happen to be so."

"I have heard these stories from abroad," I said. "And I have also heard very different reports from others who have witnessed land reform, and who speak as you do. What I am interested in is not this report or that report but in what is really happening."

"Then this can be written down. Some have been killed, without any doubt. More have been jailed. But most have been left free with a portion of land. If you like, I can tell you of some Struggle Meetings where the peasants gave full vent to their anger against the landlord. If you seek something of that, I am not afraid to tell you.

"In a village outside Foochow I was at a meeting where the local landlord was called to account. This landlord, Yung Min, was accused not only of theft and beatings and rape, but of many murders. In that village I can tell you, there are more widows than women whose husbands have survived, more fatherless children than those with two living parents.

"Murder had become a habit with this man. He was related to a high provincial Kuomintang official, and so was beyond the law. Widows, orphaned sons and daughters one after another confronted him and told, with tears and cries of grief, how he had had their husbands and fathers killed by the guns and clubs of his hired men. Murder was his solution for everything. Some of his victims could not pay all the taxes he demanded; others had owned a pig or an ox that he wanted; others had begrudged him their daughters.

"As the excitement of the Struggle Meeting mounted, someone fired a shot. It was an eighteen-year-old boy, a son of one of the landlord's victims, who had found an army revolver discarded after a battle at Nan An, nearby. The shot struck the landlord in the stomach, and he died two days later. The boy was arrested and tried, but no one would testify against him. In that village he is now a hero.

"Or perhaps you would like to hear of Chen Shao-yun, a landlord in a town near Yangchow in North Kiangsu. He was accused of murder, too. But he had other ideas of pleasure as well—he was fond of variety in women. Hardly a home in this little town has escaped his desecration. One woman after another, to the number of over forty, some hanging their heads and others shouting and spitting in his face, told of his violence to them. Some had been seized by his bullies and carried into his bedroom, others he had raped in their own homes in the presence of their husbands whom his ruffians beat and tied up. Some of the younger girls he had kept in his home reported abuses that I will not describe. But they were told in public by these miserable children.

"No, Chen Shao-yun did not live to undergo a trial. Cries of 'Kill him! Shoot him!' rose from the crowd as the story of his villainy unfolded, until at last they fell on him, the women foremost, and with their hands and fingernails tore the flesh from his body. We of the Rural Service Corps had little stomach for defending him, but we had no choice. However, we were swept aside and almost trampled for our pains."

Wang paused and glanced at my notebook.

"Tell all this to your friends if you so desire," he said. "This is the manner of land reform in new China. The peasants who were starved and abused are now receiving land of their own, to till as free men. And as they raise their heads to face their oppressors, some of these— perhaps one in many thousands—meet with death for their crimes. Write it wherever you wish—it is not bad to let it be known."

A few months after this encounter there appeared on the bookstalls in Shanghai a new novel called *Sun Over the Sangkan River*. It describes the land reform in a village of north China from the writer's two years' intimate experience of it. For years before the changeover the author, Mme. Ding Ling, had been one of China's most widely read novelists, and she continued to write with even greater success under the new regime.

The book describes the difficulties faced by Pin, the earnest young chief of a Rural Service Corps, in restraining the fury of a group of small villagers in North China, about to confront their landlord after years of suffering at his hands:

"Pin started thinking hard again. He could not think of a good solution. He was used to working in villages and understood the psychology of the peasants: either don't attack or attack to kill. They did not like going through legal procedure, fearing that if they did so someone they thought deserved death might only be imprisoned. . . ."

When he has at last thought his problem through, Pin speaks to the assembled members of the Peasant Association:

" 'Killing people at will isn't good. We can collect statements of his crimes to give the law court. Execution ought to be legally carried out. In agitating nowadays we defeat landlords on political grounds, wanting them to bow to the people, not necessarily wanting to destroy them. . . . As long as they submit and mend their ways, and are willing to work, they should be given land. You don't want them to become beggars and thieves, do you? If we don't give them land to cultivate they'll have nothing to do, and if they beg won't that mean eating our food?'

"When he explained this everyone laughed, and no one insisted on their original idea of leaving nothing to the landlords."

Pin's sentiments, expressed in a book widely circulated in China at the height of the land reform movement, did not conflict with the attitude of the government toward landlords.

❦ 12 ❧

PEASANTS INTO PEOPLE

The overriding significance of land reform was in its paving of the way for modern methods of agriculture to replace the old primitive system. The productive possibilities of China's rich, and to a considerable extent uncultivated, soil could not begin to be realized as long as the holdings of even the largest landlords, living off the labor of apathetic tenants, were split into dozens of scattered plots.*

The distribution of land to the peasants was the indispensable first step in modernizing agriculture. The common notion in the West that

---

*The potentialities in China's unused arable land were described in a publication called, "A Statistical Analysis of China's Land Problem," compiled in 1946 by the Comptroller-General's Office of the Nationalist government. It included the striking statement that more than seven billion kung mou of Chinese land (about 175,000,-000 acres) was tillable but uncultivated. The amount of land under cultivation, according to this report, was only 8.06 percent of the total land area. Huge areas of the uncultivated land, the survey reported, could be reclaimed and used to increase the country's agricultural output.

It will be news to many that the first comprehensive land-reform program planned for China was a joint project of the Chinese Nationalists and the American Governments. The plan was inaugurated on August 5, 1948, through the signing of an agreement called the Sino-American Agreement on the Establishment of a Joint Commission on Rural Construction in China. It included projects for irrigation, soil conservation, manufacture of chemical fertilizers, and reclamation of waste land. It also included a five-year plan aimed at transforming all farm tenants in the country into farm owners within that length of time.

The Chinese and American partners in this remarkable enterprise never got around to implementing it; it remained for the Communists to carry it through to a considerable extent. Most of the blueprints in the plan have become fact since 1950. As for the unused land, more than five million acres were reclaimed during the first three years of the Five Year Plan (1953-5). Further reclamation plans call for the eventual bringing of the greater part of hitherto untilled land under cultivation. This may help to allay the fears of pessimistic souls who worry about China's ability to feed her "overpopulation."

the Chinese peasant received a small integrated farm hardly corresponds with the facts. The land owned by landlords was scattered in unconnected tracts. It was these scattered plots that the tenants had farmed, and it was these that they received. Thus, a peasant who received three mou of land might have one close to the village, another a mile or two to the east, and the third equally far to west. For that reason alone the idea of farming cooperatively with his neighbors appears practical rather than "totalitarian" to the Chinese farmer.

At the time of Chiang Kai-shek's flight from the mainland, China's economy was eighty percent agricultural. An increase in productivity was essential for two reasons: to provide adequate food supplies for home consumption and foreign trade, and to increase the farmer's purchasing power to provide an internal market for industrial goods. Such a market was necessary before a serious effort at industrialization could be undertaken.

Land reform was the only answer to these problems. The need for reform of some kind had been dimly recognized, even by the Nationalist government under Chiang Kai-shek. Although complete figures on the distribution of land ownership were lacking, a number of scientific studies nevertheless had been made in selected areas.

These had demonstrated that landlords and rich peasants, comprising no more than ten percent of the rural population, between them owned from sixty to seventy percent of the land. Thus the remaining ninety percent of the rural population owned no more than thirty to forty percent. The make-up of this ninety percent differed according to area. In some regions there were very few middle and poor peasants; most were landless peasants. Of these the more fortunate were able to rent land; the less fortunate were day laborers on the farms or coolies in the villages and small towns.

These Nationalist government surveys had determined that rent charges, while varying in different districts and in accordance with fertility, seldom were less than fifty percent for average land and in some cases went as high as seventy or eighty percent of the crop. From this system evolved a series of evils which continued and even intensified the bondage of poor and landless peasants, at the same time driving more and more of the independent peasants into the ranks of the dispossessed.

Figures issued by the Kuomintang government showed how hopeless was the landless peasant's lot. No matter how hard he worked it was virtually impossible for him to achieve land ownership.

A study of changes in status of farm laborers in four provinces—Hupei, Honan, Anhwei and Kiangsi—made by the College of Agriculture of Nanking University during the last years of the Kuomintang showed the following:

It took the hired farm laborer thirty-one years on the average to rise to tenant farmer.

It took the tenant farmer another eleven years to rise to partial landowner.

It took the partial landowner another eight years to rise to full owner.

Of all hired farm laborers in the areas investigated, only one in fourteen statistically could hope to become a tenant farmer; only one in eighty-three could hope to become a part owner; only one in 167 could hope to become a full owner. *

---

*This study may well have escaped the attention of Professor W. W. Rostow, whose book, *The Prospects for Communist China*, was published in 1954 (Technology Press, M.I.T.). No better explanation, at any rate, suggests itself for his statement that "by destroying the ambition of the peasant masses, who see clearly that they cannot safely move toward their goal of rich peasant status, the Communists may have stifled the motives of agricultural society." How "safely" and how effectively the peasant masses were able to move toward the "goal of rich peasant status" is shown by the Nationalist-sponsored survey cited above. On the other hand, the steady rise in production since 1949 and consequent betterment of the peasants' economic status do not precisely point to any "destroying" of their ambition or "stifling" of their motives.

Professor Rostow's book provides a noteworthy example of one kind of scholarly contribution to literature about post-revolutionary China published in this country. His estimate of the "prospects for Communist China" was thoroughly bleak, and quite unlike the progressively brighter picture reflected by actual events in the two years or so since his book was published. In a mood perhaps not altogether scholarly, he denounced virtually every phase of the policies and actions of the government of the Chinese People's Republic, frequently in terms of high moral indignation which sometimes verged on abuse. Listing what he termed the "destructive" effects of the new government, he included an evident reference to the 1950 Marriage Law, implying that through it the government "has worked to break up the family in its old widespread functions." Some of the "old widespread functions" of pre-revolutionary family life which the Marriage Law is indeed serving to break up are child marriage, concubinage and wife slavery (see Chapter 10 herein).

Professor Rostow listed, as his main sources of data which lead him to such darkly negative conclusions about new China, a large number of publications issued in the Far East, in Europe, and in the United States. Most of them turn out on examination to be newspapers or periodicals dedicated to the sole or principal function of disseminating political propaganda against the new Chinese republic. These are supplemented by articles from the Chinese press, in which excesses here and there in carrying out some of the reform programs are denounced. To rely upon such a body of sources for a supposedly serious work of contemporary history is to strike a new note in scholarship.

Students of Chinese affairs at more than one college in this country have informed me that Professor Rostow's book is now being used at their respective institutions as source material on modern China.

Concentration of land ownership had been growing steadily since 1930. Years of war against the Japanese accelerated the process. Devastation, runaway inflation, conscription, collection of land taxes in kind and other levies of the Nationalist regime all combined to speed up the bankruptcy of China's rural economy. The rich grew much richer and the poor much poorer. The middle classes in the countryside, the small landlords and middle peasants, were swallowed up in the ranks of the poor and tenant farmers.

The situation in the countryside became so desperate and caused such outcries that the Chiang Kai-shek government was forced to come forward with land reform laws. These, like so many of its laws, got no further than mere announcements. The government machinery was in the hands of men who were landlords themselves or closely connected to the landlord class. To carry out genuine land reform the Kuomintang would have had to destroy the very class interests to which it was pledged.

After the changeover, the new government extended the land reforms it had previously instituted in the territory already under its control. From 1949 to 1952 it took in additional areas with a rural population of 300,000,000. All in all, ninety percent of the nation's rural population now owned land free of debt. Extortionate rentals, usury, market-rigging and racketeer rule—and the landlord class itself—had ceased to exist.

The immediate result was a huge increase in farm productivity. Improved farming methods were introduced through the peasant associations and through mutual-aid teams and farm cooperatives. Chemical fertilizers, insecticides, deep plowing, more concentrated planting, scientific seed selection, irrigation and flood control modernized Chinese farming.

Fundamental changes in the attitude of Chinese peasants have inevitably resulted. Their ownership of the land has given them incentives to conserve and enrich it. Traditionally cautious, many were now ready to experiment. Their reward was an increase in purchasing power which by the autumn of 1954 had grown to 76 percent.*

The Chinese peasant has a further powerful incentive to produce more, in the reduction and regulation of his taxes. In the old days tax rates were set by the local Kuomintang boss or the landlord—often the

---

*From Premier Chou En-lai's report to the First National People's Congress, September 23, 1954.

same person—and were based generally on his estimate of the maximum that could be squeezed out of the peasant. Rates are now fixed by law at from zero to thirty percent, depending on the size of the holding, productivity of the land, and other factors affecting ability to pay. Since most farms are small, most Chinese peasants now pay a tax of less than fifteen percent of crop value, and no other tax of any kind; whereas formerly a fifty percent tax, plus assorted special levies, was considered moderate. Moreover, a ceiling in taxability is now set at normal crop value, beyond which anything produced is tax free.*

In this matter of peasant taxation, the fatuous nonsense endlessly fired at the American public with regard to China was well illustrated in a speech delivered in January, 1953, by Thomas E. Dewey. Mr. Dewey's qualifications as a China expert derived from a few days' visit to Formosa about the middle of 1951 when, it is safe to hazard, he got no closer to the soil of China mainland than Mme. Chiang's landscaped garden on the "island bastion." About taxes paid by Chinese farmers he averred, according to the Associated Press, that these were now collected "in larger sum than the total of the taxes plus rents they used to pay in the past."

I found this pronouncement especially startling since, at the time I discovered it in a New York newspaper, I had recently returned to Shanghai from a trip through areas of China separated by as much as two thousand miles. From the Northeast (Manchuria) to the far south near Canton I had visited farms and talked to farmers, who had been eloquent on the subject of their current tax rates, calling them the lowest within memory.

Politically, as well as economically, the completion of land reform brought a vital change in the character of Chinese rural life. The peasant communities, formerly ruled by the big landlords and their strong-arm men, now govern themselves. Each community, under a system of general suffrage, elects its own administrators. Peasants hold positions from the bottom to the top in these local governments.

No one who has actually seen the changes in the Chinese countryside could think of notions current in the United States as anything but grotesque and dangerous delusions. The American interested in what really goes on in China might well ask himself what truth there can be

*In a report to the People's National Congress, as summarized in a Reuters dispatch from Peking dated June 15, 1956, Finance Minister Li Hsien-nien stated that "peasants' taxes would not exceed twelve percent of their total output, compared with 13.2 percent in 1952."

in reports of widespread "peasant discontent" when the peasantry throughout the country, with the assistance of the central government, now sustains an armed militia force of some 15,000,000 men against the possibility of invasion. The Kuomintang never dared, and never dreamed of daring, to organize a peasant militia and let them bear arms.

Improved agricultural methods alone could scarcely have accounted for the thumping rise in farm productivity and purchasing power during the first years after land reform. Another ingredient was present, and played an important part in making possible the use of new farming methods. That ingredient was organized, or cooperative, farming. Despite time-hallowed notions, the Chinese peasant never has been a fanatical individualist. The idea of cooperative effort with his neighbors for their common benefit is not such a radical departure as is frequently supposed outside China.

For years, in the old "Red" areas in the Northwest, many of the peasants who had received land had expedited their planting and harvesting by forming mutual-aid teams. They pooled their labor and worked the scattered plots in turn. There was no pooling of ownership, and when the busy season, whether plowing or harvesting, was over, the teams disbanded. The efficiency of working cooperatively was obvious.

Later, as the advantages of this kind of cooperative labor became more apparent, the peasants in many districts began organizing long-term or permanent teams and bigger units. Eventually some of the teams numbered several hundred men and women and nearly encompassed whole villages. In these there was opportunity for diversification of work to take advantage of individual members' special skills.

Besides routine farming, mutual-aid teams were encouraged by the government to carry on regional improvements calculated to increase land fertility, such as irrigation, water conservation and flood control. Many organized classes in agriculture and raised common reserve funds and welfare funds.

Organization of the teams was on a voluntary basis, each family being free to join or stay out, or to drop out at any time. The teams elected their leaders and made decisions by membership vote. The rugged individualists who elected to stay out did their farming on their own; and that is considered their own business. However, as years have passed, the advantages of cooperative effort became more and more evident in the equipment purchased by the teams and the greater rise in per capita production compared with individual farms.

A more advanced form of present organization is the producers' cooperative, in which numerous small plots are consolidated into larger units for more efficient cultivation. Each peasant member pledges his tract of land for his share in the cooperative, and each contributes his work and the work of the animals he owns, if any, to the common effort. The proceeds are divided up according to the contributions in land and labor.

As with the mutual-aid teams, membership is voluntary, officers are elected and policies determined by vote. Members may withdraw at any time. In the cooperatives, however, a withdrawing member may receive a different piece of land equivalent in value to his original land investment, since the land he originally pledged may be in the middle of the overall farm or may have become the site of a new farm building belonging to the members as a whole. Similarly, contributed tools and livestock are usually paid for in cash, since tools may have deteriorated, while animals may either have multiplied or have lost some of their working value with age.

The producers' cooperative is a manifest improvement as an organization over the mutual-aid team. In the latter the individual farms remained small separate units and had to be cultivated as such. Since each family raised primarily the crops it needed for its own use, each small plot was subdivided to grain, cotton, vegetables—an uneconomic form of production closer to gardening than to farming. Moreover the Chinese peasant, like his Western counterpart, was apt to worry most about his own farm during the planting and harvesting, and dissensions arose as to priority in getting the services of the team.

In the producers' cooperatives, on the other hand, the land, while still individually owned, is pooled and cultivated in a unified way. Hence the choice of crops can be determined by the character of the soil. Larger tracts can be sown in a given crop, and all the advantages of large-scale planting, tilling and harvesting can be realized. At the same time, since it is all one big farm, no trouble arises as to whose portion is tended first.

Peasants who work the land through producers' cooperatives do not all share alike. The government, in fact, opposes what it calls "equalitarianism," feeling that a greater contribution should bring a greater reward. Sharing is on the basis of a point system: credit is set at ten points a day for ordinary labor, the same for men and women. Skilled or difficult work is allotted extra points. In distributing the proceeds of a crop, it is usual to pay fixed rates to members in accordance with the quantity of land, animals and implements they contributed. Then, after expenses have been paid and a small portion set aside for reserve and welfare purposes, the remainder is divided according to points earned through work.

To encourage producers' cooperatives the government gives them priority in securing state loans and obtaining improved farm tools at low prices, as well as choice seed, insecticides and sprayers, and technical guidance.

Coordinating with the producers' cooperatives are supply and marketing co-ops for large-scale purchases of seed, implements, etc. and sale of crops; also credit co-ops for arranging loans.

The next higher step in agricultural organization is the collective farm in which all the land, animals and implements are owned in common by members of the collective, with the peasant's share of income depending almost solely upon his contribution of work. This type of collective farm—commonly-owned rather than state-owned— is now usually referred to in China as "higher-stage cooperative farming."*

Finally, as a goal still somewhat in the distance, is the state-mechanized farm. This form of agriculture, the culmination of the socialist aim, is best adapted to huge tracts of land, and therefore must necessarily await the time when China's industrial plant is able to turn out the heavy farm machinery necessary for its efficient operation. When that time comes, thoroughly mechanized farming on a large scale can be expected to produce a higher yield per acre—and per peasant farm worker—than any of the agriculture forms yet practiced.

The government at first pursued a go-slow policy on the organization of collective farms. But it has sought to show the way toward this ultimate stage in large-scale agriculture by establishing a number of state farms and experimental farms run on a fully collective basis. One of the best known was the *Shin Juang* (New Village) Collective Farm, established by poor peasants and landless farm laborers settled on newly reclaimed government land in Northeast China in 1948. This particular farm differed from others in that the government owned the land, which formerly was wasteland. After a slow start the

*Present terminology in China divides cooperative farms into two classes: the "lower-stage" involving individual ownership of land worked collectively as one big farm, and the "higher-stage" which amounts to fully collectivized farming except that the land, instead of being owned by the state, is owned in common by the peasants belonging to the collective.

farm was operating at a profit, within five years, with fully mechanized equipment. By that time each peasant member had accumulated from ten to fifteen times as much worldly goods as he had started out with in 1948.

Until 1954, while I was in China, the mutual-aid team was still the backbone of China's organized agricultural effort, but producers' cooperatives were clearly about to overtake them. The year 1955 saw a phenomenal advance in cooperatives. By the year's end approximately sixty percent of the peasant households in China had gone into co-operative farming, and it was expected that eighty-five percent of the nation's 110,000,000 farm families would be in cooperatives by the end of 1956.

In all forms of agricultural cooperation, membership is, as I have said, on a voluntary basis. The number of those who have elected to stay outside remains considerable, and no coercion is attempted. This may come as news to Americans in view of newspaper accounts of "peasant resistance" to the "collectivization program." There is no "peasant resistance" because there is nothing to resist. It is basic to the "step-by-step" policy of the government that the adoption of new social forms cannot and shall not be undertaken until the people indicate that they are ready and willing.

This policy has been pursued from the beginning by the Chinese Communist Party, which is officially recognized as the leading, though not exclusive, political force in the national government. In a widely circulated manual the Party has proclaimed that "in dealing with any of the problems existing within the mutual-aid teams and agricultural producers' cooperatives, two principles must be absolutely observed; i.e., the principle of voluntariness and the principle of mutual benefit." Further,

> "Only under the call to produce more grain and to increase income can the peasants be mobilized to organize themselves. And it is only by really achieving these aims that agricultural mutual-aid teams and agricultural producers' cooperatives can be said to be truly serving the peasants and hence be welcomed by them, thus consolidating them and making their influence felt by the peasants far and near, who will then begin to organize themselves.
> The criterion for the work of mutual-aid teams and agricultural producers' cooperatives is, therefore, whether they have raised productivity, produced more grain or other crops than individual peasants and increased the income of their members."

This statement, particularly noteworthy because it also expresses the policy of the government as a whole, is even more explicit about the rights of individual peasants not affiliated with cooperative farm‐ ing systems.

"They [party workers] must remember that individual farming is lawful, as stipulated in the Common Program and the Agrarian Reform Law. They must refrain from scoffing at the individual peasants or calling them backward; furthermore, any attempts to frustrate them by means of intimidation or restrictions are for‐ bidden.

Agricultural loans shall be reasonably issued both to the mutual‐ aid and cooperative organizations and to the individual peasants. Such loans should not be given exclusively to the former while the individual peasants are refused them or given small amounts.

Even in a village where the overwhelming majority of peasants have joined the mutual-aid teams or cooperatives and where only a small minority of peasants remain individual farmers, the attitude of respecting and uniting such a minority should be adopted. We must realize that our present concern for and proper care of the individual peasant will make it possible for them gradually to join the mutual-aid and cooperative organizations in the future and will also make it possible for us to reach our ultimate goal in the countryside—leading the whole peasantry to socialism and com‐ munism."

This statement was contained in a public document issued by the Communist Party of China, later reissued, and widely circulated. Like all such public documents, whether issued by the government or by the Communist Party, it was easily accessible not only in China, but also in Hongkong and other "listening posts," to any reporter interested in the facts. Nevertheless, in presenting it here I have the distinction of achieving an important scoop—only because my astute colleagues have chosen to look the other way. *

---

*In October, 1955, a New China News Agency dispatch from Peking reported a new resolution on agricultural development in China. American newspapers, such as the *Christian Science Monitor*, covered the new information under such headlines as "China's Peasants Being Herded Into Cooperatives."

A reading of this resolution reveals that while peasant membership in cooperatives had increased rapidly it was not because the peasants were "herded" but "reality has taught the peasants that they cannot continue their former way of life—individual farming, working on scattered, tiny pieces of land—and that the only way out is for a large number of people to unite and adopt the method of joint labor and collective management."

And as to "forced" speeding up of agricultural cooperatives: "Patience is required

In October, 1952, while covering the Asian and Pacific Regions Peace Conference in Peking, I took occasion to visit some small villages outlying the capital.

In the village of Bai Yen I found a busy farming community of slightly under 400 families, numbering 1,720 souls in all. Tang Te-yu, the village head, told me that the total farmland belonging to the village was 4,150 mou, a mou equaling one-sixth of an acre. Of this, he said, 1,485 mou or a little more than a third had been owned by nine landlords and eight rich peasant families. Another 1,285 mou had belonged to 104 middle peasant families. The remaining 279 families, consisting of poor and landless peasants, had owned only 1,380 mou. This distribution was fairly typical of farm areas in north China before liberation.

In the land reform the landless and poor peasants had been given an average of two mou per person, or about one and a half acres per family, to work for themselves. While this is a pathetically small amount of land by American farm standards, it can provide a living for a Chinese peasant family and represented a tremendous rise in their economic status. Along with the land three carts, four draft animals and some farm tools and utensils had been confiscated from the land-lords for common use by the peasants.

In the three years that had elapsed since land reform, Tang told me, their production of grain had increased from 100,000 catties a year to 1,200,000. Nor did he consider this strange. In the past, he explained, the landlords had done nothing about fertilization and ir-rigation, even on the land they occupied themselves. After land reform a mutual-aid team had dug irrigation ditches; and new methods of intensive plowing and planting had been introduced. Government loans had been received for seeds, fertilizer, new carts and draft animals.

Walking about the farm, he proudly pointed out the community's nine insecticide sprayers, eleven modern plows and twenty-four water-wheels. Before land reform, he said, there had been only two water-wheels, and no modern plow had ever been seen. Tang also pointed out several houses that were being repaired and two new ones under con-struction, and reminded me that neither repairs nor new buildings had

for those who, for the time being, do not wish to join cooperatives, even if they are poor or lower middle peasants. No attempt should be made to violate the principle of voluntariness and drag them into cooperatives against their will. A peasant may put forward and withdraw his name for cooperative membership repeatedly before he reaches a final decision with plenty of time to consider the matter."

been known in the area before. Some peasants were also making minor repairs or improvements on their own houses and barns. There were literacy classes one could attend in the village.

Later in the day I looked in at the village cooperative store, more or less equivalent to a general store in an American country town. The head of the cooperative there informed me that the store had been opened in the summer of 1949, immediately after land reform had been instituted. At that time, he said, more coarse than fine grain was being sold, but this had been reversed within two years. The village people were now consuming more rice as well as more white flour, the best indication of improved conditions.

The stock on display gave further evidence of a rise in peasant purchasing power. Goods ranged from shoes to shirts, notebooks, bottled beer, cooking oil and cotton cloth. At the cloth counter the round-faced woman clerk pointed out the quantity of colored and patterned cloth on hand along with the traditional plain blues and blacks. "Where four people were able to buy such cloth at the time of liberation," she said, "fifty can buy it now."

I wandered out into the road and talked to some of the villagers. One told me that the head of the cooperative store, Tsuei, had been the first elected village head after liberation, and later had been elected head of the cooperative. The latter job paid him a salary equivalent to 102 catties of millet a month, or two catties more than he received as village head. Both jobs paid less than the earnings of the average peasant, on the theory that neither was strictly productive work.

Farther along the road I talked with a young married woman who boasted that she was one of forty members of the Democratic Women's group which was part of the village government. She was also, she said, among the women who made up half the number of representatives from this village to the district people's representative conference.

Another woman, a forty-year-old peasant wife named Meng Shu-fang, told me that she and her husband, along with her mother-in-law and her younger son, lived on a farm of seven mou. A son of twenty had a job in an electric bulb factory in Peking. Prior to land reform the Mengs had worked as hired farm hands, and the family of five had lived in two rented rooms. After receiving land they had built a three-room house.

While we were talking, Mrs. Meng's husband came by, a tanned, sturdy-looking man with his head shaved bald. He insisted on telling me about his wife's new occupation which had brought her considerable note in the village. After they had acquired their land she had attended a course in chicken raising, and had then launched into that enterprise. Using her newly gained knowledge, she had built a two-story chicken coop. In the approved scientific manner she kept her chickens free of dirt and disease on the upper floor of the coop, had had them vaccinated, and kept their food receptacles sterilized. By these means she had avoided the huge losses through disease which plagued other broods in the vicinity.

Mrs. Meng was proud of the laying record of her twenty-eight hens, which averaged twenty-five eggs a month. She had gone on to mobilize other wives as chicken raisers, and was considered the leader among the fifty who were now using her techniques. A government training class had taught them how to inoculate their hens.

Mrs. Meng, who did most of the talking, suddenly broke into a wide smile that was motivated by more than mirth. She poked her finger at a gleaming incisor. "See my new tooth? I got it last summer at a dentist's in Peking, after needing it for many years. Yes, we have a little money left over to spend now. My husband and I can even buy new clothes once in awhile—something one only dreamed of in the old days!"

❧ 13 ❧

WAR AGAINST DISEASE

On a pleasant June morning in 1950, while walking along a Shanghai street, I was challenged by a uniformed nurse who asked to see my anti-cholera inoculation certificate. Unable to produce one, I was ushered into a street-corner tabernacle and given a shot on the house.

This arbitrary forty-five-second abridgement of my liberty and application of a sharp metal instrument to my person might, in hands more skilled than mine at a certain kind of reporting, have provided stimulating headlines for the home papers and conceivably another diplomatic incident. What had actually happened was that China's all-out public health drive had caught up with me and forcibly deprived me of my individualistic right to be a victim and carrier of cholera.

The inoculation campaign was only one phase of a comprehensive public health drive that began in the autumn of 1949, shortly after the adoption of the Common Program. Article 48 of that document declared: "Public health and medical work shall be expanded and attention shall be paid to the protection of mothers, infants and children." The drive had been launched in October on a broad front which included programs of education in medicine, nursing and midwifery as well as hospital building, intensive public health propaganda, diet instruction and a sanitation and refuse-removal drive.

All of this had been urgently needed in China for ages. While the civil war was still being fought a program of health education, sanitation and medical training had been going on in the old liberated areas. The job that remained to be done throughout China was of staggering size.

Under the old Nationalist government there had been a department labeled "Ministry of Health," but no organized health service. People interested in public health had referred to its paper program as "building hospitals in the air." Health institutions were confined to the large cities, and even these were inadequate except for the most privileged. No attempt was made to extend even rudimentary health services to the poorer classes in town or country.

When the new health campaign with its ambitious goals was announced, a good deal of skeptical comment was voiced among foreigners and unreconstructed Chinese of my acquaintance. "Sure, it's been overdue for centuries," was a familiar refrain at the French Club bar, "but only the Communists are crazy enough to undertake it!" My *amah*, Fu Ma, a rugged individualist in all things, dismissed it with a contemptuous, "Nobody is going to stick me with needles!" Sze Shing, the office boy at the *Review*, chuckled, "Suddenly all sickness will stop and everyone will live ten thousand years!"

I asked my friend Amos Wang, one of Shanghai's best-known physicians, what he thought about it. Dr. Wang, an obstetrician and a big man in his field by any standards, had kept pretty closely to his specialty and seldom had time to concern himself with public health problems. Armed with a Columbia medical degree, a genuine virtuoso talent and the requisite amount of personal charm, he had been baby doctor to the wealthy set in Shanghai, both foreign and Chinese. An infant who wasn't a Wang baby could scarcely have been said to have belonged.

Dr. Wang had traveled a good deal in China, and although not particularly public-health-minded he was well informed about the state of the medical profession in the country generally. He was not overcome with optimism at the prospects of putting China's people on a healthy basis.

"In Sinkiang province, with an area twice as big as France," he pointed out, "there are, believe it or not, just fifteen medically trained doctors. Oh sure, there are lots of Chinese-style doctors, but if the government wants effective medical personnel they're practically starting from the ground up. Twenty thousand Western type doctors in all China, with half a billion people—that's the story in a nutshell."

Nor were the difficulties confined to a shortage of modern physicians. Ho Cheng, Vice-Minister of Health under the new government, had issued a survey report of the difficulties that would have to be overcome in order to bring proper health conditions and medical care to the people of China.

The shortage of doctors, he reported, combined with an equally severe shortage of trained nurses, midwives and pharmacists, left the rural eighty percent of the population largely dependent on "superstitious healers and old-time midwives." The result was that an estimated six million people died every year from preventable infectious diseases—tuberculosis, smallpox, typhoid, dysentery, typhus, plague, cholera, black fever, and schistosomiasis or liver flukes.

Such medical personnel as there were practiced in the large cities. But the ordinary Chinese worker could not afford their services, and many doctors had too small a practice to get along. Hospital facilities and medical education were sadly inadequate, and the pharmacology of the country was largely dependent on imports.

Sanitary conditions were inconceivably bad. In the cities there were mounds of garbage that had not been cleared for years. The Kuomintang capital, Nanking, had seven miles of open sewers. Peking had 200,000 tons of garbage to be cleared out during the drive. In Shanghai a clogged sewer had been so long neglected that when it was rebuilt in 1950, houses were found to have been erected over the manholes.

It is therefore not hard to understand why epidemics had raged unchecked in China, while infant mortality was at the fantastically high rate of 250 per 1,000 births. For nearly a century some Western missions had labored to improve health conditions among the people, but with government indifference and public apathy they had had little effect.

The health drive was officially launched in October, 1949, by the new Minister of Health, Mme. Feng Yu-shiang, usually known by her maiden name—Li Teh-chuan. As one of the first steps in the drive, Mme. Feng organized an onslaught against public ignorance, apathy and superstition.

Medical teams were sent throughout the country to train the people in disease-prevention measures. They were equipped with lecture scripts, movie films, posters, exhibition materials, and handouts for newspapers and radio.

An eventual by-product of this drive was a nationwide uprising against rats, flies and mosquitoes. Bounties of so much apiece for dead rats and so much for a catty of winged pests were offered. During this crusade it became a common sight to see a peasant marching into his village health station with a couple of dozen rodent carcasses to collect his reward, or a city fellow weighing in a sack of deceased flies and mosquitoes. While these may sound like amusing didoes to outsiders, they were healthy indications of a widespread movement that played its indispensable part in the banishment or control of many ancient diseases.

One of the most effective means of education used was the health exhibit. I visited several in Shanghai—one during anti-TB week, another devoted to mother and child health, and another on general health and sanitation. In the large Race Course Building, once the preserve of Shanghai's foreign colony, the Public Health Bureau staged a maternity and child health exhibition in cooperation with forty hospitals. It was a show in a dual sense: whole families from outlying farms, who in all likelihood had never heard of a germ before, mingled with substantial-looking businessmen and their wives, factory workers with their broods of children, and white-collared professional people. Here a bent old peasant woman could be seen blinking at a chart that illustrated the importance of proper diet; there a self-conscious Shanghai miss gazing at life-size models showing the process of birth, and modern measures for prevention of infant diseases.

By the following midsummer the Health Ministry felt that sufficient preparatory work had been done for the calling of new China's first National Health Conference. It was held in Peking in August, 1950, and adopted these three main principles:

All health activities should be directed at serving the mass of the population, with chief emphasis on workers, peasants and soldiers;

Chief attention should be paid to preventive medicine;

Close unity must be maintained between doctors with modern scientific training and the old-style herb doctors, many of whom had a rudimentary pharmacal knowledge and rough common-sense skill at simple healing which provided a basis for modernized training.

A five-year medical training program, calling for medical institutions throughout China, was outlined. It called for a health center in each county with five to seven graduate doctors and medical assistants; and a health station in each district, with an assistant medical officer, a nurse, a midwife, and if possible a graduate physician. To carry out this program, in addition to providing adequate medical staff for factories and mines, 20,000 more doctors would be required, 30,000 assistant medical officers, 3,000 chemists and 1,500 dentists. Army medical personnel were to be given additional training or refresher courses and fitted into the program.

In addition, village schoolteachers were to be drawn into local health work, and materials for general mass education in health and sanitation were to be distributed. These were to include hygiene textbooks, pamphlets, posters and films.

The program was immediately set in motion. Two years later, when I made an extended trip to the Northeast and then down to the south, I saw health officers and clinics in almost every town of any size.

While a program of medical education takes years to carry out, mass health teaching and wholesale sanitation measures can, and did, bring early results.* During the first year of the general health drive the accumulated garbage of years or decades was removed from scores of cities and towns; sewers were newly installed or rebuilt; and stagnant pools were drained all over the country. Peking's three lakes and miles of moats received a badly needed cleaning, and her 600-year-old sewage system, clogged up and discharging into an open ditch in the heart of the city, was cleaned out and modernized.

Meanwhile the spring of 1950 saw the launching of a mass inoculation campaign in all the larger cities against cholera, for centuries one of China's worst plagues. In Shanghai it was undertaken with the help of the trade unions, the schools and several private hospitals. Twenty-five hundred medical workers took part in the drive, including several hundred nurses employed to perform the inoculations. The campaign was carried into the countryside, and newsreels soon appeared in the movie theatres showing peasant families being inoculated by field teams.

Besides the usual publicity apparatus of posters, street-corner lectures, newspaper stories and radio talks, loudspeaker trucks toured Shanghai calling on everybody to be inoculated. A power launch equipped with a loudspeaker and decked with bright banners and

---

*In June, 1956, Mme. Feng Yu-hsiang, Public Health Minister, announced that a number of major diseases including malaria, from which China had suffered for centuries, were gradually being brought under control to a point where their complete elimination could be predicted "in seven to twelve years."

graphic posters sailed up and down the Whangpoo River and Soochow Creek to reach the tens of thousands of boat dwellers.

Shanghai's people, thoroughly advised as to what anti-cholera inoculation could accomplish, came crowding to the stations that had been set up all over town and received their shots and their certificates. Passers-by who evinced no interest in the proceedings were stopped by sidewalk scouts and asked to produce their certificates of inoculation. If they had none to show, they were gently but resolutely urged inside and given a shot. No excuses accepted.

Thus a number of people who had neglected to keep their certificates handy received more than one shot. If you were determined to escape inoculation, you either had to be a powerfully convincing talker or else stay indoors. It was, on the whole, a vastly successful demonstration of mass obedience to official propaganda—almost as successful, in fact, as the parallel achievement I had witnessed in New York during a weekend visit in 1947, when the entire populace was calmly submitting to vaccination in a campaign to forestall a threatened smallpox epidemic.

14

UNFINISHED BUSINESS

One of the foremost figures in Shanghai of the Kuomintang days was a gentleman named Shiu Lin-chi. He enjoyed the popular title of King of the Buttock Burners.

Shiu Lin-chi's specialties were blackmail, kidnapping and extortion. Whether he was the biggest operator in his particular line of business I am not sure, but he was without doubt one of the most successful. Shiu's method of assuring a steady influx of revenue was simple. He would select a likely prospect, gather together a force of trusted thugs, surround the victim's house, and force an entry. The victim could yell for the police until his cheeks were purple; the police heads were Nationalist lodge brethren, as it were, of Mr. Shiu, and they could not in all decency interfere.

When Shiu had achieved the hospitality of his selected prospect's home he would not be so impolite as to ask him for his money. That, for one thing, might have yielded only partial results. Shiu had a more subtle way, the way that had earned him his unique sobriquet. He would relieve his host of a portion of his clothing and apply a lighted candle to the most prominent part of his person thus exposed. This was apt to bring prompt results.

If it appeared to Shiu that his victim was not reacting quickly enough or handsomely enough, he had a surefire finish to his act. He would direct his men to douse other members of the family with gasoline and set them ablaze. This invariably brought results, and Shiu

Lin-chi would depart richer than he had come. Of course many re-
cipients of his treatment died or were scarred or crippled for life, but
that was all a part of the business. And Shiu's business was not one in
which the occupational hazards are borne by the entrepreneur.

Shiu was in his late thirties when his fame first reached my ears
while I was working on the *China Press* in 1948. He had then been
operating for at least a dozen years—first under the Kuomintang, then
under the Japanese occupationists, and then after 1945 under the
Kuomintang again. Parallel with his extortion activities, and of great
importance both to the Japanese and to the Kuomintang, went his
services as an informer and a strongarm boss in keeping down popular
unrest and dealing with complaints.

When the People's Government took over in 1949 he was not
immediately apprehended. Instead he was given a chance, no doubt
foolishly, to improve his ways. Having no more Kuomintang friends in
the government to protect him, he had to operate more circumspectly.
But he continued to observe his fealty to China's former rulers by
spreading dark predictions and alarming rumors about the new regime.
This brought him the inconvenience of occasional arrests. But each
time Shiu Lin-chi went back to his old habits as soon as he was
released.

At last, in the spring of 1951, Shiu Lin-chi was arrested again along
with many kindred characters. This time he was brought to trial, found
guilty of many crimes including murder, and executed.

In Shanghai, as in more than one large American city, gangs and
gang leaders were powerful in municipal affairs. The power of the
hoong-bang (Red gang) and the *ching-bang* (Green gang) was openly
acknowledged, and their bosses were honored and rewarded by the municipal government for services rendered. Tu Yueh-sen, called China's
Al Capone because of the magnitude of his operations, was a respected
figure in government circles and an indispensable ally to Shanghai
officials. The connection between these gangs and the Nationalists was
well appreciated everywhere; Chiang Kai-shek himself was a member
of the Green gang in the early twenties.

There were also the great superstitious societies which flourished
both in the cities and in the countryside. In north China the dominant one was the Yi Guan Dao; in the great hinterland of the southwest it was the Ge Lao Huei (Elder Brother Society). While purvey-

ing mystic charms and secret rites for the propitiation of the gods, and other mumbo jumbo, these societies also engaged in blackmail and sold "protection" to the poor in town and country. The Yi Guan Dao, in fact, had a record of shootings, kidnappings, and poisonings reminiscent of the armed desperado bands of medieval Europe.

All kinds of private and public activity required the sanction and payoff of these gangs, from the granting of a pedlar's license to the building of a house or the negotiation of a labor agreement. Their control of the transport workers was particularly notorious. No transport worker could get a job unless he bought the "protection" of a gang. Thus the gangs served the Kuomintang officials both as strong-arm terror squads and as collection agencies.

Shiu Lin-chi the buttock burner and Tu Yueh-sen were by no means the only men of distinction in Shanghai's community of racket bosses.

There was Cheng Wei, forty-year-old leader of the Thin Dagger Gang. During the Japanese occupation he had formed an alliance with the puppet head of the Shanghai secret police. After V-J Day he had transferred his services to the Kuomintang secret police and carried on as before.

The Japanese, and later the Kuomintang, gave Cheng immunity from the law, allowing him to extort and bully to his heart's content. In return he served them as an informer; and as a "wang," local underworld "king," he helped keep the people quiet despite oppression and hunger. His gang was always at hand to beat up a newspaper editor or a leader in the student movement or anyone else who might be suspected of stirring up trouble.

As a sideline, Cheng dealt in the lucrative prostitution racket and owned three brothels of his own. When he was finally arrested and tried, one of the principal witnesses against him was a former nurse who charged that he had abducted her and forced her to become his concubine. She had been working in a dental clinic at the time she caught his fancy, and he had simply carried her off, no one daring to complain to the police.

In addition to this and other rapings, Cheng was charged with two murders and with being implicated in many others. It was brought out at his trial that he had been connected with the notorious extortion house at 76 Jessfield Road in Shanghai, a Japanese counterpart of the Nazi *braunhauser*, where many people had been tortured and killed by the Japanese and the Chinese puppets working under them.

Then there was Sun Wen-liang, another extortionist and the leader of a gang that practiced its own specialty in the art of terrorization— burial alive. His victims numbered well over a hundred. Like most of the gangleaders he had hired out first to the Japanese, then to the Kuomintang.

Hwang Kwan-fu, another gang murderer, convicted of eight kill- ings, had merited special fame through his habit of chopping up his victims' bodies.

Literally thousands of local terrorist leaders like these, including hundreds in Shanghai alone, had held undisputed sway in old China.

One of the most venerable of these gang rulers, known as the Tiger of Bao-an Road, gave his age as sixty-eight when he was finally hailed before a People's Court in Shanghai. His history went back to the early 1920's, when he had lent his services to the British police in the old International Settlement. In return for their protection and non- interference, he had provided them with information about people in his district who he thought might profitably be accused of a connec- tion with the Sun Yat-sen nationalist movement. Since those days Shanghai had seen many political shifts and changes, but the Tiger of Bao-an Road had survived them all, effortlessly shifting his allegiance from the British to the Japanese gendarmerie and then to Chiang Kai-shek's secret police.

In general, as with Shiu Lin-chi, the buttock burner, the new gov- ernment did not get around to cracking down on these racketeers for some time. Most, though not all, of them were known to have direct ties with the Nationalists and to be promoting fear and uncertainty in the community. They were advising workers not to exert themselves above their minimum work quotas, and not to carry out the Common Program because Chiang would soon return to oust his usurpers. Many also were thought to be agents of the continuing American campaign of psychological warfare against the new regime. Announcements from Washington about sums of money allocated for precisely this kind of activity did nothing to allay such suspicions.

Nevertheless, save for occasional arrests, some of which led to convictions and more to releases with warnings, no real effort was made to clean up this state of affairs for nearly two years after the changeover. Just what accounted for this delay I do not know. I suspect, however, that it reflected overconfidence on both sides.

The gang leaders, having operated with impunity for many years, could not believe that this situation was going to be changed even by a revolution. In addition, many believed their own propaganda about the early return of the Kuomintang. The new government, on its part, was so confident of the completeness of its victory that it left the solution of the problem to time and patience with perhaps a dash of moral suasion thrown in.

It is quite possible too, though I saw no tangible proof of it, that Nationalist agents had penetrated the new government to an extent where they were able to divert vigorous action against the counter-revolutionary nuisance (which is what it amounted to) by minimizing its importance. Both national and local adminstrations under the new government contained officials who had held posts under Chiang Kai-shek. Because experienced personnel were badly needed, they had been assimilated into the new People's Government after declaring their change of allegiance. Most undoubtedly meant it, but by no means all.

In any event, the overconfidence shown on both sides proved mistaken. The government was wrong in its belief that the gangsters and saboteurs would change with a few arrests and admonitions. And the racketeers were misguided in their hope that they could get away with it indefinitely or that a rebirth of the old regime would save them.

By the time the situation was resolved, however, it had become thoroughly serious. People were writing letters to newspapers complaining that gang activities in their neighborhoods made life as hazardous as in the old Kuomintang days. Gossip could be heard about it in restaurants, in the buses, on theatre queues. In Shanghai delegations visited the police stations to demand action.

Finally, in April, 1951, the Shanghai city administration lowered the boom. In a roundup lasting several weeks, heavily manned police vans trundled out to the racketeer haunts and collected all known gang leaders and henchmen. The move, when it finally came, had been thoroughly planned. There was little resistance, and few of the gangsters and agents escaped. Some managed to hide out in the city and some drifted into the countryside. Mopping-up operations, lasting several more weeks, brought most of them in.

Similar roundups took place at about the same time in cities and towns throughout China. The national government, having at last decided to deal with the mess, made the cleanup nationwide. In Shanghai alone several thousand major and minor thugs were arrested and brought to trial. I do not know what the total number was in China as a whole, but Shanghai's situation was by far the worst.

When word got about that the gangsters were safely in custody, many people who had suffered at their hands came to the station houses to offer testimony. Hoodlums like Cheng Wei of the Thin Dagger Gang were confronted at their trials by scores of surviving victims and by relatives of those they had murdered.

Not all of those arrested in this drive were gangsters or terrorists. Some were Nationalist counter-revolutionary agents who operated on loftier levels. There was, for example, a talented stage director named Chu Shi, head of the acting and directing section of the Shanghai Dramatic School. He had held this position under the Kuomintang and was kept in it under the Peking government.

Through my interest in the Chinese theatre I had come to know Chu, and had been impressed with his lively and original mind and his scholarly knowledge of Chinese drama. When the new government took over in Shanghai he had made the transition smoothly. Still young, and at home in the politically advanced student movement, he had always been regarded as more sympathetic to the new ideas than to the old.

One evening in April, 1951, I met Chu Shi at a party in the home of some American friends. There he held forth on a new motion picture called *Between Husband and Wife*, whose theme was the need for compromise between marital partners in order to adjust their relationship to the new conditions under the 1950 Marriage Law. Chu, taking the approved political stand, thought the picture had educational value and suggested that it could have gone even farther in asserting the new rights of women.

He left the party shortly after midnight, apparently in excellent spirits and unaware, as was everyone else, that this was the opening night of the big cleanup drive. Next morning came the astonishing news that Chu Shi had been picked up on the way home and jailed on the charge of counter-revolutionary activity over a long period as an agent of the Kuomintang.

At his trial, details of which were avidly followed by Shanghai's theatrical community, Chu was accused of having been one of the Kuomintang agents who had infested the student movement during

Nationalist days. He had been directly responsible, according to the testimony, for the deaths of a number of students whose names he had turned in and who had subsequently been executed.

Chu Shi was convicted of the charges and, because of the student executions laid at his door, sentenced to death. But he was granted a two-year probationary period for education and reform, at the end of which his sentence was commuted on the basis of achieved rehabilitation. When I left Shanghai for home, six months after this, Chu was free and working again in the Shanghai theatre, though in a lesser capacity than before.

In the trials of those arrested in the cleanup drive, ordinary criminals were tried in the regular criminal courts. Those against whom there was evidence of activity as Kuomintang agents were tried in special courts, political, not military in character. The trial procedure in these cases was elaborate and provided for a review of the trial record and decision by a public board of examiners. In Shanghai the Examination Committee, as it was called, was appointed by the Municipal Council which in turn had been established by a city-wide People's Representative Conference.

The Shanghai Examination Committee included Wang Yung-seng, editor of the *Ta Kung Bao* (called the *New York Times* of China), which continued to be published as a privately-owned daily; Miss Hu Tze-yin, a well-known Shanghai business woman and general secretary of the Federation of Industry and Commerce; Professor Lu Yi-tao, an eminent biologist; Yung I-sen, one of the owners of the privately-operated Sung Sing Cotton Mills; Wu Yun-tsu and O. S. Liu, local manufacturers; Chang Chin-yi, dean of the University of Shanghai; Chen Ren-bing, professor of government at St. John's University; Y. T. Wu, publication secretary of the National Committee of the YMCA; Cora Deng, general secretary of the National Committee of the YWCA; Han Shueh-chang, a prominent Shanghai woman lawyer; and seventy-four-year-old Jiang Yung, one of China's best known jurists, a justice of the highest tribunal in the Ching Dynasty before 1912.

The trials were not open to the public, but the Examination Committee had the right to be represented by one of its members as an observer. He was empowered to examine documents offered in evidence and to demand additional facts from either side. In addition, the committee in important or complicated cases had the right to designate one of its members to sit as an associate judge in the trial.

Chen Ren-bing, the St. John's University professor who was on the Examination Committee, was one of my Shanghai acquaintances. He had spent several years in the United States studying law and other subjects, and had taken degrees at the University of Michigan and the University of Southern California. Discussing the trials with him, I pointed out that the denial of admission to the public was perhaps the one thing most difficult for Western minds to accept.

Chen seemed unimpressed. "I am aware that political trials in the West—those in which political dissenters are convicted for what they believe or teach or propagandize—are open to the public.

"But what does that achieve from the standpoint of justice? Your trials could be attended by the public in limitless numbers without in the least affecting the conduct of a judge who happened to be prejudiced, or of a biased jury chosen from a special class. And if a prosecutor wished to bring forth perjured testimony from witnesses who had been told what to say, the presence of the public could not prevent him.

"Nor is your press likely to raise an outcry or even give passing attention to such injustices where the victim has been sufficiently denounced beforehand. In contrast, it is the duty of our Examination Committees, as the people's representatives, to seek out and correct any abuses in a trial, and we have the power to do so."

Chen maintained that the arrests and trials of these gangsters as Kuomintang agents were based not on their "thoughts" but on specific crimes charged against them. When I asked him about trials before "howling mobs," such as had been reported abroad, he laughed.

"Have you seen any such trials?" I admitted that I had not.

"No. Neither has your housekeeper, and neither has my secretary. Neither has the rice dealer or the book vendor or the pedicab driver. And that is so for two reasons. First, these so-called trials-by-mob are not trials, not intended as trials, and not represented by the government as trials.

"Secondly, they are not held before 'mobs.'

"They are meetings held after the regular court trial and conviction of important criminals, in which the evidence is repeated to an audience of government functionaries and the testimony re-enacted. Those present at these meetings are members of the local People's Representative Council, and some specially invited guests who represent people's organizations. The meetings are held to demonstrate to the men and women of the Representative Council what kind of crimes have been committed in the name of the Kuomintang counter-revolution, and to demonstrate to the public that the criminals are at last being dealt with."

What happened finally to those found guilty in this 1951 cleanup drive? A good many of the racketeers, as I have indicated, were guilty of murder or rape or other capital crimes on the basis of massive evidence. These were sentenced to death. But in all except the most extreme cases they were given a two-year probationary period, according to the custom in new China, to prove their capacity for rehabilitation by "reform through labor."

If at the end of that time they gave evidence of repentance and a willingness to fit into the new social organization, their sentences were commuted to prison terms in work camps for varying periods of time according to their records. Lesser criminals were sentenced to "reform through labor," the term used in China for what is called "imprisonment at hard labor" elsewhere.

When I questioned Professor Chen about the Western conception of Chinese "slave labor camps," his answer was that they are no different from prisoners' work-camps in other countries, except in one respect.

"Convicted criminals do not lead a life of idleness in any country," he said. "It is my understanding that they work for their upkeep. The difference is that when our criminals are released after a period of 're-form through labor' they have been re-educated and made ready for a decent life, whereas in other countries they often go on where they had left off."

The 1951 drive rid new China of a double disease: a long-standing criminal element and a troublesome counter-revolutionary force. The popularity of the former achievement was evidenced by the number of people who came to Shanghai police stations to express their relief and gratitude. The cleanup of the Kuomintang agitators removed a persistent obstacle to China's advance toward the new goals she seeks.

15

UNFINISHED BUSINESS II.

Another item of unfinished business, less dramatic but no less urgent, was taken up a year or so later. Its effects became visible to me one evening in a rather startling way.

On the evening in question I went to one of Shanghai's popular theatres, the Lyceum, which at the time was still British-owned. As one of the few foreigners who regularly frequented this place, I had formed a speaking acquaintanceship with its Chinese manager, who incidentally was the husband of one of Shanghai's most popular movie actresses. It was his habit to stand in the lobby and greet arrivals; but tonight he was not at his usual post. Another face smiled at me as I passed through the doors.

I found my friend however, inside the theatre. He took my ticket and courteously, though a little self-consciously, directed me to my seat. He was the manager no more; he had become an usher.

During the intermission I sought him out and broached as tactfully as I could the subject of his precipitate demotion. He talked frankly, though more than a little ruefully, about it.

"I am being disciplined," he said. "I was caught last month pocketing a portion of the theatre receipts. In fact I had been doing it for some time."

He paused, waiting for some comment. I couldn't seem to think of any.

"It is the *Wu Fan* movement," he continued. "I suppose I should

128

have known that they would catch up with me. Besides not being honest, I have not been intelligent. I ignored the warnings, and now this is the manner of my punishment and reform. For six months I must do this humble work, and then if my fellow workers decide that I can be trusted perhaps I will get my old job back again."

I asked him why he had decided to try embezzlement. Wasn't his salary adequate? Wasn't his wife earning a good income? The former manager shrugged.

"Old customs are not easy to cast off. Before liberation, as you know, everybody helped himself to a percentage of any money that passed through his hands. It was the thing to do. When the people's government took over it was frowned upon and became unpopular. But since then many people I know have gone back to the old way, despite the people's government. When I saw others again enriching themselves without extra work, I though I might as well do it too."

"And what about those others you saw?" I asked him.

He broke into a pleased grin. "I will mention no names, peng yeou, but a man I know who used to come here often—he was the purchasing agent of a large printing plant—is now cleaning and oiling the presses because he was found to be accepting gifts from paper manufacturers in return for contracts. He wishes he had been more wise— at least sufficiently so to be more honest."

The Wu Fan movement, of which the ex-theatre manager had spoken, was a drive against corrupt business practices. It was then in full swing throughout China. His plight and that of his friend, the printing executive, was being shared by many others in positions of responsibility who had not been able to resist temptation.

Along with the Wu Fan campaign another vigorous movement, called San Fan, was combating corruption or laxity among civil servants. Both drives were sponsored by the government. Both were felt to be necessary to counteract a tendency toward the return to old habits. It was partly, as the former manager of the Lyceum Theatre had intimated, a swing-back of the pendulum from the austerity which the new government had brought with it in the first days of liberation.

In any country where the people have little to say about their government, the civil service tends to become a power unto itself, preoccupied with the protection of its own interests. In China, from ancient times down to the fall of the Nationalists, a class of paper-workers numbering hundreds of thousands had operated within the safe walls of officialdom, skilled in the techniques of delay, buck-passing, playing politics for status or prestige, getting and holding office through pull. Educated and in some cases technically skilled, they made rituals of documents, protocol and record-keeping, were adept at foozling the files and crossing the cross-references so as to keep themselves indispensable.

This folderol was done away with by the new government, but many petty bureaucrats were held over in their jobs on the promise to reform their ways. As it turned out, this was more easily said than accomplished, and the old abuses gradually returned.

San Fan means literally "Three Anti's"—in this case anti-corruption, anti-waste and anti-bureaucracy. These were the government objectives in its *San Fan* drive. *Wu Fan*, or "Five Anti's," was directed against uneconomic or anti-social practices in private business—bribing of officials, evasion of taxes, theft of public property, selling adulterated or substandard products, and ferreting out official information for the purpose of private speculation.

The campaign, carried on simultanously in government and private business, was generally known as the *San Fan-Wu Fan* movement. It had begun toward the end of 1951 in Peking. Immediately following Chinese New Year's 1952, it was extended throughout China.

In private business, as in government, the prevalence of graft and corruption in old China is a thrice familiar story. During the last hundred years the influx of foreign investors and operators bent on quick fortunes intensified such practices. In the two decades following the First World War they reached their peak, with Kuomintang-allied financiers and industrialists using modern big-business methods to conduct graft on a tremendous scale.

In the last days of Nationalist China the evidences of this were to be seen on every hand. In the metropolis of Shanghai graft had become literally the chief industry. The fortunes amassed by the Chiangs, Kungs, Soongs and Chens in those days, even without America's largesse, must have put them among the world's richest families.

The changeover brought with it a set of new practices. Many of the revolution's leaders were men and women who had never known personal wealth, and their ideas of achievement had little if anything to do with it. A fanatically rigid set of regulations were put into effect against graft and malfeasance in private business on the one hand and in the public service on the other. You could still make money in business if you produced goods the people needed—really needed—but the cut, the tip, the bribe, the "special service charge" were out.

This worked well, and to most people it made sense. For most people, to the extent of perhaps ninety-five percent of the population, had always been the victims rather than the beneficiaries of corrupt practices. The Spartan honesty of the new public servants brought a shock of surprise to people nurtured in the old ways; but without this the initial steps toward reconstruction could scarcely have been accomplished so quickly or successfully.

But as times improved, a certain relaxation of standards set in. This was true both among government officials and in private business circles; but it was much more prevalent in the latter. While the revolution has brought a new breed of men into the government, China's businessmen under the new regime were still generally the same who had operated under the old. They had lived all their lives under a system where bribery at every step was taken for granted, where nobody except the peasants ever thought of paying taxes, and where such practices as shortweighting, adulteration of goods, and any kind of theft that could be brought off, were considered merely good business.

It was doubtless too much to expect that these people would suddenly reform under the new government. As my theatre-manager friend reminded me, "old customs are not easy to cast off." It is unlikely that many of them tried very hard once they realized that they were still being permitted to stay in business, or even that they understood very clearly what the new regulations were all about. Whoever heard of paying taxes? Whoever heard of fair competition or honest dealing?

And so the old practices continued or, where they had been temporarily dropped, reappeared. And to some extent they involved government workers, too. For where a bribe is passed there must be a taker as well as a giver. Like the old-line businessmen, plenty of Kuomintang holdovers in the civil service began reverting to their ancient customs.

Nor were all the revolutionary stalwarts, many of whom had spent more than a decade in the old Communist areas, able to withstand the temptations placed in their way. Yet at no time did the relaxation of civic morality among public servants reach epidemic proportions. Po Yi-po, a member of the Central Committee of the Communist Party, in a speech delivered late in 1952 reviewing the accomplishments of the *San Fan-Wu Fan* drive along with other movements, said that "4½ percent of the government workers were found guilty in varying degrees of corruption, waste and bureaucratism and dealt with accordingly. . . . The most serious cases were given judicial punishment," the implication being that minor offenders got off with an admonition or public exposure.

In contrast, Po Yi-po reported that among private business firms investigated in nine major cities including Peking, Shanghai, Tientsin, and Canton, "Seventy-six percent were found guilty of various illegal transactions." These "illegal transactions" included tax evasion, which had always been automatic on the part of businessmen.

When the *San Fan* drive got under way (the movement to correct civil service practices) the commonest crime was found to be not bribe-taking or theft, but that wide calendar of offenses which the Chinese call "bureaucracy."

Included under "bureaucracy" in China, and in the new regime particularly, are such malpractices as red tape, undue officiousness, obeying the letter but not the spirit of a law or a directive, keeping aloof from one's colleagues, and petty tyranny.

Aloofness not only from colleagues but from the people at large is considered the gravest of these offenses. Government servants are constantly exhorted to keep close to the people they serve, to be familiar with their desires and opinions. If this sounds never-never-landish to anyone in a Western country I can't help it; it is what happens in China. Government employes, from bureau heads to petty officials, who neglect to seek the ideas of their subordinates and of the townspeople and villagers are considered guilty of "bureaucracy." In the *San Fan* drive some of them were sharply dealt with.

The devices used in the drive were the familiar ones of mass publicity and self-correction. It doesn't take much to popularize a movement against public graft or inefficiency. Through articles and cartoons in the press, through posters in the streets and on trolleys and buses, the people were exhorted to demand a tightening-up of standards among their officials.

At the same time, within the government departments and bureaus, a campaign of criticism and self-criticism was launched. Staff meetings were held at which executives were required to give their subordinates an account of their administration. If these reports were not deemed sufficiently full or self-critical, the underlings had the right to demand further facts and franker analysis. But proof of any charges was required to forestall squabbles motivated by petty jealousies. There was no need to fear retaliation from superiors, because anyone had the right to carry charges higher up.

In the Wu Fan movement, the "Five Anti's" directed against bribery, tax dodging, theft of public property, cheating on product quality and theft of official information, the chief target was the bribery of government officials for the sake of business favors. Not only money was used for this purpose, but gifts ranging from a suit of clothes to the favors of the enterprising businessman's wife or daughter.

All this followed a well-established etiquette of the old days: first came the initial feeler, then the invitation to drinks and a simple dinner, then a sumptuous banquet or two to seal friendship, then gifts and commissions, and finally the regular payment of bribes. In return the businessman naturally felt entitled to special influence, special information and, when possible, the direct placing of advantageous contracts.

The alertness of this type of business go-getter was astonishing, and sometimes amusing. Once an official in the East China Ministry of Industry lost his fountain pen and posted a notice on the office bulletin board. Within three days he received ten imported Parker 51's from brokers doing business with his office, each of whom with a straight face claimed to have found the missing pen.

Other old-time practices that reappeared, now that businessmen were feeling their oats again, were price gouging, the supplying of inferior materials on government orders, and the surreptitious altering of specifications. Some of the bigger firms even began forming combines to corner raw materials and do in their competitors. Most of these shenanigans required the collusion of one or more government employes, but with the powerful inducements offered many such were found.

When the Wu Fan crackdown came, with the arrest of some of the influence-buyers and other chiselers, general business ethics tidied themselves up with alacrity. The government still depended to a large extent upon private business and had no interest in inflicting widespread punishment upon it, but in reforming its methods. Extensive government orders, in fact, continued to be placed with private business firms, including some that were under investigation, even at the height of the *Wu Fan* movement.

Inevitably, reports of the drive reaching the ears of American and British journalists outside China set off a series of comic-strip stories about a "business purge" accompanied by "mass suicides" of luckless victims. These made interesting reading for me after I had noted the thriving plants owned by some of these "victims," and after having seen the owners in the theatres, restaurants, dancehalls or shops, looking quite healthy. Such stories, always predictable in pattern, remind me of the Western press reports in 1951 of the "suicide" of Miss Wu Yi-fan, head of the one-time American-missionary-sponsored girls' school, Ginling College, in Nanking. In the fall of 1952, when I was in Nanking, I looked up Miss Wu, found her well and happy at her old job, and had dinner with what was presumably her highly animated corpse. This kind of journalism, I suppose, does no harm except to truth and to the prospects for peaceful living and survival among nations; and it does keep the home papers lively.

Where the names of specific persons were mentioned in these newspaper accounts it was always fun to check and compare the stories with reality. Usually, however, the victims dispatched in these stories were anonymous, like the "informants" or "sources" to which the stories were attributed. But when our subscription copy of *Time* magazine for March 24, 1952, arrived at the *Review* office, we found on page 24 a tale with names and an address.

It appeared that in Shanghai, at the corner of Canton and Fukien Roads, there had flourished the Unsurpassed Prosperity Medicine shop, owned by a Mr. Chang Kuo-liang. Mr. Chang had borne the nickname of "The *Lungyen* King" (*lungyen* meaning "Dragon's Eyes") because of his fame as a brewer and purveyor of tonics made with a syrup of *lungyen* nuts. But now, alas, Mr. Chang had to be spoken of in the past tense. According to the story, he had been driven to kill himself and his wife, his five children, his seven employes and all of their wives and children because the employes had denounced him to the authorities as a private-business malefactor.

Bill Powell and I, impressed with this grim story of massive retaliation composed in *Time*'s throbbing style, dropped in at the address given in the account, a bare five-minute walk from our office. Entering the shop, we encountered a substantial-looking citizen standing near the door, wearing a grey Chinese gown. We asked him if he could tell us anything about the late Mr. Chang Kuo-liang, the *Lungyen* King.

"I am Chang Kuo-liang," said the man. "What would you like to know?"

Suppressing an impulse to ask him whether he was dead, we showed him the *Time* story and translated its macabre curtain line: "Before the meal was half-over, all the banqueters were dead. The *Lungyen* King had killed them all and himself as well, with a liberal seasoning of potassium cyanide."

Mr. Chang looked at us a little strangely, looked at the magazine, and asked me to repeat what I had read to him. After I read it again he shrugged. "I don't understand. I have killed no one. And as for me, here I am!"

"What about your seven employees?" Bill asked him.

"Why, they are here," Chang said, waving his hand toward the interior of the store. "There are my four clerks. Two others, apprentices, are working in the back, as is my bookkeeper. Would you like to meet them?"

We looked over at the four clerks, who stood staring at us from behind their counters.

"Never mind, thanks. So your employes haven't been informing on you?"

"Yes, they have," Chang said calmly. "I dodged my taxes for this year and last, and I had been selling colored water for tonic. Two of my employees said they didn't think I ought to do such things under the people's government, but I told them not to concern themselves. So they went to their union and complained."

"What happened?"

"I paid my taxes and a fine and promised to run an honest business. So now we are all on good terms, and I feel better."

Bill glanced at a display of dark brown medicine bottles. "That tonic of yours," he asked Chang—"is it really good?"

"It is truly excellent," said the *Lungyen* King solemnly. "You can trust me; there is no water in it."

We assured him we would like to try it some time, and left. Mr. Chang gave us a friendly wave as we departed. I waved the copy of *Time* in reply. Somebody, it struck me, had been spreading poison around. But it wasn't Mr. Chang.

The truth about China's "business purge" is that by the end of 1953, nearly two years after the Wu Fan movement, thirty-eight percent of China's industrial output was still being produced by private business. This proportion, just 4.3 percent under that of the preceding year (when the cleanup drive was in full blast) reflects the government's long-range plan of *gradual* steps toward socialization, and hardly indicates a "purge." The privately-owned thirty-eight percent, incidentally, was in much healthier condition through the elimination of graft, and was making higher profits than ever before, in common with the increasing prosperity of the country as a whole. Half of China's retail trade also was in the hands of private enterprise at the close of 1953.

When I was getting ready to depart for home toward the end of that year I was given a farewell dinner at Sun Ya, one of Shanghai's largest restaurants, by three Chinese friends, two of whom happened to be well-to-do businessmen. One was Mr. Hua, the owner of an elevator manufacturing concern inherited from his father after the new government came to power, and the other was "Fatty" Chien, who had a large fabric shop at the corner of Szechuan and Peking Roads. They seemed to be in high spirits, shared with me rather more yellow wine than was prudent, bore no discernible scars or bruises either on their physiques or their psyches, and had no pathetic stories to tell me, a newspaperman returning to the United States, about their sufferings as businessmen in Red China. I suppose the whole thing may have been an optical illusion, but I doubt it.

⪻ **16** ⪼

SPEAKING OF WORKERS

China has a special kind of national celebrity today. He (or she) is photographed for the newspapers, interviewed over the radio, handed bouquets in the newsreels, acclaimed in "personal appearances." He (or she) is not, as once upon a time, a statesman or a general or an opera singer or a movie star.

He (or, again, she) is a *lao doong moh fan*—a "model worker."

After we Western sophisticates have had our snicker over this, it might be well to reflect on its meaning. I can testify, for one thing, that the public adulation now showered upon Chinese industrial eager beavers and quota-busters is neither synthetic nor imposed. The Chinese people happen to feel that way. They are as intelligent as any other people, and they have become convinced that more production means a better living.

Believing that their whole future will stand or fall by the industrial progress of their country, they have become thoroughly production-happy. Whatever anyone else may feel about it, at the rate she has been developing since 1949 China is virtually certain to become the leading industrial nation in the East by 1960, and quite conceivably will have surpassed most West European nations by a decade or so after that.

This very sizeable statement is based on the achievements already realized toward fulfillment of the country's first Five Year Plan, and on the steadily accelerating pace of progress toward the goals set in the fifteen-year program. A report of the United Nations Economic Commission for Asia and the Far East, issued in October, 1955, cited an increase in industrial output of seventeen percent in China during the previous year, while most Western countries showed little or no increase. The first Five Year Plan calls for a minimum increase in production of fourteen percent each year—or at least seventy percent for the first five years—an unprecedented rate of industrial growth.*

But my theme at the moment is not industrial growth; it is people. In China, as elswhere, it is people who make news; and by the fall of 1952, when I made a swing around the big eastern cities from what used to be called Manchuria in the far northeast to Canton in the south, working people and their accomplishments were big news everywhere.

There was, for example, Wang Wen-shan at the Number One Machine Tool Factory in Mukden, who had developed a new method of cutting oil rings. It enabled him to increase his output a dozenfold and won him the title of model worker.

There was Ni Chi-ying, twenty-year-old foundry worker at the Changshientien Railway Works near Peking, leader of a production team that was regularly knocking off six days' work in five.

There was Ho Chien-shiu, seventeen-year-old textile worker in Tsingtao. By her new spinning technique developed on the job, she had made it possible for workers to tend twice as many spindles with the same expenditure of energy and to cut waste by more than eighty percent.

There was Liu Fu-chi, waterworks engineer of Tientsin, who had just won his model worker's badge by building the town of Shinshiang its first sanitary water system.

There was the celebrated Tien Kwei-ying, China's first woman locomotive driver, who had ignored the protests of her family and the gibes of old-fashioned males to learn her unconventional trade.

There was Lin Tsun-ching, an installation foreman at the Ho Chi Elevator Company in Shanghai, whose team of workers could install elevators faster than anybody had ever installed them before.

There were thousands more in factories large, small and middle-sized. Taken together, and added to the twelve million other indus-

---

*According to a survey issued by UNECAFE on February 1, 1956, China's increase in industrial output since 1952 was the highest in Asia. "The increase in industrial production was achieved," it stated, "by a fuller utilization of existing capacity, installation of new capacity and improved labor productivity."

trial workers for whom they were setting the pace, these labor heroes were carrying forward before the indifferent eyes of the Western world a production boom such as America might be proud of.

View it however you may, the story of the workingman in post-Chiang China is a thoroughgoing success story. On the average, though still a poor man in terms of accumulated wealth and current earnings, his income is from two and a half to three times greater than in 1949. And in other respects he is correspondingly better off. He works a normal eight-hour day instead of ten, twelve or even sixteen hours. He now has employment stability for the first time in his life. The value of his money, too, has been stabilized. He is covered by life, health, accident and old-age insurance for which he pays no premiums. He has the protection of a highly-organized union whose grievance and negotiating functions are encouraged and protected by the government, whether in private or in state employment. And he enjoys a position in society comparable to that of the doctor or the lawyer in the West.

The millenium, it is needless to add, has not overtaken the Chinese workingman. He lacks many luxuries and conveniences enjoyed by his counterpart in the United States and Britain, though less noticeably so in Italy or Spain or Latin America or the Middle East. It will be a long time before he acquires the blessings of mechanical refrigeration, television or the automobile. But his lot has immensely improved, and and there is every sign that it will continue to improve.

The reasons for the change are manifold. They have to do partly with the ending of the civil war and the resumption of industry on a full-time basis, but with many other things as well. Essentially the change results from a new outlook and morale shared by everyone in present-day China from the Minister of Heavy Industry down to the unskilled laborer. The ingredients of this new morale include national pride, new incentives for personal effort and ambition, sweepingly new methods of work, and improved social status. These have made possible significant, and sometimes spectacular, increases in production and, in turn, have had a beneficial effect both on the national economy and on the wellbeing of the individual worker.

Heard everywhere during the beginning years of the new People's Republic were the words "rationalization of industry." The term "rationalization" means exactly what it says—the bringing of logical order into a field where chaos existed before.

When the new government took over, China's factories were in a state of backwardness and neglect. Neither the Chinese entrepreneur nor the foreign investor had much interest in modern industrial methods. Labor was cheap; hours were long. To get more production you worked the help a little harder. Labor-saving machinery, short-cut methods, safety devices were academic considerations, something for "advanced" countries.

Add to this the effects of the Japanese war and occupation, the civil war and the irresponsible misrule of most of the country by Chiang Kai-shek's government. By the time the Kuomintang was swept from the mainland China's industry either was ruinously damaged or, at best, was decades behind the times.

The first year or so of rehabilitation under the new regime was strictly an Operation Bootstrap. I have already described, in the chapter on early recovery in Shanghai, the quick measures which the government undertook to get the wheels of production going again in the face of economic breakdown, shortage of capital and raw materials, and foreign blockade. Such rapid recovery would have been impossible without a new spirit on the part of the workers, hitherto indifferent or resentful.

What caused this new feeling? There is no mystery about it. After the fall of the Kuomintang, workers worked better and produced more simply because, for the first time, they felt that it was in their interest to do so. This compelling reason had been absent during the Japanese occupation and under Nationalist rule.

And yet the common Western notion about the alleged technical backwardness of the Chinese workingman had been refuted long before the change came about. China's finely wrought metal household utensils, her intricate looms, the delicate glazes on her early pottery, some of her home-created mine engineering equipment testify to skills both ancient and contemporary that the West would find hard to surpass. During the Japanese war and the civil war, when Chinese guerilla forces were fighting for themselves and their own land, miracles of ingenuity were performed by truck mechanics in repairing equipment with nothing but metal scraps—feats that an American automotive engineer could not afford to sneer at. Today Chinese technicians design, build and install every conceivable kind of engineering equipment from machine-tool dies to locomotives, operate every kind of machine from power lathes to jet planes.

When the reconstruction of factories was begun, every worker was encouraged to put forward his own suggestions for new working methods and even new tools and machines. Workers who contribute important ideas, like those who achieve significant increases in production, are elected model workers and are awarded bonuses and other benefits. The call for suggestions yielded some useful ideas in almost every plant. In some of the bigger factories they numbered thousands.

Intelligent workingmen had long been aware of possible improvements in their working operations or implements; but the pressure was to keep one's mouth shut. A worker was supposed to stay in his place. And in any case, increased efficiency at his work could benefit nobody but his boss.

In Mukden in October, 1952, I talked to a model worker in the Number One Machine Tool Factory whose story is typical. The man, named Ma Ming-ho, aged twenty-six, had devised an ingenious new welding tool. I asked him how he had happened to think of his idea.

"It did not happen suddenly," said Ma. "Actually I began to think about it during the Japanese occupation, but put it out of my mind since I was sure no good could come of it. I would have received nothing for suggesting it. And I surely had no reason for wanting to help the management."

In this same factory no less than seventy-five percent of the workers were credited with usable ideas in the rationalization program. Not all had been earth-shaking—some merely had to do with the elimination of a single work motion or a simple rearrangement of machines. Not all entitled their authors to the status of model worker. But some, like Ma Ming-ho, had contributed ideas of basic value.

While in Peking I went to the Cultural Palace for a look at the exhibit of inventions and new working methods developed by workers in the rationalization drive. The exhibit occupies several floors of the building. You wander along from a display of new cutting tools and perforating machines to a diagram of a new cotton-ginning device, an improved iron smelting method, a new type of truck-engine cylinder, a photo layout of new mine safety devices, and new efficiency ideas introduced within the past two years in paper mills, cement factories, waterworks, railroads and chemical laboratories.

The Workers' Cultural Palace in Shanghai had a similar exhibit. Here were to be seen examples or pictorial representations of improved wire and cable stretchers, cigarette-rolling machines, an ingenious system for handling deep-sea fishing nets, a method for prolonging the life of grain-milling rollers, a large variety of safety devices, and an entirely new process for preparing pigskin which makes possible its mass production at low cost.

There was also an exhibit of industrial pottery, showing how Chinese ceramics craftsmen have applied their legendary skills on flawlessly glazed tools and machine parts of earthenware, fashioned with such precision that they could replace highly complicated metal machines. Because of their corrosion resistance many of these were actually superior to metal implements. They were a boon to the chemical industry and to technical research where corrosion often makes metal tools undependable.

Many of these innovations seem so logical and apparently simple that one was frequently tempted to ask, "Why didn't anyone think of this before?" The answer was always the same: "Why should one? Nobody cared about such things before."

❦ 17 ❧

"SEE YOU AND RAISE YOU"

Interviewing the factory workers or wandering through the plants of China, one is bound to hear a good deal of talk about "emulation." What is really meant by the word is "competition"—competition between factory teams or individual workers to equal or surpass production goals. In the campaign to increase output and income, such contests are as important as the modernization drive. They engender about the same kind of excitement as do the fortunes of the local baseball club among the workers in an American plant.

The emulation drive is officially encouraged and propagandized with a vigor characteristic of new China. But it could never have achieved more than token results unless the workers themselves were behind it. The records chalked up by thousands of competing workers' teams show that it has been as important as the innovation campaign in boosting output. It would be nonsense to suppose that such reports, posted in factories and widely published in newspapers, could be fabricated with the acquiescence of the workers themselves. Actually, emulation and rationalization are closely related, for the breaking of production records also results from the competing teams' use of the new methods.

The occasion for my 1952 visit to Peking was the Asian and Pacific Regions Peace Conference, which I reported for the *China Monthly Review*. The conference lasted about two weeks and was attended by unofficial delegations from all of the Asian and many

143

Latin American countries, and a delegation from the United States whose status was excruciatingly unofficial. (This was in the days before the idea of peace won security clearance and was given at least probationary good-conduct status by some nations of the West.)

Correspondents representing the press of five continents also were there in large numbers, and I had a chance to make acquaintanceships, some of which became lasting friendships, with journalists from England, France, Italy, India, Pakistan, Indonesia, Burma, Mexico, Chile, New Zealand and Australia. Some newspapermen covering the Conference for *Hsinhua* (New China) News Agency were on hand, too, and among these I was delighted one day to run into my old colleague "Scoop" Liu, whose *Time*-tortured prose had complicated my problems as city editor of the *China Press* in Shanghai.

Scoop was at a table in the press room, laboriously translating into English a story in the *Peking Daily* for the benefit of an Indian newsman who wanted to get off a summary of it to his paper. We greeted one another briefly and made a date for dinner that night.

At a Mohammedan restaurant we hashed over the old days, and I asked him about his present job. "I've got one big complaint," Scoop said. "I don't get much chance to write English any more, except when I do a little translating. For some reason they didn't find a spot for me on the English-language news bulletin."

Offering no opinion as to the possible reason, I told Scoop that I was interested in surveying the progress of the industrialization drive and asked him what would be a good-sized factory in Peking to look at.

"There are quite a few big plants in town here that are said to be turning out stuff at a fancy rate of speed," Scoop said. "But I'll tell you what. If you'd like to meet a real big-time model worker, there's the Changshintien plant about a dozen miles south of here where Ni Chi-ying works."

Ni Chi-ying at that time was one of the most celebrated model workers in North China, and the idea of an interview with him interested me. Scoop said he would apply for a day's leave to go with me.

The Changshintien Locomotive and Wagon Repair Works is a rambling place near a small station on the Peking-Hankow line. It consists of several long, low shop buildings, a recreation hall, a nursery, a school, and a hospital. Scoop and I presented ourselves at the plant manager's office, explained our errand, and asked to be introduced to Ni Chi-ying. A secretary summoned him by telephone.

A chesty youth of twenty, Ni Chi-ying the labor hero had the beaming look and bustling air one associates with an extrovert junior executive in the States. For my personal taste he was almost too dynamic; he made me seem to myself even lazier than I normally do. After shaking hands with Scoop and me he propelled us briskly into the plant, gesturing, smiling and answering our questions in rapid-fire Mandarin.

Ni was the head of an eight-man production team which included three who were at least in their forties. It was not inventions or innovations that had earned him his model worker's status, but energy and drive on the job, and the ability to impart it to his teammates. "Since last June," he told us, "we have fulfilled every month's production plan four or five days ahead of schedule. This is not done merely by going to one's bench and making faster motions. We have studied hard, planned each day's work, and tried to make use of all the advanced methods that are now becoming available."

I asked him what was his interest in working so ardently. Was it pride in his team, in his plant, in his country? Did bonuses have something to do with it?

"We receive extra pay," he said, "for what we achieve beyond the normal plan. Some of the men on my team have large families—they can make good use of the money." Then he broke into one of his ear-to-ear smiles. "As for me and many others, we have another purpose besides. The better we work, the sooner we will achieve the socialist industrialization of our country."

In his tool shop Ni Chi-ying showed us the bulletin board on which team challenges are posted. One, bearing his signature, read, "We pledge to overfulfill the monthly production plan by five days, to improve our safety standard, and to permit no production breakdowns." Other points were added, relating to such matters as punctuality, elimination of waste, care of tools. Posted under Ni's challenge, in black ink on red paper, was scribbled a counter-challenge by another team, saying, in effect, "We see you and raise you." Hence, apparently, the term "emulation"—one team pledges to do so much, another team offers to equal or beat it.

I asked Ni about his wages. "For normal production," he said, "all of us on my team receive the wage norm for this kind of work. It is 600,000 yuan a month" [the equivalent of about twenty-six dollars].

"Do you consider that a good wage?"

"It is a little more than twice what we were being paid in 1950," Ni answered.

Scoop remarked that besides wages the workers got free medical care and insurance, free school facilities, and low-cost government housing.

"What about the bonuses?" I asked Ni.

"They differ according to the work we achieve. The bonus earned by my team has never been less than ten percent of our month's wages, and sometimes has reached as high as eighteen percent."

I asked him how the general wage scale compared with that of the old days, when the railroad was operated by the Nationalist government.

"I did not work here before liberation," said Ni. "I was in the People's Liberation Army then. But ask any of the old timers here, and they will tell you they are receiving more than twice as much pay as under the Kuomintang."

As we proceeded through the plant I did ask other workers, and their answers confirmed what Ni had said. This tallied, too, with what I had heard from workers in other factories, as well as with official reports and with accounts I had received from people in other parts of China whom I had known since the old Nationalist days.

Conditions varied considerably in different industries and in different localities, but from what I had been able to gather, the increase in money wages under the new regime ranged from 75 to 150 percent above the old in addition to the substantial "fringe" benefits now enjoyed by a great many workers.* In some industries notoriously underpaid in the past, a rational readjustment of pay scales had brought the workers almost a threefold increase. Civil service white-collar workers are generally paid less than industrial workers, but many receive free housing. Another new factor is that many women who had never worked before were now supplementing their husbands' incomes with equal pay earned by themselves.

------

*Liu Ning-yi, Vice-President of the All-China Federation of Trade Unions, in a review of the Chinese wage picture since 1949, wrote in April, 1955: "In 1952 the average wage of workers in state-operated enterprises throughout the country was 60 to 120% above 1949. In 1953 it was again increased by 5.5% above 1952, and in 1954 the state plan again succeeded in raising wages by another 5.2% above the previous year."

From 1953 through 1955, according to a report by the Chairman of the State Planning Commission, wages rose by another 20 percent, while real wages taking into consideration increased productivity and some minor price rises, increased by 12 percent.

A week or so after my visit to the Changshintien Locomotive Repair Works I was to spend a day in the mining city of Fushun, but had no adequate chance to investigate wage scales. However, the report rendered to his union by John Wood, Vice-President of the Scottish Area, National Union of Mineworkers in Great Britain, after a two-day visit in the Huai-Nan mining district made at about the same time, is interesting:

"Basic wages are 500,000 people's yuan a month, while those on piece rates earn 700,000 and the model miner 1,400,000 yuan a month.* The 700,000 yuan are sufficient to maintain four persons on a high standard of living."

With regard to the "people's yuan" (people's currency) it should be pointed out that since early 1950 this had a value of about 23,000 to one United States dollar. Seven hundred thousand yuan therefore equalled, in American terms, about thirty-two dollars a month. But because of wide differences in prices and in traditional standards of living, such analogies mean little. Thirty-two dollars a month would be a beggarly wage for any American, though not bad by the standards of many European workers. But in China, where food, rent, clothing and taxes are correspondingly lower and where medical services and insurance are now generally free, a monthly income of 700,000 yuan in 1952 was, as Mr. Wood observed, "sufficient to maintain four persons on a high standard of living." Some workers earned less; some earned twice as much. As to the significant point—how they fared in comparison with the old Nationalist days—they were vastly better off.

In the spring of 1955 China's currency was converted—but with no devaluation—to more rational proportions by a new note issue with a ratio of one to 10,000 of the old. The purpose of the change was to provide a more wieldy unit of currency, so that bills could be used in smaller denominations.

The intrinsic value and buying power of Chinese money, however, remained unchanged. With the new currency the unit of Chinese money (jenminpiao), in relation to American currency, is no longer measured in thousands or tens of thousands. It is worth two and a half to one American dollar. Up to the time I left China, however, the jenminpiao issued in 1949 was still in use, and payments of any size had to be calculated in hundreds of thousands or millions.

---

*Most miners are now on piece rates but are protected by a wage "floor."

❧ **18** ❧

ON A FUSHUN HILLSIDE

Under the new Trade Union Law in effect since June, 1950, all Chinese workers are entitled to a voice in the operation of the plants where they work, through representation on what is known as the "democratic management committee." This committee is divided evenly between elected representatives of the workers, and management. It is headed by the manager of the factory, but he cannot vote on any disputed issue. The workers' representatives do not include trade union officials; they are chosen from the factory.

The democratic management committee in state-owned plants has final authority on all questions both of management and of worker relations. It sets production goals and methods, and within the provisions of the Trade Union Law it determines wages, hours and working conditions and handles management-labor disputes. If the two sides cannot agree on any disputed question it is referred to the government Labor Bureau for adjudication, with the right of appeal to the People's Courts.

Under the Trade Union Law the workers have the right to negotiate for wage increases both in state-owned and in private businesses. Their rights are spelled out in detail. In the event of a dispute management is forbidden to suspend operations, cease paying wages, or withdraw any benefits such as meals, housing or health service, during the period of arbitration.

"If one party to a labor dispute," the law reads, "in a publicly operated or privately operated enterprise or in an enterprise operated by co-operatives disagrees with the award rendered by the Labor Bureau, it must inform the Labor Bureau thereof within five days after the award has been rendered, and must lodge an appeal with the People's Court for a verdict." In practice the People's Courts have been notably—some managers would even say notoriously—inclined to see the workers' viewpoint in cases that have come before them.

Thus the Chinese trade unions, despite the fears expressed in some quarters (usually by the same people who bemoan the condition of private enterprise in China) are in no sense "captive" organizations or "organs of the state." They are more thoroughly protected than any other element in the social structure. It is apt to be pointed out skeptically that the law makes no provision for their right to strike—but whom they would want or need to strike against is the real question. In an industrial organization where the workers are an integral, active part of management a strike on the part of workers would be, in large part, a strike against themselves. Despite the continued presence of private enterprise China is avowedly a workers' and peasants', not a capitalist, society; labor in that sense, as well as in the sense of an already realized improvement in its economic status, is working for itself. This situation has nothing in common with a society where it is the recognized goal of management to get as much from labor as possible, for as little pay as possible; and of labor to get as much as possible on as favorable terms as it can exact.

The Chinese workers like their Trade Union Law. They regard it as a practical charter of rights that pays off. In much the same way American union members once swore by the Wagner Act. But they like it for other reasons besides.

One of these reasons became evident to me on a hillside in Fushun, one of the big coal mining cities of the Northeast, where I visited a workers' rest home and home for the aged. This building, erected to house Japanese officials during the occupation, had been wrecked by them on leaving in 1945 and had remained an unused hulk during the ensuing three years of Nationalist rule. After the Kuomintang departed in its turn, the building was repaired and an extension added. Now it housed retired workers and provided vacation quarters for active ones.

Walking through a high-ceilinged clubroom in the section for aged male workers, I saw fifteen to twenty old fellows playing checkers, reading newspapers or books, or swapping opinions. The front windows looked out over a trim lawn; the side windows faced a newly built greenhouse which now was catching the late rays of an autumn sun.

I approached a man who sat by himself, peering with aged eyes at a Shenyang (Mukden) newspaper. After he had recovered from his surprise at hearing Chinese from a visitor of my outlandish appearance, he talked affably. His name was Tsai Yu-lin; he was seventy-six, and had worked in factories in that part of the country for more than thirty years. I asked him how he passed his time now.

"There is a great deal to do here," said Mr. Tsai, smiling an all but toothless smile. "You can read?" He pointed to a wall bulletin announcing an illustrated lecture that evening on the history of ancient China. "On Wednesday nights we have a movie. Some of them are old—but to me they are all new. Sometimes a dance troupe comes up from Peking; other nights we sing people's songs, all of us together, led by the recreation director. And there is always the game of checkers for those foolish old heads who love to play it."

"What about the daytime?" I asked him. "Are you able to keep occupied?" Tsai looked me up and down, and chuckled.

"When you have lived and worked for seventy-five years, you *nien ching de* will not worry so much about keeping busy in your seventy-sixth. To sit and think, knowing that here I am at home, that the evening meal will come on time and that my bed is upstairs waiting for me—isn't that enough? But for those who like to work with their hands there is a carpenter shop down in the basement. As for me, I prefer to amuse myself in the garden—there is a little plot over there beyond the greenhouse which I share with a few others."

But the thing that really excited him was his room. He interrupted our talk to show it to me. Moving along briskly in spite of a game knee, he guided me up one floor and past a row of open alcove doors into a room about ten by fourteen feet. It had just enough space for its two small beds, one easy chair, one small chest of drawers, and a little round table that bore a vase with flowers. The paint looked fresh, and the floor was swept clean.

"Two—just two of us in our own room," said Tsai. "Never did I think it would happen in my old age. For six years when I worked in Shenyang I shared a room with five, sometimes sleeping on a shelf under the ceiling. Even when I was a young man with good employment, two rooms for myself and my wife and our four children and my mother was the most we ever had."

He sat down on his bed and patted the quilt beside him. "Now that I can work no longer and my wife is gone, it is good to know that I am not a burden to my children."

Tsai Yu-lin was paying for his keep at the rest home, but he could afford it. For he was drawing a pension and would continue to receive it for the rest of his life. Under the Trade Union Law male workers over sixty who have worked for twenty-five years or more, including five years in the same establishment, are eligible to retire on a pension of fifty to seventy percent of their wage at the time of retirement. Some get more, some less, depending on their length of service. Women who have worked twenty years or more can retire at the age of fifty on the same terms.

Other benefits, adding up to a comprehensive system of labor insurance, are provided by the law. If one of Tsai's sons were injured or had become ill at his job, he would receive free medical or surgical treatment, and free hospitalization if he needed it. Full wages would continue during his treatment. If total disability resulted, he would receive a pension of from sixty to seventy-five percent of his wages; if partially disabled, he would be given a light job and receive a small pension.

On the other hand, if Tsai Junior were to suffer illness or injury away from his job, he would still receive from sixty to a hundred percent of his wages, depending on his length of service, during absence up to six months. If absence were necessary beyond six months he would still get paid, but at a lower rate—from forty to sixty percent. His medical costs would also be paid, except in the case of unusually expensive drugs. His dependents would also receive partial benefits in case of illness.

Life insurance likewise is provided under the Trade Union Law. The family of a worker who dies of injury or illness sustained on the job receives a monthly pension of twenty-five to fifty percent of his wages. Funeral expenses also are paid. In the case of a worker whose death is caused by injury or illness not sustained at work, or one who dies after retirement, funeral expenses and relief benefits are also paid. Old Tsai Yu-lin's eventual burial thus was provided for, but his pension would die with him, for he had no dependents.

Women workers are entitled to fifty-six days' absence as maternity leave, with full wages and all medical expenses, from prenatal period to delivery.

Where does all this money come from? It comes neither from the state, directly, nor from the worker's pay envelope. Pension and insurance funds are accumulated through a payroll tax paid by management. If the enterprise is a private or a cooperative one, the fund comes out of profits. If it is a stated-owned enterprise the state provides the insurance fund directly. In no case does the worker contribute from his earnings.

~~ **19** ~~

WHAT, NO PENTHOUSES?

"Time stands still in China," the Old Hands used to say. And for a long time this must have sounded true. But when I revisited some of China's big cities at the start of the new republic's fourth year, I was struck by certain changes in their aspect—changes which the emergence of the workers as the dominant urban class had clearly brought about.

This was especially striking in Peking, venerable seat of China's culture, which had looked the same, sounded the same and behaved pretty much the same for hundreds of years. Now, in the four years since I had seen her—my last visit had been made in August, 1948—she seemed to have shaken off her old somnolence and assumed a new, purposeful look.

Her ancient glories that had always left the visitor breathless—the Temple of Heaven, the Summer Palace, the White Pagoda, the magnificent parks and lakes—were still there. But around them, all over the city, new buildings were going up—homes, hospitals, and schools as well as public edifices. Historic landmarks were being restored or renovated. Everywhere were stacks of bricks, mounds of cement, piles of lumber, and builder's scaffolding. In the northwestern suburb at the foot of the Western Hills the construction of a new educational and cultural zone had been started, and new university buildings and technical schools were under way.

The thousands of *hutungs*, the lanes that make up the residential areas, were clean as I had not seen them before. In 1948 beggars still swarmed through the streets; dealers in contraband dollars were still making their deals; and the poor were still bartering their possessions for food that their worthless paper currency could not buy. Now the beggars, the dollar-traders and the barterers were gone. In their place were throngs of shoppers armed with negotiable money crowding in and out of stores that had not been there before. Clean water now filled the four big lakes after noisome decades of neglect. And yes, the flies—those famous flies that have provided Western writers subject matter for so much whimsy—had become comparatively scarce. Save for a few wobbly survivors, the Peking flies had been exterminated in the sanitation campaign.

The factories, too—for Peking is a great industrial as well as cultural center—showed new life and new numbers. But that was the story wherever I went in China on the eve of her first five-year industrialization plan, which was to start at the beginning of 1953.

Shenyang, for example, whose skyline for many years had presented an imposing array of factory chimneys, now had one vital difference— all the chimneys were issuing smoke. It was in Shenyang, too, that I saw the Number One Machine Tool plant, devoted now to mass production of what China had never made for herself before—the basic tools of industry. Here also I saw something new in China—two huge workers' housing developments under construction, with such innovations as steam heat, hot water, modern kitchens, and double glass windows against the bitter Northeastern winters.

There were workers' housing developments in the coal city of Fushun, too, as well as the rest home where I met Mr. Tsai Yu-lin. And outside Canton, as the train from Shanghai carried me across the flat Yangtze Valley countryside, I could see clusters of newly built houses for workers' families each with its little garden, and dormitories for workers without families. In Canton proper, where in early 1949 I had found a row of dilapidated shacks, there is now a development housing three thousand railroad workers, with a clubhouse, primary school, kindergarten and nursery.

In Nanking, a beautiful city with many fine houses and spacious streets, the change was even more marked. Nanking, Chiang Kai-shek's capital, had been insignificant as a production center; now there were factories turning out hundreds of products from electronic equipment to steam turbines and machine tools.

For decades in Nanking the working people had lived in slum areas like the notorious district along the railroad tracks, called Wulao. In the old days, as Mr. Wang Wei-hua, the district Director of Hygiene who showed me the place, put it, "the area was filthy from one end to another, and the ditch that ran through it was a great stinking pool." The story of what has happened since contains no element of surprise, for it happened in other cities of China. The district has been cleaned up, the "great stinking pool" drained and filled, electric street lighting and modern sewage disposal were installed for the first time, and finally new workers' houses were built. "Not long ago," said Wang Wei-hua, pointing to a large green cabbage patch behind one of the houses as we walked through Wulao, "this was marshy ground with a black, stagnant pool."

Back in Shanghai my friend Peter Tang took me to see his nephew who lived in the largest of the city's new housing developments, on the outskirts of the town. Guan Li-ming is a young textile worker, with a wife and two small children.

The first section of the new development, housing 4,000 families, had just been opened. Eventually the project was to house a community of 100,000. The development, built on more than a hundred acres of land, is laid out in groups of two hundred houses, each two stories high and containing six apartments. The apartments have electric lighting, running water, and a private lavatory. Each two families share a kitchen. Down the street were a park, a cooperative store, a small clinic and a bathhouse.

Guan Li-ming introduced me to one of his co-tenants, a Mrs. Wen, the mother of a young woman who worked in a weaving mill. The family, occupying an apartment similar to the Guans', consisted of Mrs. Wen and her daughter, the daughter's husband and their six-year-old son. Mrs. Wen told me that she had lived for more than thirty years in a windowless straw hut which was damp all the year 'round and where no sunlight was ever seen. "We cooked out of doors when we could, but when it rained we had to move the little stove inside and then the hut filled up with smoke and soot. Of my seven children three died in childhood; the others lived, but were seldom well."

Such dwellings were the typical lot of the average Shanghailander before the change; many were still in evidence when I left China, for housing takes time to provide, and the new government was virtually

starting from scratch. The new homes, such as those I was now looking at, were an incalculable improvement over the old, but they were
still far from being a paradise.

Guan Li-ming's apartment, occupied by two adults and two children, consisted of two rooms, the larger about ten by twelve feet and
the smaller about two-thirds that space, in addition to the shared
kitchen. These are smaller quarters than in many American apartments, but larger than others still to be found in the crowded cities of
the United States and Europe. Most of the workers who occupied these
apartments had known neither modern plumbing nor electricity nor
even glass windows before. Crowded though they still are now, their
condition amounts to privacy compared with what they had always had.

Shanghai's housing problem, tragically desperate and wholly neglected for decades, has yet to be overcome. So has that of most other
Chinese cities. But the problem is being energetically tackled, and at
a rate that is not the slowest among the nations of the world. The
houses are going up thousands at a time, year by year, where formerly
they went up one by one, if at all.

20

PRIVATE BUSINESS IN RED CHINA

Peter Tang, who turned to the shirt business as a refuge from
Shanghai newspaper work during the Chiang era, was one of a number
of small businessmen I knew in China who ran retail or wholesale
stores or small factories. Peter never employed more than forty workers
in his shop, including cutters, machine operators, a packer or two, a
part-time machinist and a foreman.

As far as I could see, he lived on about the same scale after the
changeover as before. Always a taciturn man, he talked little about his
business, but allowed that he was making money steadily and doing
a little better each year. That is, until 1952, when sudden prosperity
visited him.

Like most businessmen in China, Peter Tang found himself in
serious difficulties during the general demoralization that led up to
the final Kuomintang collapse. When the new government set up its
takeover commission in Shanghai he applied to it for aid. He was
given a deal accorded to many small manufacturers at the time. The
state furnished his raw materials and guaranteed to buy all his finished
product at a fixed rate of profit.

He was thus, in effect, working for the government, but he continued to own his business and to manage it. His employes had a say
in the running of the factory through their representation on the
"democratic management committee." But since he was working on a
cost-plus system, Peter could afford to be receptive toward their demands on wages, hours, safety equipment, and so on.

Peter was an undemonstrative man, and it was difficult to know at any given time whether he was happy or unhappy. But he was obviously pleased with his income and his respected position as a "national capitalist." However, he came of a solid middle-class family of merchants and old-style civil servants, and I suspect that he never quite got used to the idea of working with Communists.

As a devoted reader of the conservative press before the changeover, and an occasional listener afterward to the Voice of America broadcasts (which the new government never bothered to interdict) it is possible that he expected, sooner or later, to have his business confiscated. But he had not seen this happen to any of his fellow businessmen, although a few were sent to jail during the Wu Fan anti-corruption crackdown in 1952.

Curiously enough, that supposed campaign of persecution against capitalists was what brought direct prosperity to Peter. Being congenitally honest, he had never gone in for bribery or chiseling of any kind. When some manufacturers in his line were convicted of irregularities and had their government contracts cancelled, their orders were often transferred to more reliable quarters, and Peter Tang benefitted. With the additional business thus shunted his way he found himself, late in 1952, renting another factory loft and nearly doubling his operations, with a corresponding boost in his profits.

I had the acquaintance of a few other people in Shanghai who continued to operate their own business after the changeover. One was the owner of a small chemical factory; another was "Fatty" Chien, the prosperous fabric dealer and bon vivant. But there were many other manufacturers and tradesmen who operated on a larger scale. There still are, and will continue to be for years to come, not only in Shanghai but throughout the country. Taken together, they form the class known in modern Chinese society as "national capitalists."

The presence of a healthy capitalism in this country avowedly being led by Communists toward the goal of socialism is a curious phenomenon, and the Chinese are the first to admit its curiousness. On a closer look this contradiction turns out to be not quite so bizarre. The capitalist class is fostered and protected because present-day China needs it. At the same time, government spokesmen have made it painstakingly explicit that they anticipate the day when they will no longer need it, and then there will no longer be a place for it in China.*

*By the end of 1955 the transformation of private industry had arrived at the stage where Peking could predict its end in a step-by-step process during the course

This does not signify, however, that the entrepreneurs and managers who are now making an indispensable contribution to the modernization of China's economy will suddenly and unconscionably be "liquidated." On the contrary, detailed plans have been laid for the gradual absorption of private business into the state-operated socialist economy which is already dominant; and for the equally gradual absorption into it of private owners and managers. On this subject Liu Shao-chi, vice-chairman of the Central People's Government, said in 1954:

> The capitalist, provided he realizes the march of events, provided he is willing to accept socialist reform and provided he does not act against the law or wreck the property of the people, can enjoy the concern of the state and will have proper arrangements made for his life and work in the future; nor will he be deprived of his political rights.*

The temporary status of private enterprise in present-day China has been well understood by the national capitalists; in fact, they would have to be deaf and blind not to understand it, for it has been emphasized at every turn. Nevertheless, there is little evidence that they are unduly concerned either about their present condition, which is a highly respected one, or about their future, in which they seem to have an abounding confidence.

The biggest private capitalist I met in new China also turned out to be one of the most complacent. He was introduced to me by a Chinese newspaperman of my acquaintance in Canton, and we sat down in the lobby of the Ai Chun Hotel on the banks of the Pearl River for a talk. Mr. Pang Yung-gang knew no English and I am innocent of Cantonese, but despite his heavy Cantonese accent we got along satisfactorily in Mandarin.

Mr. Pang is not a very big businessman by American, or even by modern Chinese, standards. In 1952, when I met him, he was the manager and one of the directors of the Ching Hwa Battery Factory in Canton, turning out dry-cell batteries for flashlights, radios and

---

of at least ten years. In his June, 1956 report to the National People's Congress, Finance Minister Li Hsien-nien estimated that 63.8 percent of total 1957 industrial production would be by state enterprises, indicating an estimated 36.2 percent still privately or part-privately owned.

*Report on the Draft Constitution of the People's Republic of China, September 15, 1954.

telephones. The plant had been founded some twenty-five years earlier with thirty workers, and by now it employed upward of three hundred. Pang, a man in his early forties, who had kept the factory going continuously through the revolution and the changeover, had evidently not bothered to alter his outward appearance under the new regime. He looked the part of the prosperous big-little businessman anywhere, with his starched collar and regimental-striped necktie, his gold-banded wrist watch and his flat straw hat. His figure was somewhat portly, his face round and smooth, and he carried himself like a man of consequence. His chauffeur was waiting to drive him off in his British-made car.

I asked Pang how he had managed to stay in business during the troubled days of the turnover. He replied that the difficulties had been tremendous, but that he and his brother, who between them owned a majority of the shares, had been determined to keep it going at any cost.

"The market for our goods had dwindled to almost nothing, and the wild inflation made business almost impossible to carry on. But we kept going, hoping that things would change for the better. One heard all sorts of rumors as to what would happen after Canton fell, but things were already so hopeless, we were ready for almost any change."

After the change in government occurred, he related, they had gone on for awhile pretty much as before. Their workers had demanded increased wages, but they were unable to meet the demands. The new government paid little attention to them until the beginning of 1950.

"By that time," Pang said, "the new currency was in use and it was quite stable. Communications had been reestablished with the entire country, and the demand for goods was increasing. In other words, business was improving. Representatives of the government asked if we could supply an increased quantity of batteries for Canton and some of the cities in the north. We told them this would mean expanding our plant, and we would need capital. As a result we obtained two loans—one long-term and one short-term—and were able to increase our output."

But didn't he have to contend with government competition? Pang's answer was simple. So far the government had not gone heavily into the manufacture of batteries, while the demand was increasing so rapidly, both in the cities and in the countryside, that the Ching Hwa factory was constantly being pressed to step up production.

"It will be a long time before this growing demand can be met," Pang said. "That is why the government considers us national capitalists so important. We are not only getting further loans, but the government has also helped us procure raw materials. It is also helping us with the erection of a new building. We have worked out our own factory 'Five Year Plan,' and our aim is to increase production fourfold in that period. This is an ambitious plan, but in the last three years we have earned enough to make it feasible."

Just how much money he was making Mr. Pang did not say. In private business enterprise ten percent of the net profit after taxes is set aside for reinvestment. Dividends not exceeding eight percent annually are paid out of the balance to shareholders. If anything is left over—and in his case there had been considerable in the last two years, Pang said—it is distributed in the following way: sixty percent for remuneration to directors, bonuses to supervisors, superintendents and managers, and bonuses to shareholders; not less than fifteen percent for plant safety and hygiene; fifteen percent for welfare funds and special bonuses to workers; and the remaining ten percent as a general reserve fund.

"The level of profits in factories handling government processing orders," said Pang, "runs from ten to thirty percent, and that gives a good index to the profits of private business in general." He settled back comfortably in his chair, then added, "You know, we private businessmen now have our own organization. A conference of national capitalists from all over the country was held recently in Peking. Its chief purpose was to organize to protect the interests of private business and to help develop its scope."*

I asked him how it felt to be a capitalist in a society which looked toward a day when no such thing as capitalism would exist. Pang's face broke into a grin which, if it was not an expression of self-confidence, was at least a highly convincing imitation.

"You may be surprised," he said, "but I personally have no qualms. Before, in the *jiou sheh hwei*, the old society, what did we strive for?

---

*At the National People's Congress session of June, 1956, eight leading Shanghai businessmen, all of them deputies to the Congress, joined in criticizing government price policies on orders placed with joint state-private industries. The businessmen, led by Jung Yi-jen, known as "China's biggest millionaire," complained that prices paid allowed them insufficient profit margin to operate with maximum efficiency. They also took emphatic issue with Vice-Premier Li Hsien-nien over his estimate as to the reasons for unsatisfactory performance by the trade administration in failing to reach its profit goal in 1955.

To make as much money as we could, both for our children and for the sake of position. Some of us were more interested in the one, some in the other. But in the present society there is no need for either. Social position is measured by other things.

"As for my children, it is true that they can still inherit my money. But what would that make of them? I would rather that they make something of themselves, and for that they will need my money less and less as time goes on. My oldest son is now studying radio in a technical school in Hankow; I think he will make a good technician. My oldest daughter is a civilian employe of the air force in Peking; whether or not she marries, she has a good job and can support herself. I have two other sons and one little girl, all of them now in school. By the time they have grown up there will be even more opportunities for the young in China than now.

"However, I expect to keep on working for a long time to come. True, the government will doubtless buy into my business gradually, until I no longer own any of it. But I will still have the skill and the experience of running it, and will be needed as much as ever. People like myself will always be in demand to serve as factory managers and administrators, and even if we do not make fat profits we can always make a good living."

When the People's Government came to power in China it unceremoniously took over all properties belonging to "bureaucratic capital," by which term it identified the Big Four families of Chiang, Kung, Soong and Chen plus their close political, economic and familial adherents who, in sum, made up the so-called Kuomintang clique.* These properties included many factories, most banks, some shipping, and all public utilities that were not foreign-owned. They also included some picturesque but profitable fringe activities such as prostitution, gambling, opium, organized beggardom, and other rackets, which the new government broke up as fast as it could.

Below the Kuomintang level lay another stratum of business enterprise, ranging from petty to quite substantial, which had no connection with the Big Four group and in fact was almost as much victimized

---

*The total wealth of the Kuomintang insiders at the time of the changeover has been variously estimated. In 1954 Chien Chia-chu, a Chinese economist and deputy director of the Central Administrative Bureau of Industry and Commerce, placed their total accumulation during the twenty-odd years of their regime at $20,000,000,-000. Much of their convertible property was sent out of China before the Chiang Kai-shek government fell.

by it as were the plain people. These were the business interests which the Kuomintang crowd had nothing to gain by absorbing, and which hence had to compete precariously with its monopolies on raw materials and markets, tax favors, control of the police and military, and other conveniences it enjoyed. The dominant role played by foreign industry was another important factor in retarding the development of China's small business.

The government has enlisted this lower stratum of business enterprise, which it calls the "national bourgeoisie," as its ally in the rehabilitation and industrialization of the country. The government has protected it against expropriation or discrimination, and provided it with economic and other kinds of aid. At the same time it has been made unmistakably clear, as I have already said, that this liaison is for the benefit of the nation in its aspirations toward a socialist economy, and not for the benefit of the owners of private enterprise.

The Constitution of 1954 spells all this out:

> The policy of the state towards capitalist industry and commerce is to use, restrict and transform them. The state makes use of the positive sides of capitalist industry and commerce which are beneficial to national welfare and the people's livelihood, encourages and guides their transformation into various forms of state-capitalist economy, gradually replacing capitalist ownership with ownership by the whole people; and this it does by means of control exercised by administrative organs of state, the leadership given by the state sector of the economy, and supervision by the workers.

The forms of cooperation between government and private enterprise are various. They have been worked out to suit the conditions of many different types of business. But in general it may be said that they fit into two wide categories. In one the business remains entirely in the hands of its private owner, while the government supplies it with either some or all of its raw materials and buys either some or all of its finished product, with profits guaranteed but limited. This is the form under which Peter Tang operated. It is considered by the government to be a "lower" form of cooperation, since it includes no direct participation by the state in the process of management or production, and in the last few years it has been rapidly disappearing.

The other involves joint private and public ownership, with the government investing funds and participating in management. The private capitalist continues as owner to the extent that he retains an investment in the business, with the government as his partner. The extent of the government's share (for which it pays cash by buying into the business) varies widely among different enterprises. But it is the government's stated objective to buy out ultimately all such businesses in their entirety.

The willingness and even enthusiasm with which businessmen take part in this program naturally puzzle many Western minds. Nevertheless I found little evidence of fear or concern, and little of reluctance, on the part of China's capitalists. They are not a wholly dedicated class; there is a fair proportion of chiselers and boondogglers among them, as there is among workers and doubtless among professors, five-star generals, physicians and judges everywhere. Yet from 1949, when they produced more than sixty percent of the country's total industrial output, to 1955 when they were still producing more than a third of it, their contribution to their country's rebirth has been great. It is unlikely that they could have done this, even from motives of self-interest, had they been beset by resentments or fears or boredom.

In many Western lands the idea of abetting and even embracing socialism is as unthinkable as the idea of participating in a Black Mass. But in China, as in many other countries both east and west where individual enterprise is regarded as one form of social organization but something short of ultimate perfection, even capitalists can view the coming of a socialist society without altogether losing their composure.

In any case, China's businessmen are not bound to participate in the program if they do not choose to. They can pick up their marbles, sell out to the government, and either live on the proceeds or take jobs in private or state-owned industry. Some have done exactly that, but they are a small minority. As for the rest, those who operate their businesses with and for the state, the possibility must be reckoned with that they like what they are doing—that a normal feeling of patriotism impels them to play their willing part in the rehabilitation and modernization of their country. That, plus a seemly rate of profit over more than a decade, may seem a sufficient reward. As to the future, they appear to feel that, if they have the ability to make a good living by working for themselves, they will also be able to make it through employment in state enterprise.

In 1950, speaking before the National Committee of the People's Consultative Conference, Chairman Mao Tse-tung made this promise:

> When the time for nationalizing industry and socializing agriculture arrives in the distant future, the people will never forget those who have made contributions during the revolutionary reform of the agrarian system, and during the many years of economic and cultural construction that lie ahead. Their future will be bright. . .

Most of the businessmen of new China seem willing to go along with that.

❦ 21 ❦

THE UNRECONSTRUCTED

New China has its troubled and unhappy people, like any nation in the wake of a revolution. While the new regime's popularity is obvious, there is unquestionably a segment of the population to which the change brought real distress, or at the very least perplexity and disorientation.

I am not referring to the active combatants on the Kuomintang side, who played a desperate game and lost. I am thinking of those people who shared neither the misery of the workers and peasants nor the anarchic privileges of the ruling group. They belonged mostly to the intellectual and the middle classes. Unlike many of their class who supported the revolution, they were ignorant of its meaning and unable to make themselves a part of it when it became an accomplished fact.

Consciously or unconsciously, many of them had also developed a feeling of inferiority about Chinese culture and ways, and felt that they could be civilized or "advanced" only to the extent to which they imitated Western, and especially American, ways. To a few of the more obvious expressions of China's ancient culture, such as her classical literature and Peking opera, they retained some loyalty; but in anything contemporary the Chinese way to them was the backward way, and the Western way the enlightened.

These were the people "in the middle," undoubtedly decent and well-disposed according to their lights. They did not attribute China's

166

woes to Chiang Kai-shek's government but to immutable fate; and they thought the desperate condition of the laborers and the landless peasants was either due to their own fault or to the will of heaven. They felt no urgent need of change.

It would not be hard to prove that they were grossly uninformed or morally obtuse, or perhaps both. People who desired no ill and worked no active harm, they merely swam with the tide and were incapable of understanding why that tide should ever turn. Now they go their way bothering nobody and being bothered by nobody, sighing for the old and ill-at-ease because the people who are now in charge of the nation's affairs are not their kind of people.

How many of these passively disaffected there are in China I don't know. But I should not be surprised if they numbered millions. Yet it is doubtful whether, all in all, they aggregate as much as one percent of the six hundred million population.

Their picture is not one of unrelieved gloom by any means. Many, like my housekeeper Fu Ma and others I knew, have found fresh opportunities for employment and even pleasure which outweigh their philosophical troubles. Many others have succeeded in abandoning certain old habits of mind, realizing that they conflicted with the observable facts of life. As time goes on and the remaking of China brings her increasing dignity and prestige in the world, this process becomes easier for them.

Yet a considerable number remain who, I suspect, will never adjust, or at least not for a long time. These are destined to live their lives more or less as strangers in their own land, misfits in a world they cannot comprehend. They are people who absorbed old lessons so well that their minds exclude new ones—people, in short, who can never be happy in a time of change. I came in contact with a number of such persons and I think their story is worth telling. I want to tell, at all events, about three of them—two of whom I knew quite well and the other only briefly and casually.

Yang Mu-shien is a slight, quiet-spoken, neat young man whose father is a stocking manufacturer in Soochow, a city not far from Shanghai. Yang Mu-shien majored in Chinese literature at Ching-hwa University in Peking after the Japanese war, and then went to work for the Nationalist government as a translator in the Office of Information at Nanking. In the last hectic weeks of the Kuomintang regime, he was sent down to Shanghai to join the corps of government press censors there.

My first acquaintance with him came about through a brief argument over a line or two of a cable dispatch he had red-penciled. The cut was not important, and I did not carry the discussion beyond a routine protest.

The next time I saw him was about two months after the change-over, when he called on me to ask whether I knew any foreigners who might want to take Chinese language lessons. I suggested a friend of mine, Douglas Forman, at the American consulate. Like many other employes of the Nationalist government, Yang had decided to stay in China and see what fate might bring.

It was well over a year later when I saw him again, this time through a chance meeting in the streets of Shanghai. He was now wearing the blue-colored short coat that was the popular style of the day. But in Jimmy's restaurant where we went for a cup of coffee, he shed the coat and appeared in the Western-style double-breasted suit and bow tie he always had worn before.

Yang had problems, and there were few people to whom he felt he could talk about them. He was not working and his money was running out. He didn't know what he was going to do.

"Couldn't you get a job with the government where your experience as a translator would be useful?" I asked him.

"Very likely I could, if I cared to apply. But holding a government job in this regime would mean that I would have to attend many meetings. And this I object to as a matter of principle. I feel that a man's time after working hours should be his own.

"Besides, while I don't think it would be held against me, I feel that I would lack prestige as an employe of the new government after having worked as a censor for the Kuomintang."

"I see your point," I said. "But in that case what else is there to do?" Yang had no answer, but stared glumly into his coffee through his heavy-lensed glasses.

After this encounter Yang began dropping in at my apartment one or two nights a week, and would sometimes help me translate some of the knottier passages in a Chinese book I might be reading. Now and then we would go to a restaurant. Yang liked his yellow wine, and after he had got started on it would begin talking about his troubles.

He was obviously suffering from that schizophrenic state of mind which may assail an educated and sensitive person anywhere when caught in conflicts between treasured old values and new ideas. Yang was proud of China's growing importance on the world scene. He was pleased, too, that the old condescending attitude of foreigners in China had come to an end. But he was also proud of his English-speaking accomplishment, and felt the new rule against carrying on official business in any language but Chinese was going too far.

He conceded that land reform had greatly benefited most of the peasants, and was glad of this; but he deplored the mutual-aid teams and farming cooperatives, which he regarded as forms of regimentation. Had the old life of the peasant under his landlord's heel also been a kind of regimentation? That was no concern of Yang's; he was no peasant. Besides, two wrongs did not make a right.

What bothered him most was the joining habit. Everybody was joining organizations—unions, study groups, youth clubs, women's groups, professional people's organizations, shopkeepers' associations and what not. Meetings, meetings, meetings, motions and resolutions, programs of activities, plans and reports, with no one minding his own business. Yang considered this childish and undignified. For himself, he preferred to think and act as an individual. Yet it worried him that he had virtually no friendships and seemed to fit in nowhere.

By now Yang Mu-shien was earning a little money through selling translations of articles from foreign periodicals to Chinese newspapers and magazines. Now and then I would suggest that we take in a Chinese movie, a practice I had followed since my earliest days in China as a means of improving my knowledge of the colloquial speech. But Yang always demurred. Chinese movies, even those made in the old days, were a little beneath him. Only the better foreign product was worth his while.

He was, however, a great devotee of the Peking opera. To this we went quite often. But he found that the Peking opera, too, had changed. He thought the singing and acting as fine as in the past, but the old stories had been altered. The high dignitaries or army generals who had once been the heroes now were often supplanted by common folk.

As time went on he grew increasingly morose, complaining that there was nobody with whom he could exchange ideas or who would understand his feelings. He was troubled, too, by letters he occasionally received from relatives in the countryside, onetime landlords now dispossessed, complaining that they were having a hard time. An uncle had been convicted of extorting money from his former tenants and had to pay it back or go to jail. "If he is guilty," said Yang, "hasn't he already suffered enough by being deprived of his land, without being made to pay out money as well?"

In the spring of 1953, about eight months before I left China, Yang called me on the telephone after an absence of some time. I met him for afternoon tea at Sun Ya's, still one of Shanghai's fanciest restaurants and his favorite. He greeted me with expressions of embarrassment at his failure to show up for several months. The news was that he had a job, teaching Chinese literature and history at a private high school across the river in Pootung. The pay was sufficient, he said, but the work was very hard. Still, he had found a niche at last.

From then on I saw Yang infrequently; but when we did get together it seemed to me that he was growing a little more settled. Some of his colleagues on the school faculty seemed to be decent fellows and friendly, although there was one supercilious fool who ridiculed his reserved manner. Yang had joined the teachers' union and even attended meetings, but he felt that few of the members were his equals in education or intellectual depth. He still wore Western clothes; and now that he had a regular income was again indulging an old fondness for made-to-order shoes.

I saw him for the last time about two months before I left. He presented me with a large fan inscribed in his own calligraphy, of which he was quite proud, with a poem by Tu Fu, one of China's classic poets of the eighth century.

We did not expect to meet again, and he expressed his thanks for what sympathy and companionship I had shown him. I asked him whether he thought the worst period of his difficulties was over. He managed a cheerful little smile, and said, "A creature that is transported to a strange climate can often come to terms with it, perhaps by growing a coat of different thickness or by learning to eat new kinds of food. If such a one can do that, so can I."

He added that he had become interested in reading the works of modern Chinese political writers, including the philosophers of the current revolution. "Since I am going to live in the midst of it," he said, "I might as well try to grasp it with my mind even if I cannot receive it into my heart." He was by now well entrenched in his job and had received a raise in salary. But he was not entirely satisfied with his progress and was thinking of trying to get a job in Peking, perhaps one with the government where he could put his knowledge of English to better use. In Peking, too, he would be close to the most ancient cultural reminders of China's great past.

I wished him luck; and as we shook hands for the last time he said, "Perhaps I shall see you in America some time when I go there as a representative of China's liberated masses." Yang Mu-shien laughed as he said it, but his heart was not in the joke; and he did not look at me as he went out the door.

How many Yang Mu-shiens there are in China, doing their troubled best to live peacefully in a new world they did not seek and cannot quite accept, I don't know. But the really troubled ones, as I have said, are not numerous. Yang, and others who thought as he did, could not be at ease in a society of whose basic ideas he disapproved. Others simply do not care. Having ample means and no need to take up new ways, they live on just about as before. Such a one was my jovial friend Mr. Hua.

I met Hua originally as a friend of Yu Ling, the young importer who took me to the Hoong Chang Shing Restaurant for a practical demonstration of "face." Hua was one of a small circle of convivial souls, substantial businessmen or gentlemen of leisure, whose evenings at the gaudier Shanghai restaurants I was occasionally invited to join as a foreigner who could tell them in their own language about the fabulous ways of my native land. I also happen to have a serious interest in food, and my bemused explorations in Chinese cookery gave them considerable diversion.

I never learned Hua's given name, or if I did I have forgotten it. In any case I knew him simply as Hua *shian sheng*—Mr. Hua. At the time I met him he was about thirty-five, and owned a prosperous elevator manufacturing business which he had inherited, along with a good deal of other property, from his father. Under the new regime he prospered even more, for the government needed elevators in new buildings it was erecting and old ones being remodeled. Thus profits came easily to Hua, who ran his business with a minimum of exertion, letting subordinates do the work.

Mr. Hua and his friends, and many others like them, had no political theories, nor any other theories I could discover that did not have to do with the comparative excellence of foods and wines and the joys of companionship with the other sex. He had a wife and three children with whom he lived in considerable style, but he was out on the town several nights each week. He also acknowledged one concubine whom he continued to support, as was legal provided she consented—and she did. Whether he had other concubines was a matter of conjecture.

Hua had nothing, on the surface, to gain from the social change that was going on around him, and had little sympathy with it. But he could not get passionately worked up about the subject. He had the good luck to be able to pursue the life of ease and self-indulgence indefinitely without being bored. If he felt the need of anything else I never heard him express it. Only once did I hear him talk seriously about the future. That was one evening when he and I, having nothing else to do, lingered on after the others had departed. Hua, mellow with food and wine, fell to musing.

"What have I to look forward to?" he said. "Aparently nothing. But if these bumpkins who are trying to change everything do not interfere with me I will be content to go on as I am now, and I have enough with which to do it for a long time.

"Some say that I should worry more about the future of my children. But worrying will do no good. If things must change, let them change. Besides, if my children have any capacity at all they should have no trouble finding something to do in new China."

It was the only time I ever heard Hua use that now prevalent expression, "new China."

Yoong Feng-rei, one-time landlord, was not a friend of long standing. In fact, I met him just once in a suburban wine shop outside of Shanghai.

An American friend of mine had taken a snapshot of the wine-shop proprietor during a day spent in this suburb of Kao Chiao, on the other side of the Whangpoo River from Shanghai. He had promised his subject a print, but shortly afterward had gone home to the States. He entrusted me with the negative and the mission of getting it developed and delivering the result to the wine shop man. With one thing and another it took me several months before I got around to the forty-minute ferry ride to deliver it.

The place was an ordinary country wine shop with the usual dirt floor and five or six small tables. There was nothing about it to tempt me to spend any time there. But as I handed the photograph over to the proprietor and assured him that it did him little justice, an elderly man walked in and the atmosphere of the place changed abruptly. Although Kao Chiao is a small community and at least some of the patrons sitting at the little tables must have known the newcomer, they all ignored him ostentatiously. The proprietor's face clouded, and he failed to greet the arrival, who shuffled to a corner table and sat down.

I asked the proprietor who the fellow was, and was informed in a low voice that he was Yoong Feng-rei, a former landlord whose land had been distributed.

"I wish he would drink his wine somewhere else," added the proprietor. "He brings a chill into this place when he comes in. Nobody likes him and nobody wants to talk to him. And after he has had five or six cups he begins making loud speeches about the injustice he has suffered."

"Why don't you refuse to serve him?"

"He is an old man, and one can't help feeling sorry for him, even though he is still better off than most of his former tenants. Nobody complains when he starts cursing about the bungling district government, but it is an unpleasant business and it does not bring customers into my shop."

Meanwhile he had been ladling out two ounces of bai gan, and took it to Mr. Yoong in his corner. When he returned I asked whether he would mind it if I engaged the ex-landlord in conversation. He made a gesture of indifference, and I approached Yoong Feng-rei and asked permission to join him. The old man looked me up and down closely. Whether because he felt that he had nothing to fear from a foreigner or thought it unwise to refuse, he motioned me to sit down.

I asked him how things were going. He replied that they were not going well. As a result of the land distribution he was left with only six mou out of the forty he had owned. He still had his big house, but without servants its care was a burden. Whereas he and his wife had lived sumptuously on their rents, they now had to get along on what they could raise themselves on their little plot of land. And they were getting old.

"Have you any children?" I asked him.

"I have two sons. Both are married and live in Shanghai. The elder has a hardware shop, and the other is a dealer in electrical goods. I am proud of them both, but now I have become a nuisance to them, for instead of sending them gifts of money as I used to, I must ask their help in supporting their mother and me."

What galled Yoong Feng-rei most was the memory of the "accusation meeting" that had preceded the confiscation of his land. It had been a bitter experience. He felt that he had been ill used. It was when he talked of this that his resentment flared up.

"I am not an evil man," Yoong said. "Some landlords have been dealt with harshly, and perhaps some of them deserved it. But I am not of that kind. I stole no one's property, I committed no crimes against anyone. True, I employed an *eh ba*, but I would not let him beat my tenants, even when their rent was unpaid. Yet one after another rose up and accused me.

"Of what did they accuse me? Not of brutality, not of theft, but of charging them high interest rates when they needed to borrow money! The rates were not low—but they were not of my making. Throughout the province landlords were charging as much as thirty percent interest, or even more. I kept my rates down to twenty-five percent. Was that a crime?"

He emptied his cup, called for another two ounces, and went on.

"There was another kind of accusation against me, and it was even more unjust. Some of the tenants seized me by the arm and made me accompany them to the graves of their young children. Then they pointed fingers at me, screaming, 'You stole our land and left us with nothing!' But truly I had stolen nobody's land. When they could neither pay their rent nor the money I had loaned them, the land became mine. That was the law. Should I have said, 'Go, keep your land even though you are too lazy and too stupid to pay your debts'? Who would have done such a thing?"

Had he pleaded this defense at the accusation meeting?

"I tried with all my might to reason with them," said Yoong, "but they had one answer for everything: 'You have more than you need, we have not enough.' When I appealed to the Rural Service Corps people they would only say over and over again, 'Shall twenty families starve in order that one may prosper?' That is foolish nonsense eight ways—I did not create the twenty families and I was not responsible for their poverty.

"But when I tried to protest this they would only say again, 'Shall twenty families starve that one may prosper?' Finally I had to give in and promise to reform, though never in my life have I committed a crime."

Yoong had been subjected to other penalties besides the loss of his land. He was not permitted the use of the village cooperative, which meant that he had to buy his necessities at another store and pay higher prices. And in accordance with the common practice he was deprived of citizenship rights for five years, partly for the purpose of making sure that he, as one of the few literate persons in the community, did not exert an undue influence on the conduct of its affairs.

Yoong Feng-rei's voice had risen considerably and people at the other tables were beginning to look in our direction. One man gave a little laugh, another scowled and spat on the floor. I rose, won— or rather lost—a brief clash over the privilege of paying the bill, and said goodbye to the proprietor as I settled with him. As I left, Yoong Feng-rei was calling for more *bai gan* and cursing his miserable lot. It seemed likely that he would go on cursing until the day he died.

Some of Generalissimo Chiang's admirers have suggested that the dispossessed landlords, together with the unhappy members of the middle class, might form an effective core of counter-rebellion. I think it would be a grave mistake for anyone to entertain such hopes.

In the six years since the institution of land reform on a national scale and in the twenty-odd years since it began in the Old Liberated Areas, millions of former landlords have willingly embraced their new status and accepted their position of equality with their former tenants. Many had been guilty of much worse offenses than Yoong Feng-rei, and perhaps for that reason have been better able to recognize the irrationality of their old existence.

Among the scholars and intellectuals who have found the new life difficult—and these are by no means a majority of their class— many are now learning to accept it because the alternative of moral isolation is even worse. As to the middle-rich or idle set like my friend Mr. Hua, they are a small and conspicuous minority who, if they wished to start playing rough, are not apt to get very far.

The stories of counter-revolutionary "uprisings" in China which have appeared from time to time in the Western press, gleaned at second or third hand from Chinese newspapers, have nothing to do with these malcontents or dissidents whose problems time eventually is bound to solve. The "uprisings" are the work of professional counter-revolutionaries. Some were left behind by the Kuomintang to wait for their brief moment of activity; others were smuggled in by foreign governments on behalf of the wistful ruler of Formosa. Nobody in China considers them a serious threat, and time will, I think, eventually take care of them too.

❧ 22 ❧

FRUITS OF DEMONOLOGY

In 1920, a talented young American journalist named Walter Lippmann set out to analyze the news coverage given by the press of this
country to events in Russia since the Revolution of 1917. He had
as his collaborator another rising editor of the day—and his colleague
on the staff of the *New Republic*—Charles Merz.

As their subject for a sample analysis they took the daily issues
of the *New York Times*, partly for the convenience afforded by its
easy accessibility and partly because they regarded it as America's most
complete and efficient newspaper representing the press at its best.
In their findings they were at pains to make it clear that they intended
no assault on the integrity or worth of the *Times*, which they considered in all respects "the greatest" newspaper in the United States if
not indeed in the world. With this judgment many unprejudiced journalists still would agree.

The results of the study by Messrs. Lippmann and Merz were published in a long, closely documented article called "A Test of the
News," which formed a special supplement to the August 4, 1920 issue
of the *New Republic*. This report excited considerable attention, at
least in journalistic circles, at the time, but it has seldom if ever been
referred to since in any newspaper. Nor has either of the authors shown
much interest in recalling it. The passage of years has brought both
authors to a state of eminence where quite possibly they are ready to
forget the whole thing. For Mr. Lippmann is now an institution of

conservative American journalism. As for Mr. Merz, he and *The Times* have so far forgiven each other that he is now its editor.

Nevertheless their "Test of the News" regarding Russia in 1917-20 has an obvious and, in a literal sense of the word, a terrible significance for the present day, when another vast new nation is in its beginning years. "In the large," they concluded, "the news about Russia is a case of seeing not what was, but what men wished to see. . . . From the point of view of professional journalism the reporting of the Russian Revolution is nothing short of disaster. . . . On the essential questions the net effect was almost always misleading, and misleading news is worse than none at all."

Substitute China, and these statements would be as true today.

Lippmann and Merz found some of the reporting from Russia "passionate argument masquerading as news." Quoting from *The Times* of May 20, 1919 a front-page headline whose effect was to advocate American armed intervention in Russia, they commented:

"This in our judgment is a clear and flagrant example of the invasion of the news by editorial opinion. We are not overstating the matter when we say that a great deal of the news about Russia in the period under consideration is marked by such propaganda methods."

Commenting on the reporting of a policy statement by the Russian government on the question of peace, they wrote: "The published summary is not only abbreviated, but it omits entirely the one point in the complete document which in our opinion is most relevant."

In their historic survey the two authors traced the beginnings and growth of the "Red Peril" cry which arose after the armistice with Germany, the obvious purpose of which was to stir up sentiment for armed American action against Russia. Analyzing the dispatches in the *Times* for one month—January, 1919—they listed stories appearing almost daily containing dire predictions of "Bolshevist invasion" in one part of the world or another, and called attention to what they characterized as the "reliance upon unidentified 'experts' and upon 'unofficial quarters' where rumor invariably finds its favorite haven . . . these sources represent in fact a fairly irresponsible assortment."

"The impression that they had their inspiration in rumor rather than in fact, it must be added, is heightened by contrasting them with what has actually happened subsequent to their publication," the authors remarked. "It is on the note of the Red Peril that this study ends. It has appeared at every turn to obstruct the restoration of peace in Eastern Europe and Asia, and to frustate the resumption of economic life."

Finally, in a section devoted to "Deductions," they again called attention to the regular use of anonymous pronouncements attributed to "officials of the State Department," "government and diplomatic sources," "reports reaching here," and "it is stated on high authority that. . . . . ."

"Behind these phrases," they observed, "may be anybody, a minor bureaucrat, a dinner table conversation, hotel lobby gossip, a chance acquaintance, a paid agent."

Thus did two public-spirited young journalists in 1920 analyze the news about a new-born nation appearing in a daily newspaper widely acknowledged as representing the American press at its best. Now, another huge nation has undergone the pangs of rebirth and is taking a non-capitalist course. And a similar test of the news would soon show a repetition of the journalistic performance so devastatingly exposed by Messrs. Lippmann and Merz.

The devices used today are strikingly similar to those described in 1920. But at least two new things have been added: a refinement of ingenuity that the press of a generation ago could not boast; and the frenetic voice of the radio-television newscaster or commentator whose shattering cries of peril and doom at breakfast, dinner and bedtime are familiar to everyone. Ever since Chiang Kai-shek was induced to yield his responsibilities on the China mainland, the "Red Peril" cry has blanketed the American atmosphere with all the insistence of a voodoo chant. The value of these devil-shouting predictions can easily be determined by the criterion used by Lippmann and Merz—"contrasting them with what has actually happened subsequent to their publication."

Infant nations, unlike infant children, cannot be done away with by violent applications of hot air. After forty years of such treatment the Union of Socialist Soviet Republics is still very noticeably alive. And the new Chinese People's Republic has gained in health, strength and world influence in her formative years at a much faster rate. But, while the demon-picture can do no vital harm to China, it is a gross deception upon the people of the United States.

"Whatever the excuses, the apologies, and the extenuation," to quote Mr. Lippmann and his colleague once more, "the fact remains that a great people [i.e. the American people] could not secure the minimum of necessary information on a supremely important event."

The distortion of news about Russia helped to make possible the disastrous Western and Japanese intervention in that country in 1919. In our own time the reckless whipping-up of "Red Peril" hatred against China led to an event which, in the perspective of only a year or two later, seems almost impossible of belief: the narrowly averted decision in the spring of 1955 to launch a nuclear war which might very well have achieved the substantial destruction of mankind.

It is, therefore, important to examine this hysteria-producing apparatus, with its devil-images and imagined menaces from which only suicidal violence could save us.

In its cruder forms the campaign conducted against China by press, radio and television has even resorted to race antagonism as one of its weapons. The "Red Peril" has been made to sound doubly sinister by combining it with the Yellow Peril, in association with other emotion-charged terms like "Oriental cunning," "the inscrutable Asiatic," "barbarian hordes," etc.

Even the noted liberal, Max Lerner, did not scorn to invoke Bret Harte's racist phrase, "The Heathen Chinee are peculiar," and add a remark about "Oriental duplicity" when Chou En-lai's diplomacy displeased him.* And on September 27, 1955, when Chinese-American talks at Geneva seemed to be making progress, the *New York Herald-Tribune* launched a syndicated series of articles by an American ex-prisoner of war in Korea, heavily sprinkled with anti-Asian epithets headed by those two most offensive of all, "Chinks" and "gooks."

Here, from a long list at hand, is one final example of the race-hatred technique for saving civilization: The distinguished columnist, Robert S. Allen, in October, 1954, began one of his syndicated newspaper columns with the words, "Blood-drenched history is being repeated among the Red moguls of Peiping."

The effect of such journalism on at least a segment of public opinion was apparent in the answers to a *New York Post* "inquiring reporter" who, on Bastille Day of 1954, solicited comparative opinions of China and Russia. One of his respondents declared, "I wouldn't even consider Red China a member of the human race. . . . They deserve no better treatment than a mad dog." Another: "The leaders of Red China and their followers are guilty of many crimes against humanity

* *New York Post*, April 25, 1955. Mr. Lerner specifically applied these epithets to Chou En-lai, and added his staunchly patriotic warning that Premier Chou would "gobble up" China's neighbors "tomorrow—if he dared."

but we must never forget that Red China is a backward nation and takes her cues from Russia."

More general and persistent than the racist invective has been the use of the kind of "Red Peril" fright-terminology that Lippmann and Merz identified as serving to "obstruct the restoration of peace" in Asia. "Red Dictatorship," "Purge," "Terror," "Slave Labor," "Hunger," "Famine," "Chinese Aggression," and a dozen other stencils of hate or fear incitement have greeted the eye of the newspaper reader almost every day.

What degree of actual truth or untruth this kind of journalism reflects is not a matter that I propose to go into here; but I will demonstrate how bits and pieces of fact have been used to draw conclusions about as far from the truth as it is possible to get.

In his preface to the 1947 report of the Commission on Freedom of the Press, Dr. Robert M. Hutchins, now director of the Ford-endowed Fund for the Republic, remarked that responsible journalism means reporting "not only the fact, but the truth about the fact."*

Thus, if the American press reports that most of the top government leaders of the Chinese People's Republic are Communists it is reporting a fact. If it reports that some officials have been removed from office for incompetence or dishonesty, and that many armed insurrectionists have been captured and some of them found guilty in court and executed, it is again reporting facts.

But when government officials, armed insurrectionists and other violators of the law are all lumped together, and the number of those merely removed from office is combined with those jailed and those executed to produce the headline, "Reds Purge Millions," it is both misstating the facts and falsifying the truth behind those facts. But it is, thereby, achieving a certain calculated effect.

Whether it is the calculated effect or the facts that interest our newspapers can be determined by a simple test. The test is how much they are really concerned with freedom, justice, democracy and similar values allegedly absent among the Chinese. As to this, Dr. Hutchins had a few pithy words to say to the members of the American Society of Newspaper Editors which had invited him to address its convention in April, 1955.

"You have filled the air with warnings of the sinister figures on

*"A Free and Responsible Press," Univ. of Chicago Press, Chicago, 1947.

the Left, but have printed almost nothing about the fat cats on the Right. You have allowed things to get to such a pass that some Government departments now have guidance clinics in which the employe is taught how not to look like a security risk. Look at the Passport Division . . . at the Attorney General's list, ruining the lives of thousands on the basis of hearsay; at the Post Office Department, saving us from *Pravda* and Aristophanes; at the State Department. . . . See the blacklist spreading in industry. . . . Listen to the wire-tapping, to the cry of Fifth Amendment Communist, to the kept witnesses roaming the land. The most distressing part of it is not that these things happen, but that the free press of this country appears to regard them as matters of routine."

And, it might be added, look abroad to the jammed political prisons in Madrid, Taipei, Seoul, Johannesburg, Ankara, Athens and other capitals of the Free World, and the slaughtered thousands of colonial "natives" in Africa. Such spectacles, when they are noticed in the American press at all, are treated as normal manifestations of life. By this test freedom and democracy, as such, hold little interest for our editors and publishers. But as special terms to be used in cold war propaganda, they see constant service.

A full documentation of the character of American news coverage about China since 1949, even if limited to a single newspaper, would involve a much heavier task than the one so brilliantly discharged by Walter Lippmann and Charles Merz. Here I can only give some characteristic and significant samples. For this purpose the *New York Times* again will serve. I will rely chiefly upon it and upon another highly respected daily, *The Christian Science Monitor*. From the other, less glorified newspapers, the press associations, a few periodicals, and radio-television, I will use a few particularly relevant exhibits. My radio and television illustrations are quoted verbatim, noted down at the moment by me or by others in whom I place full reliance.

At first, when the revolutionary government had gained control over much of the China mainland, the handling of news by the American press was fairly objective. Dispatches had reflected frankly the corruption and bankruptcy of the Kuomintang regime as well as the loyalty which American diplomats and investors continued to show to Chiang. While evincing no particular admiration for Mao Tse-tung and his forces, the China correspondents and their editors did not yet raise horrified cries about them. The exemplary behavior of their advancing troops was even mentioned with approval and the plans announced by the new regime were reported as matter-of-fact news.

True, there were limits to which the foreign editors felt they could safely go in depicting Communists as human beings. More than one correspondent omitted important facts from his cables about the progress of the takeover for fear that he would jeopardize his status. "I can't afford to stick my neck out," became a familiar refrain.

During that early summer of 1949, a certain amount of unbiased news continued to flow from China to the United States and to get printed in the American press. The correspondents were not particularly sympathetic; as neutral reporters there is no reason why they should have been. But their reports were not yet garnished with the invention and distortion which later began to feature them.

Then the situation changed. There had been some hope among foreign businessmen in China that the new government might extend to them some of the generous privileges they had enjoyed under the Kuomintang, or might even invite them in to help it run its affairs. Among American diplomats, especially the wishful thinkers who hoped to see rivalry for power between the Russians and the Chinese, there had been an assumption that the leaders of the Chinese revolution would "betray Moscow" and join with the West in the cold war. This proved a bad guess. Before long it became clear that the Chinese (quite sensibly as it turned out) reciprocated the friendship and support they received from the Soviet Union.

It was then that the China reporting in the America press showed a marked change. The verbal onslaught was well under way by August, 1949. This was a couple of months before the Chinese government was to withdraw accreditation from foreign correspondents until such time as diplomatic relations should exist, with Chinese newsmen permitted to work in a country which desired permission for its correspondents to operate in China.

On the fifth and sixth of August, American newspapers featured an Associated Press dispatch datelined Shanghai. "Chu Liang, 'Little Jolly Fellow,'" read the dispatch, "has been arrested for anti-communist propaganda. Chu, a vaudeville actor who first came into disfavor for a skit containing the line, 'people like to eat,' was criticized violently by the pro-red press for subversive activity. The *Liberation Daily* says the arrested man now is being questioned."

It sounded pretty sinister—unless you happened to know what the AP dispatch had omitted. The truth, as almost everyone in Shanghai knew, was that Chu Liang had been arrested not for "anti-communist propaganda" but because a number of radio actresses had lodged personal complaints against him for having acted as a procurer for Nationalist army "brass" before the changeover and having forced them to *wei lao* ("comfort") some of Chiang's generals.

The truth was, further, that the new government had no political charges against Chu but that he had, in fact, come into "disfavor" with the old Nationalist government a year earlier. It was then that he had performed his skit containing the phrase "people like to eat," coupling it with a reference to the city's rice merchants as "rice worms." For this he had been denounced by the rice dealers to Shanghai's economic czar, Chiang Kai-shek's son, and he had extended his procuring services as a means of "clearing" himself.

Thus easily can a few facts be altered and distorted to mislead the outside world. The falsification of routine local crime stories picked up from Chinese papers to make them look like instances of political persecution—reports of the arrest of persons guilty of anything from petty theft to crimes of passion—soon became a common practice.

Before long some China correspondents were giving their imaginations free rein in the reporting of what went on inside the country. I recall sitting in a wine shop in Shanghai surrounded by Chinese and foreigners engaged in normal imbibing late at night, and puzzling over the papers from home with their United Press and Reuters dispatches which informed the world that the town had been blanketed by an early-to-bed curfew. Similarly, it was not unusual to spend an hour listening to a Voice of America broadcast, and then to pick up a newspaper and read a press association dispatch announcing that the Voice of America had been banned by the new Chinese "totalitarians."

The practice of doctoring news stories about procedures against criminals to make them sound like political arrests or convictions has since become a ritual pattern through frequent references to the "terror" and "purge of businessmen,"—phrases with which Western journalists and scholars still characterize the *San Fan-Wu Fan* anti-corruption drives of late 1951 and early 1952. I have already related how *Time* magazine served up a horror story in which Mr. Chang, a Shanghai herb dealer, poisoned himself, his entire family, and his seven employes and their entire families; and how Bill Powell and I, several weeks after this fable appeared in print, were startled to find Mr. Chang and his employes alive and at their accustomed places in the herb shop. This blithe little fiction by no means exhausted the ingenuity of *Time*.

In May, 1952, a fourteen-member Indian cultural mission visited China, headed by Mme. Viyayalakshmi Pandit, former Ambassador to Washington and later to serve for a term as President of the United Nations Assembly. On their return to New Delhi Mme. Pandit told the Indian Parliament that China's new government was bound to endure because it commanded "the respect and loyalty of the people." This, she added, was because the government was responsive to the people's needs and had released tremendous energy which was being utilized in rebuilding the country. Wherever the members of the delegation went, Mme. Pandit said, whether to one of the new industrial plants, to the Huai River flood-control project, or elsewhere, they noted a feeling of cooperation with the new government among Chinese people of all degrees. Mme. Pandit's report was released officially by the Indian government.

Hard on the heels of Mme. Pandit's report came press "interviews" with other members of the delegation, all of whom averred that conditions in China were simply dreadful and all of whom, for some unexplained reason, chose to remain anonymous.

It remained for *Time*, however, to attempt the coup de grace. "For public consumption," that magazine announced, "Mme. Pandit said a few kind words: 'We were greatly impressed by the fine creative efforts of the new China.' " (She had said a great many more kind words than that, but *Time* often is crowded for space.) Then, relying for support on its own anonymous member of the visiting delegation who happened to be conveniently on tap, *Time* went on to say: "Red China has made substantial material progress but only by using armies of slave laborers. One huge dam visited by Mme. Pandit was being built by 2,000,000 peasant conscripts."

Ordinarily such controversies end at that point, with the publication in possession of the last word and the majority of its readers, in the absence of any rebuttal, satisfied that that word is gospel truth. But Mme. Pandit was not disposed to let the matter rest there, and on June 26 she issued another statement characterizing the press reports of her mission's visit as "incorrect and misleading." She called attention to the anonymity of the sources of these reports, plainly casting doubt on their genuineness.

"One such anonymous statement," she declared, "refers to 'strict control of members of the mission from the time they reached China to the time they departed.' This is completely misleading. A number of interpreters were assigned to the mission . . . since none of us knew Chinese.

"Reference has also been made to conscription of 'forced labor' for the purpose of building the Huai River dam. . . . It is a well-known fact that the Huai River dam was built through the willing cooperation of about 2,000,000 peasants who were paid." (This was corroborated by my own observation of labor conditions at the Huai River flood control project in North Kiangsu Province, made during a visit a few months later. I spoke with men and women workers there, and learned that much of the work was being done by peasants from the areas which had time and again suffered from Huai River floods; and that many of these men and women had volunteered to participate in this effort because it would mean an end to floods and misery; that they often worked on the project during the slack season on their farms; that in addition to pay they received free housing, medical services, transportation, and the opportunity to shop at low-price cooperative stores; and that any necessary work on their farms during their absence was done free of charge by their village mutual-aid team.)

But the nailing of one press fabrication about China meant little, for another usually came close behind. Almost at the same time that Mme. Pandit was laying to rest the whimsies of *Time* magazine—on June 23, 1952 to be exact—readers of the English-language press arriving in Shanghai were fascinated to learn from a United Press story datelined Taipei, Formosa, that "Shanghai is a city of hungry millions. . . . There is no rice for the vast bulk of the population," and ". . . the average Chinese is afraid to buy meat."

What was the source of this peculiar fear? Well, it appeared that anyone "who has enough money to buy meat is immediately visited by the neighborhood Communist 'tax commissar' who accuses the family of having a hoard of cash and orders them to hand it over as a 'special tax from the wealthy classes.' "

No rice in China, that is, but plenty of corn from Taipei. . . . Having ridden a bus past the Tihua Road marketplace on my way downtown just a couple of hours before, and seen housewives and amahs milling about the scores of open-air stalls buying pork, beef, rice, vegetables, eggs and other foods on ample display, at prices that would have cheered an American shopper, I thought this story rather curious.

Just to check my eyesight, I suggested to Pang Chen, an office colleague, that we drop over to one of the restaurants serving Western food for lunch, the Chocolate Shop on Nanking Road. On the way we passed a dozen restaurants large and small and a score or so of cheaper sidewalk eateries, all of which displayed their usual stacks of pork chops, sausages, roast duck and other meats to which Shanghailanders are partial. A large bowl of noodle soup could be had for the American equivalent of about five cents; *ke fan*, the counterpart of the blue-plate special, sold for from ten cents to a quarter.

At the Chocolate Shop the customary crowd of Chinese interspersed with Westerners were launched on American-style meals beginning with soup, proceeding to meat with vegetables and salad, and ending with dessert and coffee. Nobody seemed worried about where his next cut of meat or bowl of rice was coming from, and nobody seemed "afraid" to eat it when it came. As for the neighborhood "tax commissar," he bothered no one because he never existed.

I found myself wishing that the gifted author of the United Press dispatch could have been there as our guest, for the Chocolate Shop is only a hoot and a holler from the old UP office on Yenan Road. But the UP scribe was now doing his hooting and hollering from Formosa.

It is from such apocryphal beginnings, nevertheless, that popular myths take root and flourish. The United Press fantasy about hunger in China, having achieved the dignity of print in numerous places, entered the general fund of misinformation about China and was used unquestioningly in newspaper and radio-television comment, and even in learned tomes written by scholars.

The effect of such outpourings upon an American living in China, and regularly perusing the newspapers and magazines from home, was of an eeriness not readily to be described. Among the publications we were then receiving at the *Review* office through subscription or exchange were *Time, U. S. News & World Report, The New Yorker, Harpers, The Nation* and *The New Republic*. In addition I read the daily Associated Press, United Press, Reuter and Agence France Presse dispatches which were carried by the *Hongkong Standard*, a Chinese-owned English daily, opposed to the new government, which arrived every day. I also read clippings sent from the States relating to China which appeared in the *New York Times,* the *New York Herald-Tribune,* the *Washington Post* and the *San Francisco Chronicle.* From these one might conclude that there were, in fact, two places called China—the place where one lived and the place they were writing about, to which it bore no faint resemblance.

~~ 23 ~~

NEWS FROM NOWHERE

It was from Hongkong that by far the greatest bulk of such press, material issued either at first, second or third hand. For it was to Hongkong that most of the China correspondents and press bureaus betook themselves when they decided, in late 1949 and early 1950, that the atmosphere in China was going to be uncongenial to their thinking. There, in the British crown colony on the border of China, they set up their "window," or at least peephole, into the awesome land they had forsaken.

And they found plenty of company there. For Hongkong had already begun swarming with "China experts" in the form of American and British diplomats, consular officials, intelligence officers, press agents, political theoreticians and economists, as well as Chinese refugees or fugitives. The Chinese refugee "experts" prospered; they found an insatiable market for their rumors and "inside information," their compilations and analyses, their "fact sheets" and "authentic reports" mysteriously gathered about a place to which they had no access.

Since the changeover, the consular offices of Western countries in Hongkong have transacted little consular business; but anti-Chinese propaganda assignments have given them plenty to do. At times the personnel of the United States Consulate in Hongkong has been the largest of any in the world. The special agents, publicity experts and "idea men" in some cases have been indistinguishable from the "working newspapermen" in Hongkong for one very good reason; they have given signs, in some cases, of being the same person thriftily holding down two jobs.

The Hongkong sources on which American correspondents and press bureaus rely almost exclusively consist of:

(1) *Western Governments.* Official statements or unofficial gossip from employes of the American, British, or other foreign consulates whose job it has been, since the changeover, to prosecute the cold war as energetically as possible against the present government of China.

(2) *Anti-Peking Chinese.* Chinese emigrés who have lived in Hongkong since long before 1949 and have thoroughly absorbed the comprador mentality toward China. Most of them are British, American or Formosan subjects whose sole or principal source of income is from propaganda against the Chinese People's Republic. Among these are the compilers and publishers of "fact sheets" and "reports" which form the bases for many scholarly "surveys" of conditions in China published in the United States.

(3) *Refugees, Fugitives and Released Prisoners.* Many of these are Chinese whose enmity toward the revolution caused them to leave the country voluntarily (and without hindrance). Others are persons either of Chinese or foreign nationality wanted by Chinese authorities on charges of violating laws, or deported on similar charges. Still others are military personnel of foreign governments released after conviction and imprisonment as spies or agents of Chiang Kai-shek, who has not been reticent about boasting of his "forces on the mainland." In such cases an individual's account of life in China is not precisely unbiased.

(4) *The China Press.* Newspapers, periodicals and official government statements published in China and received in Hongkong. These, on the surface, furnish the most effective ammunition in the arsenal. They are combed minutely, day by day, for any sign of an internal problem of any sort. Since "criticism and self-criticism," or public discussion of social failings, is basic to the Chinese creed today, an abundance of such material is to be found in almost any issue of almost any Chinese publication. Whether this indicates any fundamental or serious failing in present-day Chinese society is another question.

If, for example, a regional grain harvest falls short of the predicted yield, or one item out of twenty in an industrial plan fails to achieve the stated goal, this is announced in the Chinese press and much discussion centers around it. Such "admissions" are seized upon in Hongkong, and minor or partial failures are transformed into national catastrophes. The favorable news of which such items are a small qualifying part is omitted. This has been the regular method of reporting exercised by the American press all the way from the slapdash, casually irresponsible tabloids to the *New York Times* and *Christian Science Monitor*.

The *modus operandi* of this species of journalism was already familiar to Western newspapermen in Shanghai shortly after the changeover, when the foreign press corps was still doing its China reporting from China. Since few of the correspondents or bureau heads could read Chinese, translators were employed. The translator's job was to scan the Shanghai papers along with the official Peking *People's Daily*, translate the principal headlines, and list them on a sheet of paper.

This topical list might—and during the early months of the new regime probably would—include headlines reporting progress in stemming the currency inflation, agricultural gains in areas which had undergone land reform, the reopening of factories and re-employment of their workers, and so on. The Western correspondent or editor would run his eye down the list, disregard items that reflected credit on the new government, and mark one that had to do with, say, the arrest on murder charges of a landlord's strongarm overseer.

"Okay, translate that story in full, Wang," would come the command. And presently the cable would be speeding another "Chinese Terror" story to America with the Chinese press itself cited as the authority.

When the foreign press corps moved across the Hongkong border this specialized type of reporting was raised to a high art—and a considerably formalized one—through the ready availability of a whole regiment of pro-Nationalist Chinese who could render expert assistance in the "interpretation" of these selected tidbits from the Chinese press.

An illuminating example of how this process worked—and still works—was afforded by an article in the *Christian Science Monitor* of August 15, 1955. Datelined Cambridge, Massachusetts, the article deals with the sojourn at Harvard of Mr. William Hsu, identified as "chief editor of the Union Press and Union News Agency in Hongkong—a growing publishing house that has become one of the most important sources of information about what's going on in China under the Communists."

Mr. Hsu, according to the author of the *Monitor* story, Mary Handy, had been a member of "an anti-Communist underground cell" at the University of Peking. But two of his comrades in the counter-revolutionary group had repented their course, and suggested to the others that they do likewise. Then what happened?

"Mr. Hsu and his friends," the article relates, "quickly saw that things had gotten too hot—that they would have to leave. They bought railroad tickets to Hongkong." What did they do with their railroad tickets? " 'We confessed we had been members of a reactionary organization,' Mr. Hsu is quoted as saying, 'and said we regretted this. Then, before anyone suspected what was going on, we boarded the train and left China.' "

Without pausing to wonder just how oppressive a "bamboo curtain" can be in a land where a confessed counter-revolutionist can buy a railroad ticket, hop a train and leave the country, let us proceed to Mr. Hsu's quoted account of what happened next:

"When we got to Hongkong we were nearly broke. But we joined friends and worked as writers and editors at odd jobs. We saved our money, started subscribing to publications from the mainland, and set up the Union Research Institute." Apparently all that is needed to set up a "research institute" on Chinese affairs is to start "subscribing to publications from the mainland." It is instructive to note, too, that Mr. Hsu and his associates, who started out nearly broke and subsisted on odd jobs, accumulated enough money to enter business in hardly any time at all.

"Today," the article continues, "the Union Publishing House is a thriving business with a staff of 150 and offices in several Southeast Asian cities." And, we are informed, it issues a variety of publications among which are "scholarly articles," as well as "*The China Weekly* that features a weekly report on what is happening on the other side of the 'bamboo curtain.' "

Just who are the customers for this avalanche of printed matter the reader is not told. But it is evident from the healthy state of Mr. Hsu's business that his clientele must be widespread. The *Monitor* describes his publishing concern as "one of the most important sources of information" about China. In short, the outpourings of an escaped counter-revolutionary who proclaims his enmity toward the present government of China is, to our press, "one of the most important sources of information" about China.

How trustworthy is his "information," and what this means in terms of China news reporting generally, we are able to gauge from a sample quoted in the *Christian Science Monitor* story. "In March, 1954 the *People's Daily* [of Peking] reported that 200 million people—or a third of the population—lacked food," Mr. Hsu told his interviewer. This is the repetition of a myth that has become a classic in the library of anti-Chinese demonology. It was promulgated in the news columns of the *New York Times*, and through the medium of a Reuters news agency dispatch in the *Monitor*, at the time mentioned by Mr. Hsu. And this is how it was arrived at:

In November, 1953 (a few weeks before I left China) the Chinese People's Government, because of the increased demand for grain resulting from an overall rise in national purchasing power, moved to prevent speculation and profiteering in food and took over its distribution on a national scale. Much publicity was given this move in the Chinese press, including the problems and difficulties involved. The government undertook to buy from grain growers, at fixed prices, the major portion of their grain not needed for their own use and to market it to non-food growers and to farmers growing food crops other than grain.

Now, China's 100,000,000 peasant families grow various crops. Millions of them grow rice, corn, millet, wheat, and other edible grain, and others raise soyabeans or peanuts or vegetables or fruits or other foods. Still others concentrate on industrial crops like cotton or hemp or tobacco. However, despite old superstitions entertained abroad, the Chinese eat a variety of foods and, as in most other countries, few of them raise all the kinds of food they eat. Hence the need for food distribution. Grain and tea are transported to peasant families which grow vegetables and fruit, and vice versa. And to those which grow no food at all, including both the growers of industrial crops and the urban dwellers, all their food must be transported.

Food distribution on a national scale in a country as vast and as heavily populated as China is obviously a huge undertaking. "Distribution" of food means, here as anywhere, purchasing it from the grower and delivering it to the consumer. In discussing this matter the *People's Daily* in Peking stated on February 10, 1954, that, "It is undoubtedly an extremely onerous task to guarantee food at a reasonable price to an urban and rural population of 200,000,000."

How did the outstanding organs of American journalism report this story? Seizing upon the word "distribution" to make it appear like "relief," and seizing upon the word "onerous" for its vague implications of difficulty, the *New York Times* ran a story on March 9, 1954, headed, "1/5 OF RURAL CHINA IS SHORT OF FOOD." It attributed to the *People's Daily* the statement that "About ten percent of China's rural population is living in 'famine areas.'" Also that "the state now actually had to supply food to nearly 100,000,000 persons in the countryside"—the plain inference being that they were destitute.

In the next sentence the admission was made that "this total was said to include residents of county seats, small towns and industrial crop areas as well as other food-deficient peasants." If a farmer who raises other crops than foodstuffs is thereby a "food-deficient peasant," then millions in the United States are in a state of perpetual starvation.

This hoax was repeated two days later in the news columns of the *Christian Science Monitor*, through a Hongkong dispatch attributed to Reuters under the sensational headline, "FAMINE STALKS RED CHINA."

"Communist China has conceded officially," said the opening sentence, "that almost half the country's 450,000,000 people are receiving government food relief for famine. A copy of the Peking *People's Daily* reaching here disclosed that 200,000,000 people are being supplied now with food." The author of the story did not state whether he himself had dug his breakfast out of his own land that morning, or also was being "supplied with food" and thus "receiving food relief for famine."

To this bit of deception the *Monitor* story added another, based on "unofficial reports" and "other reports reaching Hongkong." These otherwise unidentified reports brought the allegation that "the Communist government has imposed a complete ban on the sale and production of polished rice in the country," and that only unpolished rise was available. As everyone knows, with the possible exception of Hongkong dispatch-writers, the polishing of rice removes most of its nutritive value, and doctors and dietitians in the United States have been loudly beseeching every one for decades to eat unpolished rice (or whole wheat bread instead of white bread) for the sake of their health. In old China the short life span and the small stature of many of the people, particularly the rice-eaters of the south, have been attributed at least partly to polished rice as a staple diet item. China's "Communist government," singularly enough, was the only government in the world sufficiently concerned about its people's welfare to discourage an ancient dietary habit injurious to their health.

Since I was still living in China when the "complete ban on the sale and production of polished rice" supposedly went into effect, I can report from personal experience that, while most Chinese appeared to feel that the eating of unpolished rice was to their personal benefit as well as a means of increasing the total amount of rice available, there was no such thing as a "complete ban."

The entire business of food distribution at fixed prices, be it noted, is a matter of taste as to who shall do the distributing and who shall make how much profit. In the United States the wholesale price of milk is fixed by either the state or federal government and the retail price by agreement among the dairy companies. For milk that is priced for the farmer at from eight to twelve cents a quart when it issues from the cow, the housewife pays twenty-four or twenty-five cents. Grain worth a fraction of a cent a pound when harvested brings from twenty to twenty-five cents at retail under free enterprise.

It was to eliminate the middle-handling, the manipulating, the speculating and profiteering on food that the Chinese government took over its distribution. Under this system the "two hundred million people now being supplied with food" pay for what they get, just as scores of millions supplied with food by business interests here pay for it. But you would never know it from reading our newspapers.*

The "food shortage" myth was repeated a year later by the *New York Times*, and possibly will become an annual feature as regularly to be looked for as that paper's spring editorial lauding the integrity of the free press. In its 1955 version the story appeared on April 24, in the form of a Hongkong dispatch by Mr. Tad Szulc. The factual nub of this story, as cabled by Mr. Szulc, was that the Chinese government had been "announcing recently a series of measures to improve production"; that the goal was an increase of ten million tons of grain

---

*On September 8, 1955 the *People's Daily* in Peking, commenting on the purchase and distribution of grain, noted that a good summer harvest had been reaped in many areas and a good autumn harvest was in sight. "This year's grain production in China," the paper stated, "is estimated at 180,400,000 tons. The estimated figure for 1957 is 192,800,000 tons, or 12,400,000 tons more than this year. State purchases will remain unchanged for three years, even though the output of grain is expected to increase. Every peasant in China will, it is estimated, have 25 more kilograms of grain in 1957 than in 1955, or every household approximately 100 kilograms more. If the production plan is overfulfilled, the peasants will keep still more grain for themselves."

over 1954; that the newly formed Agricultural Bank of China would make loans to individual peasants as well as to farming cooperatives and state enterprises; and that peasants were being urged to use high-quality seeds in their planting.

To this report the *Times* gave the headline: "RED CHINA IN GRIP OF SPRING FAMINE." And this is the paragraph with which the story was introduced: "Signs of a spring famine in Communist China are filtering from the mainland. At the same time the Peiping Government is showing a growing concern over the long-range agricultural picture."

These alarming conclusions, and a few others like them, were based on the following sources in the dispatch: (a) "persons [unnamed] who have crossed the border to this colony"; (b) "A Canadian missionary [unnamed] recently arrived from Shanghai"; (c) "experts here" [anonymous]; (d) statements culled from Chinese publications in which government officials reiterated their basic national policy that the socialization of agriculture must proceed gradually and voluntarily.

On the basis of such statements, and of the unidentified voices whispering into his ear, the correspondent drew a picture of "food shortages" and "famine." Government officials were encouraging the peasants to produce more grain. Therefore there must be "shortages." Measures such as agricultural loans and the distribution of more productive seed were being employed—ergo, there must be a famine.

The *Times* returned to the subject three months later—on July 30, 1955—in what was essentially a rewrite of the previous year's story ("1/5 of Rural China is Short of Food"). This time the "news peg" was a report to the National People's Congress by Deputy Premier Chen Yun. What he reported, as a scrutiny of the *Times* dispatch itself would reveal, was that China had produced 1,300,000 more tons of grain in 1954 than in the preceding year despite almost unprecedented floods; that the country had "sufficient grain to eat and dispose of"; that China was able to export grain as it had been doing since 1950; and that domestic use and export of the crop did not leave, in Chen Yun's own words, "much of a surplus."

All these facts were included in the *Times* dispatch itself, but so effectively minimized, buried, or larded over with "interpretation" that they were discernible only to the trained eye of a professional journalist or a propaganda analyst. Upon this report of progress in China's agricultural program the *Times* bestowed the headline: "Many in China in Need of Grain." And the correspondent, borrowing liberally from the *Times*' "famine" story of a year earlier, began his dispatch thus: "Almost one-fifth of China's peasant population must buy grain from the state because of natural calamities or individual shortages, according to Deputy Premier Chen Yun." Individual shortages? Well, millions of Chinese didn't raise any grain—so they were "short!" And to prove that they were in desperate circumstances, they had to buy it from the "state"—the only distributor of grain since November, 1953, as we have seen!

A few weeks before the appearance of this example of responsible journalism—on May 30, 1955, that is—the *Times* printed an editorial lamenting what it termed the "spring famine" and "rural starvation" in China, ending on this lofty note: "It is clear, however, that the Chinese Communists are learning that promises of future industrial greatness cannot substitute for present food, and that hunger cannot be assuaged by government edict."

Quite so. Neither can it be created by verbal legerdemain.

Similar techniques of distortion, invention, and the half-truth-disguised-as-fact have been employed to fasten upon the public consciousness such notions as the "Red purge," "brainwashing," "slave labor," "Chinese aggression."

The foundations upon which these tales are based seldom vary: the well-coached "refugee"; the escaped counter-revolutionary selling anti-Chinese propaganda for a living; the faceless "expert" whose identity or whose very existence cannot for some mysterious reason be established; the doctored-up version of reports in Chinese newspapers or official documents. To such tainted testimony the press has thrown open its columns in a solemn-faced pretense that it is purveying "news" from China.

A massive headline in the *New York Post* of February 23, 1955, screamed: "MAO KILLED 15 MILLION CHINESE, EXPERT SAYS." The "expert" is Mr. Walter Robertson, whose main assignment as Mr. Dulles' Assistant Secretary of State at that time was to labor at resuscitating Chiang Kai-shek's collapsing fortunes. The sources for his story were unspecified "reports"; the occasion was an appearance at a Congressional hearing designed to drum up public sentiment for increased military appropriations, during which annual process traditionally anything goes. The editors responsible for this hysterical headline must have known the nature of Mr. Robertson's qualifications as a China "expert" and the probable degree of truth or nonsense in his performance. In the normal practice of responsible journalism such a statement would have been shrugged off or ridiculed. But "MAO KILLED 15 MILLION," in extra bold Gothic, makes a feverish headline. And feverish headlines not only sell newspapers, but in such matters carry a vague impression of fiery patriotism.

In its more staid manner, *The Christian Science Monitor* joined in with a series of articles by another Robertson. Basing his figures on the Chinese press, Mr. Frank Robertson added together all reports of Chinese arrested for crimes ranging from petty graft to kidnapping and murder, threw in the regiments of Kuomintang troops mopped up by the People's Liberation Army after the departure of Chiang, used the stock mistranslation of the Chinese term for destroying the military effectiveness of a body of troops—that is, killed, captured and dispersed—and emerged triumphantly with the allegation that millions of innocent Chinese had been "purged."

Along with this myth, tirelessly promoted by the newspapers and doubtless accepted by millions in Western lands, goes another: the "slave labor" legend. Like the "purge," it is useful to those interested in maintaining the impression that China is ruled by men so inhuman that there could be no possibility of living peacefully in the same world with her. This, if true, would certainly be of the utmost seriousness in a world where, as President Eisenhower has said, there can be "no alternative to peace."

For a demonstration of the technique whereby the "Chinese slave labor" story is purveyed to the American public in the guise of news and commentary, let us follow Mr. Egon Kaskaline, author of an article in *The Christian Science Monitor* of November 2, 1954, headlined:

Soviet Pattern
SLAVES PRODUCE FOR MAO

This headline, calculated to put the reader in an exorcistic frame of mind by linking the detestable idea of slavery with the Chinese leader Mao Tse-tung and then with the onerous "Soviet Pattern," need not be attributed to Mr. Kaskaline. Newspaper writers generally are not responsible for their headlines. Nevertheless it reflects accurately the tone and purpose of the piece.

That tone and purpose were set forth by Kaskaline in his leading paragraph, furnishing an admirable example of journalistic objectivity: "Communist China has adopted one of the ugliest features of Communist dictatorship by establishing a slave labor organization."

Having succeeded in crowding into one sentence of less than twenty words the time-tested fright symbols of "slave labor," "dictatorship," and "Communist" (twice), with the epithet "ugliest" added for the benefit of the dull-witted, the author proceeded to announce in his next paragraph that:

"Official documents, published by the Communist government, report that numerous forced labor camps have been set up all over Communist China. Slave laborers, counting probably millions of men and women, already are making important contributions. . . ."

In his third paragraph Mr. Kaskaline assured his readers that "Mass internment of 'enemies of the people' began immediately after the Communists took over. Yet it is apparently only now that political prisoners are being used as slave laborers on a large scale."

It was in his fourth paragraph, however, that his startling exposé mounted to its climax. Here he divulged the source of his confidential information about "slave labor" in China. "Regulations Governing Labor Service for Reform, published September 7," he wrote, "and other documents which have come into the hands of western experts show how thoroughly the Chinese Communists are imitating the Soviet model."

It was upon China's own documents, then, that he based his allegations and the atmosphere of guilt by association with the Russians —"the Chinese Communists are imitating the Soviet model." The fact that "Regulations Governing Labor Service for Reform" was printed literally by the hundreds of thousands and circulated both in and outside China seems hardly worth mentioning, since copies of it doubtless did come, as Mr. Kaskaline darkly phrased it, "into the hands of western experts," whether they got them by writing to Peking or by picking them up at the American or the British consulate in Hongkong.

But what did these Chinese documents, once in the hands of "western experts," reveal to justify Mr. Kaskaline's accusations? What secrets did they lay bare that enabled him to write about "millions of slave laborers" in China? Here is his answer: "The number of inmates of the Chinese labor camps is not disclosed."

The lack of tangible facts in paragraph five of his story did not disconcert him, however, for he had on call another sure source for this kind of journalism. "Unofficial estimates," his story continued, "place the figure at several millions, citing as their authority such statements as the following from the September 7 *People's Daily* in Peking."

He then proceeded to quote what he alleged to be passages from the newspaper mentioned:

"A nationwide campaign has resulted in the arrest of large numbers of bandits, despots, special-service agents, backbone elements of reactionary parties and corps, and leaders of reactionary societies and religious organizations. These elements have been sentenced to prison terms, deprived of their political rights, and eventually organized in labor corps where they carry out their reform through forced labor."

And so, with hardly any effort at all, the *Christian Science Monitor's* writer had taken a Chinese press discussion of the arrest of assorted criminals in "large numbers," and had blown this up into "several millions" with the aid of "western experts" and their "unofficial estimates."

What had really happened?

For years since the *San Fan-Wu Fan* drives of 1951 and 1952 and even before, the new government had been rounding up racketeers, gangsters, armed insurrectionists, business bribe-givers and bribe-takers, and intelligence agents sent in by Chiang Kai-shek and some of his friends. These had been put on trial, and those convicted had been sent to prison. The mysterious "document" produced by Mr. Kaskaline, supposedly revealing a portentous new development in what he called the "organization of a slave-labor system," was in fact a routine report by Lo Jui-ching, Minister of Public Security, on the handling of these convicts. Kaskaline's quotation from the Peking *People's Daily* (a copy of which is before me as I write, and the excerpt turns out to be not from a news report about the "Regulations on Reform Through Labor," but from an editorial) is badly translated, or perhaps successfully mistranslated, to give it imputations which it did not carry.

As a matter of fact, when one compares his quotations with the original text in the *People's Daily*, one can begin to see how the omission of a few sentences, plus a few mistranslations of Chinese characters, produces meanings quite different from what the original statements contained.

In short, just as *The New York Times'* Mr. Szulc had taken a government report reflecting marked progress in agriculture, operated on it with scissors and paste, disguised it with the grease paint of "interpretation," and presented it as a confession of failure and distress, *The Monitor's* Mr. Kaskaline had performed similar surgery on Lo's report and sought to transform it into an admission of wholesale atrocity upon innocents. What such press stories represent is an application of the technique of "Great-heavens-look-what-they're-doing-now!" What they are doing now may well be what is properly, beneficially and universally done. But pointing an indignant finger at it while uttering exclamations of pious horror couched in "Red Peril" cliches can convince many readers that it constitutes a dreadful crime.

As regards "forced labor" in China, there is certainly a system of compulsory work for convicted criminals, as there is in other nations throughout the world, including the United States, Britain, Canada, France, the Soviet Union, Belgium, Sweden, and so on. Modern penology emphasizes the therapeutic value of work for prison inmates. The laws of the United States, like those of almost every nation in the world, prescribe imprisonment "at hard labor" for most categories of convicted criminals. One difference between such "forced labor" in America and "forced labor" in China is that American prison inmates receive next to nothing for their work while those in China are paid prevailing wages and in many cases support dependents at home on their earnings.

These facts about prison labor in China are easily accessible to any Western journalist who might be interested in them.* But no doubt it is more advantageous to conform to the official mythology. Thus in "good" countries the universal institution of compulsory labor by criminals is a natural and wholesome thing; in "Communist" countries it is a crime against humanity.

---

*A *New York Times* dispatch published August 13, 1956, from Lanchow, China, strikingly answered the "forced labor" charge. The author was identified by the *Times* as "David Chipp, a British correspondent of Reuters, who has just completed a 5,000-mile round trip from Peiping to the northwest of China." Describing a huge development project in the northwest, Mr. Chipp wrote:

"If there is forced labor, then it is nowhere apparent either in attitude of the workers or in the pace at which they work." He also quoted Chinese officials as saying that in such undertakings "unwilling labor would be a drawback rather than an asset."

✎ 24 ✑

WHO "BRAINWASHES" WHOM?

One of the most heavily exploited myths of the cold war was blown up with a shattering bang in February, 1956, in the pages of the conservative weekly, *U. S. News & World Report.*

Its issue of February 24 carried a long interview with Major William E. Mayer, an Army psychiatrist who had spent four years in Korea and at home studying "brainwashing." "His conclusions," the editors of the magazine noted, "are based on detailed questioning of nearly 1,000 U. S. soldiers who were captured in Korea and underwent brainwashing at the hands of Chinese Communists."

Major Mayer was quoted in the interview as saying that American prisoners of war in the hands of the Chinese "were not subjected to physical torture, according to their own statements."

The verbatim interview, presented in the form of a series of questions and answers, continued:

"Q. So you don't count torture as an essential part of brainwashing?

"A. Definitely not."

In answering the question, "Then what is brainwashing?", the psychiatrist replied: "It is not the third degree. It is not an inhuman system of unnamed tortures and magic designed to 'detroy the mind' and will."

A little farther on he is quoted as follows:

"As long as we understand precisely that by brainwashing we are simply using a coined word to apply to an indoctrination and education process, I can say that every prisoner-holding power in every major war has engaged in this kind of activity. This is permitted under the Geneva Convention. The Communists simply went about it more intensively, more systematically."

Toward the end of the session the interviewer asked: "Did they [the Chinese] try to make prisoners into Communists?" The answer:

"Never. One of the largest areas of public misunderstanding has related to just this problem. It seems clear, from the things the prisoners said, that not only was no attempt made to convert them to Communism, but, in fact, any prisoner who even suggested joining them physically was very promptly and emphatically dissuaded. They made quite a show about this."

The article ended with a "disclaimer" stating that the opinions expressed by Major Mayer "do not necessarily represent the view of the U. S. Army." His statements can nevertheless be regarded as definitive. Not only were they made by a fully qualified authority, but it is inconceivable that they could have appeared in print without the cognizance of the Pentagon.

This official repudiation of the "brainwashing" myth, one of the harshest accusations flung at the Chinese, came after five years of its constant employment. Time and again, when conditions had begun to look favorable for some meaningful move toward settling differences and bringing order and stability into American-Chinese relations, the legend had been trotted out as an excuse for prolonging enmity. The Chinese "tortured" American prisoners; how could they be admitted into the company of civilized nations?

From the outset the "brainwashing" story had been used to stir emotional frenzy in cold war propaganda and introduce mystical elements that prevent rational reactions. Speculations on psychology, psychiatry, medical theory, propaganda methodology and even witch doctoring were flung about. Every editorial writer, columnist, and "China expert" aired his views on it.

To confuse the discussion still further, the fuzzy term, "brainwashing" with its flavor of science-in-slang was sloganized and given every sort of meaning from physical torture to mass hypnotic persuasion. "Brainwashing," like "purge," "slave labor," and other verbal stigmata, became a fright word whose mere utterance conferred automatic guilt upon the accused. As such it became a regular part of the press vocabulary.

Specific accusations of "torture" took a prominent part in this campaign. They came from the press, from diplomatic circles, even from the White House. A prominent physician turned diplomat as a member of the American delegation to the U. N., elicited headlines by announcing his conviction that American prisoners of war had been "tortured." His sole support for this theory was a learned, and admittedly hypothetical, analogy with Pavlov's dogs. The mere mention of Pavlov was supposed to prove that American soldiers had been "conditioned" by their captors—and with techniques invented by a Russian!

The accusers somehow failed to notice that many American prisoners, returning home, denied stories of mistreatment when speaking of their own free will, although not when speaking under the eye of public-relations officers. Some had no opportunity to speak at all, but were kept incommunicado on reaching American soil and hustled to military hospitals for mental "reconditioning."

Meanwhile in the mass-circulation periodical *This Week* for July 17, 1955, A. E. Hotchner, an outstanding freelance writer, quoted with evident Pentagon approval the findings of Army Intelligence that "no American military prisoner was 'brainwashed' during the Korean War." It made little difference; the "brainwashing" cry still went on. Then, in February, 1956, came the final obsequies on the myth, pronounced by an Army authority on the subject who was fully identified and quoted verbatim in the *U. S. News* article.*

---

*Still another article debunking the "brainwash-torture" myth, and based on official U. S. Army findings, appeared in *Look* magazine for June 26, 1956. Written by Dr. Julius Segal, a psychologist, on the basis of an investigation conducted for the Department of the Army, the article states that, "The Communist captors in Korean prison camps used no hypnotic powers to influence our men; nor did they in some mysterious fashion 'wash their brains' clean of Americanism to replace it with the Communist faith."

In answer to the suggestion that American prisoners of war "collaborated because they were 'brainwashed': mercilessly browbeaten and shrewdly indoctrinated with propaganda," Dr. Segal wrote, "This just isn't so." To the notion that "collaboration followed brutal, physical abuse—that collaborators signed Communist propaganda petitions, or informed on their fellows, only after they were subjected to excruciating tortures," his reply was: "This, again, just is not so."

An editor's introduction to this article states that "the research was conducted by the Human Resources Research Office of George Washington University, operating under contract with the Department of the Army and directed by Dr. Meredith P. Crawford. A full technical report has been submitted to the Army and has been declassified [made available for publication]." Of the author: "He served in the U. S. infantry from 1943 to 1945. A graduate of the University of Scranton, he received his Ph.D. from Catholic University in Washington."

Despite all of this, no real effort has been made to spread this information so that it can be effective. Books and articles continue to be published, and references continue to be made, as if the myth were a reality.

So much for the "brainwash-torture" myth as applied by the press to American military personnel. In the case of American civilians imprisoned in China, similar techniques have been employed.

Most American civilians, on arriving in Hongkong after their release, have been received into the waiting arms of State Department representatives and given some intensive coaching, after which they issued statements about their "suffering" and "mistreatment." When any declined these ministrations—and some did—their refusal to speak the desired piece was quickly attributed to "brainwashing."

Such a case was that of Mrs. Adele Austin Rickett, who arrived in Hongkong late in February, 1955 after three and a half years' imprisonment for espionage under the guise, as she related, of a Fulbright scholar.

"From the time of her arrival in Hongkong," Henry R. Lieberman cabled to the New York Times on February 28, "Mrs. Rickett has seemed calm, patient and quietly determined." And what was she quietly determined about? She had been telling reporters that she had become convinced of the rightness of the Chinese cause; that she had served as a spy against them and now considered this a crime; and (in reply to questions) that she had not become a member of the Communist party because she was not "worthy" of the "honor." She added that her purpose henceforth would be to work for peace among nations.

To have admitted the possibility that such a person might still be in her right mind would have been objective journalism, but it would have been fatal to the propaganda mission of the press in the cold war. The Times correspondent prefaced his account of Mrs. Rickett with his own interpretation, and wrote of her and Dr. Malcolm Bersohn, another released American who had spoken in similar terms:

"Their utterances still provided the most striking example of Communist prison indoctrination yet encountered here. They have come out of China not only with standardized Communist ideals but also with the whole Communist vocabulary." And, as a prop to the "brainwashing" imputation, he offered a comment from an unnamed American who had known Mrs. Rickett in Peking in the old Chiang Kai-shek era. Here is the comment which the *Times'* Mr. Lieberman, apparently unaware of its revealing nature and indeed of the whole history of political conversion, quoted:

"Mentally, she is completely different. She was a sound, intelligent person. There was never any indication that she had leaned to the left. For a person like that to have undergone such a change is a complete shock."

Here, at any rate, is naive honesty. Many millions of sound, intelligent persons around the globe have "undergone such a change" after an opportunity for first-hand comparison; and if that is a "complete shock" to an impartial American journalist or his "sources," the fact might as well be admitted in cold print. The story adds up to a simple sum: If you have seen good in new China you must be prepared to say you have been "brainwashed"—or else to give, and doubtless receive, a "complete shock."

But it is in the broader use of the "brainwashing" slogan—that is, as implying hypnotic or compulsory control of the thinking of an entire people—that the American press has done its most thorough job. The concept, as used for this purpose, is as vague as chlorophyll and as all-embracing as the benefits of the right deodorant. Anything under the sun can be explained by it or linked with it.

Thus, if the Chinese people rally around the leaders who led them to freedom from the Kuomintang, it is because they have been "brainwashed." If they follow their lead in turning away from medieval farming methods to join agricultural cooperatives and treble their income, the explanation is easy: "brainwashed." And so too with the thousands of scholars, writers and intellectuals who, having compared the despoliation of their country under Chiang Kai-shek with her new health and dignity under the government led by Mao Tse-tung, have decided to embrace the latter. "Brainwashed!"

As one more propaganda formula in the general press, the brainwashing myth is not likely to have any marked effect on general emotional attitudes toward China. But when serious organs of opinion throw open their pages to it—such as the liberal weeklies and the literary monthlies—they place a stamp of supposedly disinterested approval upon it in the eyes of many thoughtful readers.

For example, in the pages of the widely respected weekly, *The*

Nation, there appeared in the spring of 1955 an article epitomizing an intellectualized version of the "brainwashing" myth. This article was written by Mr. Kingsley Martin, editor of the London *New Statesman and Nation*. His conclusions in some respects parallel those of the staff press agents of the American State Department and the China Lobby, but he possessed the advantage of having made his observations inside new China.

From his articles it was not clear how long a time he had devoted to his first-hand survey; it may have been four weeks, it may have been six. His general report was far from being all, or even preponderantly, negative. He found no evidence to support what he identified as "the Honkong-American view of divisions, discontents, and instability in China." He discounted heavily the stories of "mass liquidations," pointing out that "liquidated" meaning killed, was a mistranslation of a speech by a Chinese general who boasted that two million enemies had been "rendered harmless," and noting the inclusion of numbers of criminals and "ex-Kuomintang soldiers in southern China who had refused to surrender their arms."

Even in the area of his main theme, that of "brainwashing," Mr. Martin discredited much of what is purveyed in the popular press on this subject. Yet he clung to his own version of the "brainwashing" slur, and did so on two specific grounds. One was the tales of dissident or partially converted intellectuals, admittedly holdovers from the Kuomintang regime, whose testimony he seems mainly to have sought on the subject. He accepted their stories of physical and mental torture though unsupported by any observed evidence. In my four active years as a journalist in China during the present regime I never encountered such evidence; and since no disinterested person has ever claimed to have witnessed any, the hearsay stories which Mr. Martin relies upon must remain highly questionable.*

---

*Lo Jui-ching, Minister of Public Security, in an address to the National People's Congress in June, 1956, acknowledged that some unjustified arrests had been made on the ground of counter-revolutionary offenses, and that some of those wrongly arrested had been convicted and jailed. "We arrested some against whom warrants might well have been withheld rather than issued, and in a few cases we even arrested some persons who should not have been arrested." Criticizing these injustices, he stated that "some have already been rectified and others are in process of being corrected." Security Minister Lo added that physical mistreatment of prisoners is forbidden by state policy.

Tung Pi-wu, President of the Supreme People's Court, described to the Congress a current policy of "greater leniency" on the part of the courts in view of substantial success achieved in combating counter-revolutionary activity.

But his chief reason for the accusation of "brainwashing" arose from broader considerations. Mr. Martin complained that political and propaganda pressures were exerted on the Chinese people in order to make them believe certain things. This is undoubtedly true—just as it has been true in every major country of the world, including England and the United States, since the beginning of the cold war. One man's "brainwashing" is another's "loyalty-security program." The American thought-control apparatus that has invaded schools, churches, the press, trade unions and the home, scandalized our allies, and excited bitter protest from courageous scholars and jurists, clergymen and plain people at home, can scarcely have escaped his notice.

The only question then, if we are to accept Mr. Martin's terms, is, who is to "brainwash" whom, and to what purpose? He noted in his *Nation* article that what he referred to as "brainwashing" was called "re-education" by the Chinese. And that, from my own extensive observation, is exactly what it is: education away from old ideas that made their country a land of misery toward new ideas that offer hope and realized achievement. This departure from the old toward the new is the path the Chinese have chosen for themselves. It is not the path prescribed for them by the Western intellectual liberal. And this is the one thing that the Western intellectual liberal, in all his self-righteousness, cannot endure.

The trouble is, of course, that the leaders of China's revolution do not happen to share Mr. Martin's opinion as to the moral superiority or even the common sense of what he identifies as the "liberal tradition." Being men and women of intellect too, they are not unacquainted with this tradition. They happen to regard it, with its abdication of active moral choice, its compulsion toward safe respectability, its well-bred suspicion of the submerged man and anxious concern for the rights of his most brutal oppressors, as a destructive and self-defeating ethic. They have noticed no deterrent effect exerted by the "liberal tradition" on the Western cycle of militarism, wars, depressions and moral decay over a period of two hundred years. Above all they have seen it ineffectual in retarding the procession of foreign gunboats to the Whangpoo River. They have chosen to believe that there must be a better way.

The Western liberal attitude toward "brainwashing" seems even more strange in view of my experience in seeking to challenge some of Mr. Martin's conclusions via a letter to his magazine: In reply I received a printed slip informing me that my communication had been received and would be given "attention." That was the end of the matter, though not, perhaps, the end of Western liberal complaints about the one-sidedness of propaganda in China.

It is not because the Chinese leaders of today exercise conformity pressures—with methods and results amateurish compared to those of the West—that liberals like Mr. Kingsley Martin accuse them of "brainwashing." It is because they are exercising their pressures in a direction displeasing to those advocates of toleration and good will. And in adding their voices to the general chorus of invective and abuse, such critics have performed on the intellectual level the same task to which the popular press has devoted itself: the building of an emotional *cordon sanitaire* against the new Chinese nation.

✧ **25** ✧

"LOGIC OF DEATH"

In a remarkable editorial in its issue of March 27, 1955, the *New York Times*, after a sober inventory of the war clouds then gathering over Quemoy and Matsu islands, wound up thus:

"It is time that the fire-eaters in Washington, whether in the Pentagon or elsewhere, went into silence. We need calmness and wisdom. This newspaper hopes and believes that President Eisenhower, hating war as we know he does, and realizing, as he said he did, that one cannot see where a war will take us, will exercise his leadership during the coming critical week to save this country and the world from irretrievable disaster."

I have called this pronouncement remarkable—and in fact it is a good deal more than that. Not every day, before or since, has it been possible to read in the pages of a powerful and conservative American newspaper an editorial enjoining "the fire-eaters in Washington" to silence, and calling upon the President "to save this country and the world from irretrievable disaster" not by waging or threatening war, but by rejecting it.

The critical events in Sino-American relations during that winter of early 1955 may have faded in the minds of many, but they are worth recalling—for it was then that the world in all probability came the closest it had yet been to the "irretrievable disaster."

March 27, 1955 was a Sunday. During that weekend there had taken place in Washington, according to Doris Fleeson, political columnist writing in the *New York Post* on the following Monday, "what amounts to the attempted 'brainwashing' of President Eisenhower and the American people by the 'China war party.'"

"If it succeeds," the columnist went on, "the United States will be in a war for two tiny islands a few miles from the China mainland which are not vital to Formosa, stronghold of the Chinese Nationalists. We would wage it alone. Every major ally of this country, including Canada, has warned of its profound disagreement over such defense."

The path toward this point-of-no-return had been paved, during the preceding weeks, by a steady outpouring of newspaper headlines and radio-TV newscasts harping on what was variously called "Chinese Red Aggression," "Chinese Communist expansion," and so on. The *Times* itself, just a month earlier, in its Sunday review of the week's news, had invoked the latter term, calling it "the most urgent foreign policy question confronting the United States," and supplementing it with other dark references to "Peiping's expansionist pressure," "Communist penetration and attack," "the overall Communist threat in Asia," and similar phrases. The *Herald-Tribune*, undisguisedly waving the "Red Peril" flag day after day, referred in its Page 1 leading story of March 26 to "information [source as usual unidentified] that Red China, possibly with Russian aid, may attack in the Far East within the next three weeks."*

A week earlier, on March 18, the eminent syndicated columnist, Joseph Alsop, urged in his column "the clear possibility verging on the likelihood, that the United States will end by having to fight an atomic war for Formosa's offshore islands." Mr. Alsop, who previously had been conditioning his readers for such an event by cool calculations about necessary "megadeaths" (a scientific term for millions of deaths), opined that we lacked "the forces needed to give us a reasonable margin," but noted comfortingly that "the use of the atomic weapon can thus become unavoidable."

Along the Atlantic seaboard, across the great plains, in the shadow of the Rockies and up and down the West Coast, newspapers informed their readers with monotonously uniform accent and pitch that any Chinese attempt to dislodge Chiang Kai-shek's forces from the "two tiny islands" would be "a threat to American security" and "an act

---

*The *Christian Science Monitor*, too, had been adding its bit to the uproar with contributions such as the giant-size headline in its Feb. 17 issue: "China Reds Build Up Challenge to Offshore Islands—and U.S."

of aggression against world peace." The cry was echoed by Mr. Ned Calmer, CBS Radio newscaster, who spoke on March 7th of "the present Communist Chinese aggression in Asia," and by most of his radio and television colleagues.

Few if any newspaper writers or broadcasters reminded their public that both President Eisenhower and Secretary of State Dulles, less than a year earlier, had dismissed the offshore islands as having little strategic significance. Now there was a hue and cry for the launching of an atomic war over them—and the press was doing its share to whip it up.

A note of questioning did appear here and there, such as Miss Fleeson's strongly worded column and an Ottawa dispatch in the *Washington Star* which quoted a member of the Canadian parliament as being "horrified" at Secretary Dulles' "calm acceptance of the possibility of a world war over islands that are utterly inconsequential." But these were isolated voices amid a full-throated nationwide chorus which, if not calling expressly for war and proclaiming that we had better be the ones to start it, plainly intimated that it was "inevitable."

Then came the *Times* editorial of March 27, like the agonized muttering of a man struggling to awaken from a nightmare. Not only did it hit back at the "fire-eaters in Washington, whether in the Pentagon or elsewhere" and implore the president to "save this country and the world from irretrievable disaster." It reviewed the chain of events that had brought us to where we were, and ended:

"So we have, as today's news describes it, a situation in which a certain kind of logic—the logic, perhaps of death and widespread destruction—goes from the defense of Quemoy and Matsu to an all-out atomic attack on the industrial potential of Communist China. What this logic means in the cost of human life and perhaps in a vast destruction of cities far outside China, the citizen may ponder."

The fact is, however, that the "logic of death and widespread destruction," which the *Times* so justly deplored, went far back beyond the crisis over Quemoy and Matsu for its premise. Had the whirlwind struck, it would have been only the bloody reaping of those winds of suspicion, fear, hate and belligerency unrestrainedly sown since 1949 by almost every American medium of opinion-formation against the new China.

The process is a familiar one, and contains its own built-in "logic." Its onward march, once undertaken, is well-nigh irresistible. It proceeds compulsively from Step One, the automatic conception of all Communists as monsters; to Step Two, the consequent classification of governments led by them as "aggressive"; to Step Three, the labeling of all international disturbances as the result of their evil plans for world conquest which threaten every home and every life; to Step Four, the inevitable conclusion that they must be wiped out by violence, whomever else that violence may destroy.

This mental process has been called "suicidal mania" by more than one thoughtful critic of contemporary events. At any rate, it is a recognizable mass expansion of the tragic case history of that American Cabinet officer whose obsession with the "Red Peril" drove him to mental breakdown and who ended his life plunging from his hospital window, screaming, "They're coming!"

This is not to maintain that the press alone is responsible. It was not the press but the Dulles State Department and its allies in Congress that took the actual physical steps to keep our relations with China in a state of continuous crisis. It was not a single-minded group of newspaper owners and writers, but the atom-happy wing of the military command, that drew up a program for immediate nuclear attack against the China mainland and nearly succeeded in selling it to the President.

But the point is that such conduct would have been impossible except in an atmosphere of such hysteria and reckless hate as to make self-destructive madness seem plausible. The creation of such an atmosphere is precisely what the press accomplished. You cannot cry up a lynching, even in the deepest South, without first creating a frenzy of hate against your victim. And if the lynching is to be done with a noose that will encompass the necks of the lynchers themselves, then you must first convince your fellows that even such a fate would be better than continued life in the same world with the hated one. That, too, the press and its related organs have very nearly succeeded in accomplishing.

That it does not have to be thus is proved by the abruptness and unanimity with which they can change their line from fury to calm, from bitterness to something almost approaching sweetness and light, when moved by some higher law, whatever it may be. The resemblance of the entire coast-to-coast press-radio-TV complex to an orchestra obeying the will of an unseen conductor has been remarked often enough to make it platitudinous.

"You," said Dr. Robert Hutchins to the publishers in his 1955 address, "are the only uncriticized institution in American life." And being almost wholly uncriticized and almost wholly unopposed, they can create with their concerted voices a deafening noise and an enveloping atmosphere of whatever kind they choose, whenever they choose.

Whether they will choose in the long run to create an atmosphere hospitable to life or will go on promoting "the logic of death," only the future can tell. What is certain, however, is that no general release from self-destructive superstition is possible without a change to rational attitudes on the part of the press and the broadcasters. If they cannot directly bring about the change, they can at least refrain from making the change impossible. A little light, a little truth, a little recognition of grave responsibilities, would go a long way.*

---

*In fairness to some newspapers, especially the *New York Times,* a distinct change in the tenor of their China reporting since the spring of 1956 must be noted. The *Times,* gradually devoting less space to slanted "dope" stories from Hongkong, began covering the news realistically from inside China. Other papers, notably the *Christian Science Monitor* and the *New York Post,* have occasionally followed suit.

The shift in the *Times* policy began with the publication of frequent dispatches from Peking by *Reuters,* a British news agency thoroughly conservative but perhaps less subject to cold war influences. Some of these dispatches contained reports of marked progress in China's industry, agriculture and foreign trade. News stories indicating improvements in the lives of the Chinese people also found their way into the *Times.* In general its new-style China coverage tended to confirm many important claims of progress made by the Chinese government.

The *Times* went still further in August, 1956, when it ran a series of several dispatches from Peking by Reg Leonard, correspondent of the *Melbourne Herald,* "who recently completed an extended tour through Communist China." These reports presented, with minor qualifications, an over-all picture of social and economic progress, personal well-being, and political solidarity in the new Chinese nation which contrasted startlingly with previous reports in the same paper and in the American press generally. They included such statements as:

"Even in the most cautious assessment, it has to be agreed that great things are happening in China."..."Building construction is fast."..."New railroads."... "New industries."..."Spectacular progress."..."The Chinese people are attacking the task with determination and unbounded enthusiasm."..."No evidence whatever to support reports that Moscow was 'running China.'"..."Nobody bends the knee in China these days."..."Stories that they are starving are false."..."Rents are absolute bedrock."

Compared to these reports in the *New York Times,* my own assessment of progress in Red China, as described in this book, is virtually conservative. These *Times* news stories reduce to unworthy nonsense that newspaper's continued use of such editorial page incantations as Chinese "crimes," "repression," etc., with which it has tried to excuse the State Department's anachronistic policies.

✥ 26 ✥

LAST LOOK AROUND

My six-year sojourn in China ended in the fall of 1953. The *Review*, which for some time had been hampered by an unofficial mail embargo in the United States, finally closed its doors with the July, 1953 issue.

We on the staff had been aware for almost a year that Stateside subscribers were receiving their copies irregularly or not at all, although no ban was ever officially—or at least publicly—announced. While the *Review* had readers throughout Asia and all over the English-speaking world, its main readership had been in the United States. By early 1953 it was evident that the invisible curtain had been considerably tightened; letters came from readers inquiring whether the magazine was still being published, and if so, why copies were no longer coming through. The financial struggle became more and more difficult, and at last impossible.

After winding up his business affairs and waiting out the two or three months normally required for a foreigner's exit visa to come through, Bill Powell left with his family for the United States. I meanwhile had entered into long-distance negotiations with some newspapers and magazines published in India and in New Zealand in the hope of serving them as China correspondent to enable me to stay on and watch the developing Five Year Industrialization Plan at close range. This failed to materialize, and I applied for my visa and began looking up steamers. The visa came through after a wait of ten weeks, and I was free to depart for home without fuss or fanfare, as fifteen hundred other Americans and thousands of Europeans had already done since the changeover.

It was early November before I was able to get passage on one of the British freighters that was making regular weekly runs up and down the China coast between Shanghai and Hongkong. Meanwhile I caught up on my diary and paid farewell visits to friends. A few evenings before my departure that light-hearted trio of restaurant habitues, David Chen, Fatty Chien, and Mr. Hua, in whose company I had consumed many a Peking duck and downed many a catty of amber rice wine, gave me a farewell dinner at a wine shop on Foochow Road which served food along with its liquid fare, specializing in Shanghai-style sea food delicacies.

As usual on such occasions we had to carry on much of our conversation at the top of our lungs. Most of the other shouting was done in the traditional *hwa chwen*, or "fist game," which we also played. This game, reminiscent of a method of choosing up sides for a ball game among American kids, is conducted by pairs of players each of whom calls out a number from zero to ten and simultaneously shoots out from his clenched fist any number of fingers from none to five. The winner is the one whose shouted number equals the total number of fingers extended; if neither does, it's a draw. The loser's penalty is having to take a drink. Unlikely though it may seem, practice increases one's proficiency at this game, and I won often enough to maintain an upright posture. But no matter who wins or who loses, a wine shop or restaurant full of *hwa chwen* players can make a lot of noise and dispatch a significant amount of wine in the course of an evening.

My companions and I called time out from the game when the swinging door to our private cubicle opened to admit an ancient, wispy-bearded gentleman with an er *hu*—a Chinese two-stringed violin—followed by his pupil, a willowy young woman singer. It was the custom of these entertainers, moving from table to table in the wine shop, to present to patrons a long scroll-like list of favorite Peking opera arias. They would sing and play request numbers while all fist-game playing and all but a modicum of dining and drinking ceased.

Enjoying this last taste of Shangai night life, I could not help reflecting that there were literally hundreds of wine shops throughout the city, not all as festive as this particular one, but all offering a place where convivial folk could come and spend an evening over a catty or two of yellow wine, a plate of roasted salty broad beans, and a dish or two of other food. And I wondered, as I was to wonder often after returning home, what could be the basis for those tragic reports one read about "darkness and gloom" over the new People's Republic.

When our dinner was over my friends were for going on to Ciro's, one of Shanghai's bigger and fancier ballrooms. But I had some final packing to do. We drank a last farewell, and I left them to finish their evening in the style to which they were accustomed.

Alone in my rooms, pawing over the accumulated clutter of six years, salvaging this newspaper clipping and discarding that, hanging on to one keepsake and sacrificing another, I began to wonder how one would go about summing up what had happened during the last six epochal years in China. Maybe the story could be told adequately in statistics, or through a sober survey of industrial, agricultural and economic changes. Or maybe there was a better way of assessing it: through what had happened to the people around me.

From their standpoint China had not become a paradise in the four and a half years since the change. Nor would it in the forty to come. Many still were poor, and would remain so for years. Many millions would continue for years to win their daily subsistence only through arduous labor. Millions would remain inadequately housed and no more than adequately clothed. Nor can I doubt that there were some victims of injustice while others enjoyed prosperity without having earned it.

These are things that could be said with equal truth of any nation in the world. The crucial difference was that now, less than five years after the overturn, these things were true of fewer Chinese than ever before. Poverty in former times had been considered normal and inevitable. Now it was thought of as abnormal and avoidable. Its conquest had already begun, and the further that conquest advanced, the more certain seemed the ultimate victory.

Most important of all, the new society had brought hope to vast numbers who had scarcely known its meaning before. For decades the expression mei yo banfa, "there is no way," had been heard throughout the land. It had now become plain that there was a way—and a good way from any rational human standpoint.

Of the workers one met in the streets, more than half had been unemployed in 1949, living under almost subhuman conditions without comfort, dignity or hope. Now, in November of 1953, all but a very few had jobs, and these few were covered by unemployment insurance for the first time in China's history. As for wages, they had risen at least to double their level at the time of the change, while prices had remained stable.

China's workers, under the provisions of the 1950 Trade Union Law, could look forward to a lifetime of productive employment, with their old age provided for and the education of their children, as well as their future place in society, assured. New advantages such as the bonus system, life and health insurance and retirement pensions had made life worth living for them in a way they had scarcely conceived of before.

Many still lacked good housing, especially in Shanghai, but tens of thousands of new dwelling units had gone up and construction was continuing. The last four years had seen more accomplished in that direction than the whole century preceding.

The redistribution of the land to the people who tilled it, had been completed in the first three years. More than four hundred million peasants, eighty percent of the entire population, now owned their own land and for the first time in their lives were reaping the benefits of their labor on it. Gradually learning the advantages of co-operative farming, they had increased their average income by nearly two-thirds at the end of 1953. They were now ready to start on the more advanced, more productive cooperative methods through which alone China's agricultural potentialities could be realized.

Another monumental change I had witnessed was the launching of the huge complex of flood control, water conservation and afforestation projects which, aided by the extension of railroads and highways, was lessening the hazards of flood and drought which from ages past had been a constant menace to tens of millions of China's people. I had seen enough to convince me that China can never again suffer any flood damage or famine remotely resembling what has happened throughout her past history.

The rehabilitation of industry, which I had observed in the factories of half a dozen cities, was the prelude to the launching of a fifteen-year industrialization drive. This vast project is designed to make China the industrial equal of any nation in the East, and to lay the groundwork for becoming a thoroughly industrialized nation.

The preliminary phase had already established in China for the first time such heavy industries as machine tools, locomotives, chemicals, textile machinery and farm equipment. Evidence of the rise in the nation's industrial output was visible in the daily lives of the people. As this is written, in mid-1956, it appears that although some of the individual goals of the first Five Year Plan may fall a little short, most of them will be overfulfilled.* A few years ago the mere undertaking of such an enterprise by China would have been unthinkable.

But the life of the Chinese people as it teemed and bustled about one in that fall of 1953 was by no means all production plans and agricultural goals. Every walk through the streets, every ride on a bus, every evening spent in a theatre or restaurant or in the home of a friend brought fresh reminders that the Chinese were undergoing a renascence in their social and cultural life, and were enjoying it hugely.

I have tried to describe the new atmosphere that followed upon the demise of the Kuomintang era. It is not an easy thing to make explicit in words. Perhaps the best way to characterize it is as a sense of release—the freeing of pent-up energy and purpose. The Chinese, despite their long history of suffering, are by nature one of the most ebullient peoples in the world. In their first years under the new government a gradual increase in personal well-being and a new sense of security, as well as the birth of reasonable hope for the future, gave them the impetus to let themselves go.

Browsing over my collection of newspaper files and clippings in my apartment on Hengshan Road, I came across a dispatch dated April 20, 1953, from the *Hongkong Standard*, a hard-core pro-Kuomintang English-language daily. It reported that, "The consensus was that Shanghai is now a dead city." As far as the absence of clip joints, gambling dives and bordellos was concerned this was quite true. But otherwise it made no sense. I dug out my copy of Shanghai's biggest daily, the *Shin Wen Rih Bao*, of the same date to have a look at what had been going on that day.

Half a page out of the six was devoted to ads for movies, stage plays and opera. Dozens of movie houses were open from two in the afternoon to around eleven at night. On that day—and it was no

*Minister of Finance Li Hsien-nien's budget report of June, 1956 stated that the overall production goal set for 1957 would be reached by the end of 1956. Total industrial ouput in 1956, Li said, would be 19.7 percent above 1955, as contrasted with the target figure of a 14 percent increase.

special kind of day—exactly forty-nine theatres were offering plays or opera.

The Chinese had always been avid theatregoers—at least those who could afford it. Now, with the general rise in income and with lowered admission prices, everybody was going to the theatre, and getting tickets was a problem. Prices, unlike the days when I first came to Shanghai, were comparatively trifling. Seats at the movies were under a quarter; tops at theatre and opera, well under a dollar. The *Ke Mon,* "House Full," signs came out early, and long lines of people queued up for future bookings.

During the previous summer the famous Peking opera star, Mei Lan-fang, who has a huge following throughout China and is known in many other countries, had played in Shanghai to packed houses. Peking opera, a highly stylized and symbolic form of the art, has a tradition that goes back many centuries. Mei Lan-fang performed a number of classical works including The Drunken Beauty, The Warlord of Chu Bids Farewell to the Lady of His Heart, and Sword of the Universe.

Shaoshing opera, named for the famous wine-producing city in Chekiang province where it originated, is likewise a great favorite in Shanghai. It is noted for its all-female casts and elegant costuming. Its familiar arias can be heard hummed in the streets of Shanghai and sung on the radio. Both old favorites and recent works were included in its repertory.

In the packed movie houses the accustomed fare of imported films, chiefly American, had given way to Chinese-produced pictures. Some Russian, Czech, East German, Hungarian and Polish films, all with dubbed-in Chinese dialogue produced in China, also were being shown. One of the newer movie houses, built in a workers' district at the edge of the old French Concession, featured a snack bar, a library and news-paper reading-room, and a lawn fronting the entrance. At the time I left China there were rumors that French and Italian movies were about to come in, as well as some Chaplin films.

But although Hollywood movies had lost favor, other forms of Western entertainment had come to enliven the Shanghai scene. One was American-style ballroom dancing, which by the time of my departure had developed into something approaching a fad among all strata of the population. Many people were taking dancing lessons, learning the mysteries of the fox trot and its infinite variations, the old-fashioned waltz and related maneuvers.

In China most dancing is done at Saturday night parties thrown by organizations or individuals, often to dance music played on records of a vintage that would quicken the heartbeat of an American collector. But Shanghai also has splendiferous public ballrooms which used to be frequented mainly by Kuomintang officials, tired but solvent businessmen, and playboys. Lately the clientele has represented a broader segment of society, although businessmen are still much in evidence. These ballrooms still offer a certain number of dance hostesses, who now have their own union. But mainly couples come to caper to the strains of popular music played by Chinese bands.

Another, less frivolous, pastime that was attracting great numbers of people at that time was peculiar to post-civil war China. This was the cultural exhibition, which can best be described as a sort of traveling museum unit in which models, pictures, charts, facts and figures tell a story about some phase of Chinese society past or present. In addition to such current subjects as agriculture, light industry, and the manufacture of machinery in China, some have been devoted to themes like painless childbirth, the story of mankind's development, the Taiping Revolution of the 19th Century, and other topics of broad educational interest.

A better measure of what I have called China's rebirth was the widespread interest in books and music. Public libraries in the Western sense, where books are borrowed to be read at home, still were few. But a huge new one of 900,000 volumes had been opened in one of the buildings at the old Race Course on Bubbling Well Road in 1952. Crowds lined up each morning an hour before opening time. Every workers' club and union hall also had its library or reading room.

In the literacy drive, aided by the introduction of simplified writing, millions were being taught to read, bookshops opening up everywhere. In 1953 Shanghai had 340 shops devoted principally to the sale of books. China has a huge network of traveling book stores, libraries and newspaper-reading circles, penetrating into backwoods villages and city alleys.

The crowds that jammed Shanghai's book stores every day, and doubly on Sunday, always amazed me. Books bound in paper and printed on cheap stock are published in minimum editions of ten thousand, and sell for a few cents. Many resemble the American "comic" book in their picturized form, but the stories they tell range from episodes out of Chinese classics such as *Shui Hu*, "Water Margin," to dissertations on how to grow wheat more productively or how to keep the neighborhood clean. Even these picture books contain a large proportion of reading matter, as do the many children's picture books that are now produced.

Among the pictureless books, translations of foreign classics were high on the popularity list. A good deal of Dickens was now available in Chinese translation, as well as *Vanity Fair*, *Gulliver's Travels* and other standard novels. A twelve-volume edition of Shakespeare was being prepared for publication at the time I left.

Other English authors published since include Milton, Fielding, Byron, Shelley, Hardy and Shaw. Among American authors widely read in China are Dreiser, Jack London, Longfellow, Walt Whitman, Howard Fast and Albert Maltz. A translation of Mark Twain is under way. A number of French and German classics have been translated, too.

Many of these translations were being issued by private publishing houses. The publishers have a sure thing, since they can count on government purchase of about ten thousand copies of any of their translated classics for use in government office reading rooms and schools and libraries.

Among the growing number of professional translators one of the most eminent was Zau Shin-mei, whom I saw frequently in Shanghai. I had first met him in New Haven in 1947. Zau had been a leading light in Shanghai literary and artistic circles in the old days, had spent a good part of his student years in the twenties in England and France, and spoke English with an Oxford accent. He was now serving as adviser to private publishing houses which specialize in translations.

Zau was a great friend of Emily Hahn, who had much to say about him in her best seller, *China To Me*. Since I was to pass through Hongkong on my way home, and he had heard that she was living there at the time, he asked me if I would be good enough to look her up, tell her that he would like to hear from her, and assure her that it would be perfectly safe for her to write to him. "She appears to think," he said, "that I would get into trouble if I received mail from Western friends outside China."

A widespread interest in serious music also was in evidence. A new form of folk opera had come into being, dramatizing the new life of the Chinese laboring man and woman. By far the most famous is *Bai Mao Nü*, "The White Haired Girl," which is performed constantly throughout the length and breadth of China. It was enthusiastically received in many countries of Western Europe when a Chinese opera troupe presented it there in 1955. The music of the new folk opera has a Western flavor, and is easier for a Westerner to listen to than the classical, high-pitched Peking Opera.

There is also a tremendous new interest in folk songs, which are as diverse as China's far-flung provinces. Much of this music had never before been written down, but scholars were now traversing the countryside and recording it from the lips of the peasants. Such recordings are widely bought for home use; they also are popular on the radio. If the Chinese radio offered a "hit parade" program, folk music would run off with the honors by a wide margin.

Chinese concert music still is based mainly on the ancient Oriental five-tone scale and uses traditional instrumentation. By 1953, however, far more Western classical music was being heard than during the old days. Tschaikovsky, Dvorak, Beethoven, Mozart and other composers familiar to Western concert goers were being played over the air several hours each day in Shanghai. The Shanghai Symphony, formed several decades ago and made up principally of Europeans, had now become a municipal organization and was composed about half of Chinese and half of Westerners when I last heard it. In March, 1953, the 126th anniversary of Beethoven's death was observed with special performances of that master's works. Since the new government was established a symphony orchestra has been set up in Peking, as well as a conservatory for the training of Western-style musicians.

When I first came to China, fresh from the study of her language and cultural history, I was filled with romantic notions about a land of quaint charm and antique graces, slant-eyed beauties posturing in jeweled robes, bearded scholars debating Confucius and happy-go-lucky coolies accepting their humble lot with philosophical smiles. A picturesque little civil war was going on somewhere in the background, important mainly as a source of dinner conversation.

What I found was a land of widespread suffering and human degradation beyond utterance, whose victims were neither smiling nor philosophical about it, but desperate to get rid of it. I found that most people regarded the men who were waging war against it not as bandits or adventurers, but as patriots.

The men and women who led that fight are now leading the reorganized society that rose out of the victory. The people's loyalty to them is nothing new; it grew up and solidified over the many years during which the fight went on. For the Chinese Revolution was no overnight *putsch* by a conspiratorial clique. It was in progress for decades, and it never could have succeeded if millions of people had not rallied to its support and voted for it with their lives. Nor were they unduly frightened by the "Communist" label that went with it, any more than were the non-Communist nations of Asia, the Middle East and Europe which have recognized the new government since its formation.

The paranoiac fear which that label inspires in some lands must seem incomprehensible to the people of non-Communist nations like Indonesia, Burma, India, and Japan, where Communists hold public office without causing nightmares, and where, as in France, Italy, West Germany and Finland, Communist parties poll significant votes and Communist newspapers are sold even in the lobbies of swank hotels.

Regardless of labels, the profound stability of the Chinese People's Republic both within and without is a condition of life that the most reluctant must get used to. That there is no future for Chiang Kai-shek or his followers is a fact now being assimilated even by his fondest friends. It is also becoming universally understood that the reuniting of Formosa with the mainland is only a matter of time. China is well on her way toward becoming a first-rate power, with a vast and lucrative consumers' market awaiting the breaking down of trade taboos and with export products of which some nations are already availing themselves, while others gaze wistfully at them across the artificial barriers.

Leaving the possibility of an all-destructive Third World War in the realm of psychopathology where it belongs, it is evident that America and China are going to live together in the world if they are to live at all. To the ordinary Chinese, whose friendliness reaches out to all peoples, this outlook is an immensely pleasing one. To the average American, if his faith in his country and its traditions is as firm as it might well be, I believe the same prospect will prove equally pleasing.

At seven o'clock on a chilly morning in late November I presented myself and my luggage at the Whangpoo River pier just off Yenan Road for customs inspection. An hour and a half later I boarded the little Butterfield and Swire steamer that was waiting to take me to Hongkong on the first leg of my voyage home. A number of other foreigners were already on board, including a Britisher, a Frenchman, and about fifteen White Russians bound for Australia.

The view of downtown Shanghai from the river, as one begins the long slow sail toward the open sea, is an impressive one. We passed the tall business buildings along the Bund, Broadway Mansions where I had lived in my days of affluence as a newspaper and radio correspondent, the power plant, Shanghai University campus.

At the foot of Garden Bridge, which crosses Soochow Creek, we passed the park which lines the river bank, with benches where people sit and look out at the water, keeping an eye on their children at play. While my last view of the city where I had spent so much time and seen so many things happen was an unforgettable one, I was interested even more in watching these last few Chinese people whom I could see in their homeland. I found myself making mental computations, as I had done many times before, of the vast change that had come into all their lives and of what must be the impact of those changes on them.

A little family group in the park caught my eye as we sailed down the Whangpoo and began slipping along past the miles of smoky suburbs. There were a young woman, an elderly one who might have been her mother, and a little girl of perhaps three or four. There was nothing very special about them, except that the little girl at the moment did not appear to be happy. She was crying bitterly as the grandmother held on to her while the younger woman walked off with a wave of her hand, perhaps, I conjectured, to do some shopping or household chore.

As the little tableau passed into the distance, I could not help thinking about the unhappy child, and reflecting that however great her momentary grief might have been, she had in the long run much less to cry about than would any child of her age in the old China. Nobody would ever be allowed to sell her into concubinage or slavery. If she married, no husband could misuse her as he pleased and no tyrannical mother-in-law could make her life a hell of submission.

When she grew up she would be compelled to go to school and

receive at least a primary education. She would be taught a trade; if she showed aptitude for it, she could continue her studies and learn an art or a profession. If she conducted herself as a normal and useful citizen, she was entitled to the fulfillment of her normal wants from the beginning of her life to its end. And she was entitled to this not by reason of any particular kind of birth or family, or of any superior personal gifts, but simply because she was a human being.

We have often been told by persons of high moral authority and great rectitude that there is a deep wickedness in all this. And yet somehow I find that hard to believe.

27

WHAT THEY ASK ME ABOUT CHINA

Since my return home, in conversations and in public talks about China, I have been asked certain questions. Few people have had access to any information on the subject except what is offered in the general press, or in books, that purvey the official line of thought.

Many Americans, I have found, are interested in the present mode of living of the Chinese people. Others inquire about the land reform, about general attitudes toward the government, and about "brainwashing" and the general *schrecklichkeit* the present Chinese government is alleged to practice. Still others ask about China's relations with Soviet Russia, and whether it is true that Red China is out to conquer all of Asia, if not the entire world.

Many of these questions I have dealt with in this book—some briefly, others at great length. In the main I have sought to tell my personal story and to write about things observed as part of my own experience. On larger issues such as the intentions of the Chinese government toward the rest of the world, it is possible to form reasonable opinions based on first-hand knowledge of the new nation and its people and the forces within it.

In an effort to answer specific questions existing in many people's minds about present-day China, I shall take up some typical ones that I have not previously gone into, with the reminder that none of these can be fully covered in a few paragraphs or a few pages.

What About Russian Domination of China?

Two contradictory theories have been persistently advanced to the American public. According to one the Russians are "exploiting" and even planning to "swallow up" the new Chinese nation. The other declares that theoretical differences and "personal rivalries" make a "falling-out" inevitable.

The second eventuality also is said to carry with it two contradictory alternatives: (1) The "independent" China will adopt a "Titoist" attitude more favorable to the West; or (2) being freed of Soviet restraint (the Russians are conceded a peace-loving character for the purpose of this theory), China would unleash her "Red aggression" upon the rest of Asia.

The Chinese to whom I talked on this subject seemed to have not the slightest fear of Russian "imperialism." They pointed out that the Russians' plain interest lies not in attempts to "swallow up" a huge neighbor with more than three times her own population, but in aiding and fostering its growth as a valuable ally. And China's common-sense interest, they were certain, lies just as plainly in cultivating friendship and collaboration.

I can testify, at any rate, that the "hordes of uniformed Russians" described by long-distance reporters have never been in China. The few Russians one sees—aside from the White Russians in the coastal cities—are technologists, helping to implement the financial and industrial aid extended by the Soviet Union toward China's reconstruction. The Russians have also contributed what China needed perhaps more than anything else: technical advice and training.

The Chinese attitude toward them was summed up for me by a young electrical engineer, Yang Kung-ming. I met Yang through his sister, Nancy, who had been a student at the Yale Drama School in 1947, and who introduced me to Kung-ming on his return to China in 1951 after several years of study in England and France. "After all," Yang observed, "foreigners came in large numbers for a hundred years or more. But most of them came to help themselves, not us! After a century of such foreign visitors China still remained an industrially backward nation.

"The Russians are doing things differently. In the first place, they are here because we have asked them to come. And they are helping us to establish industrial enterprises not for themselves, but for us.

When they go home they take no profits with them, and leave nothing behind that they claim is theirs.

"Seeing them work, or working with them, one discovers among them a feeling of respect for the Chinese people such as no other foreigners have shown us. Many have come prepared to work as equals, live with us in the same way that we live, eat the same food and occupy the same kind of dwellings. They do not act like imperialists—and we have had enough experience to enable us to tell an imperialist when we see one."

Trade between China and the Soviet Union constitutes about 75 percent of China's expanding foreign commerce. Most of her imports from Soviet Russia are capital goods—industrial and agricultural production equipment. This is not the kind of material one nation supplies to another which it is preparing to "colonize."

Since 1950 the Soviet Union has assisted China with the design, construction and equipment of 156 major industrial projects, including steel works, oil refineries, engineering works and the nation's first motor-vehicle factory. In April, 1956, the addition of fifty-five more such projects was agreed upon.

For people in the United States who are seriously interested in present realities and future probabilities in Asia, the dream of Chinese-Soviet conflict would not be a sensible one to cherish.

What About Americans in China?

There are, as I write, a number of Americans still living in China. Of these about thirteen to sixteen—the estimates differ—would like to leave but have been unable so far to obtain exit visas.

It will be news to many Americans that a number of their compatriots, including confirmed non-Communists, have been living and working in China and are in no hurry to return home. Some are busy at their jobs or professions, others are ordinary housewives; all apparently consider China a good place in which to live and bring up their children. A number, though by no means all, are married to Chinese. Some have spent many years in China.

There is, for example, Talitha Gerlach, a YMCA worker for more than twenty-five years from the mid-West. There is Sidney Shapiro, a New York lawyer who went to China early in 1947, married a Chinese writer, and is working as a translator in Peking. There is also Professor Robert Winter, well-known to Americans who have been in Peking at any time in the last twenty years, who continues to teach English at Chinghwa University. In Shanghai I knew several American women who had married Chinese in the United States, had come to live in China, and felt no regrets.

Of the Americans remaining in China who wished to leave, some were businessmen whose only difficulty was that they had not yet been able to settle their affairs. Chinese law required that any foreigner wishing to leave the country must settle all debts. Most Western businessmen have acted for principals at home, and have not been allowed to leave until the affairs of these principals were completely settled. In the West this has been often referred to as holding them for "ransom." The Chinese maintain that once the responsible person acting for a foreign firm has departed, there is no way that the firm's obligations can be met. Claims made by former employes for back pay or severance made up a large proportion of the unsettled accounts.

What hampered settlement of the debts? In most cases involving Americans it was the restrictions on sending funds to China, plus the freeze of Chinese funds in the United States, which the Treasury Department put into effect late in 1950. To send money to an American in China, since that date, special permission from the Treasury Department has been required. The Chinese government retaliated by freezing American assets in China and controlling accounts of American businesses. However, it provided that Americans living in China could withdraw the equivalent of up to 1,000 U. S. dollars in Chinese currency a month to meet their living expenses.

While Washington has permitted the transfer of money needed for living expenses to businessmen in China, permission for sums required to close down a business has not always been forthcoming. When cash has been made available to pay off debts owed for materials, rentals, taxes, services, etc., the businessman concerned has received an exit visa and has departed. But often these special allotments have been slow in coming through, and in some cases they had failed to materialize at all. This was no fault of the stranded American, no fault of the Chinese government, and usually it was no fault of the employer at home. The decision lay with the Treasury Department, which apparently has found it useful to point to the plight of American civilians being "held" in China.

American restrictions on funds to China similarly proved a two-edged sword in the case of missionaries and others operating in that country. Since most were dependent on money from home to carry on, the restrictions left them high and dry.

Businessmen and missionaries who were unable to return home but had broken no laws were not being held in jail when I was in China. Frank Price, a well known American missionary who at one time was Chiang Kai-shek's adviser, waited more than two years for his exit visa, and stories were circulated abroad that he was under house arrest. I would run into him now and then at various places in Shanghai; on one such occasion he told me he had received a cable from the States inquiring whether he was still alive because there had been rumors at home that he had been "executed." In my conversations with him, one of which took place alongside the swimming pool at the down-town Rowing Club, Mr. Price expressed optimism about eventually receiving permission to leave; and eventually he did.

I have known American businessmen in Shanghai, have seen them walking or riding in their chauffeur-driven cars by day, have met them in restaurants and clubs, have played bridge with them in their well-appointed houses or apartments. They were free to do as they pleased, so long as they abided by the law and remained within the ample confines of Shanghai. In some cases, like other Westerners, they applied for and received permission to travel to other parts of China for business purposes.

There also are, or have been, some who were held in prison—but not for the reasons commonly supposed in the West. Some, like un-adaptable foreigners in any country, found difficulty in adjusting their conduct to the laws of the land. This was particularly true in China, where some Westerners had behaved for generations as a superior race, and were abetted in this view of themselves by the Chinese officials and compradors with whom they dealt. In old China it was not uncom-mon for foreigners to beat rickshaw drivers, tear up tax bills, and ridi-cule the nation's customs and culture. In the process of finding out that the new government had illegalized such practices and really meant it, some Westerners ran afoul of the law.

Again, there were individuals in the foreign community who simply had criminal tendencies and would have wound up in jail in any country. One such character, who had been in and out of prison under the Chiang government, too, finally left China with the ardent bless-ing of the police at the end of 1953. On reaching Hongkong he was promptly enrolled in the ranks of American martyrs to "Chinese barbarism."

This fellow, whose name I forebear to mention solely from motives of charity, will readily be recognized by anyone who was in Shanghai in the last twenty-five years. Born in China of an American missionary family, he had early forsaken the teaching of his parents, and had engaged in dubious business operations. His reputation was so bad that he was the only American in Shanghai, to the best of my knowledge, ever denied membership in the American Club. He had a penchant for issuing bad checks, and issued them with such persistence that he was taken into custody first under the Nationalists before the Japanese occupation; again by Chiang's police after VJ Day; and finally by the police of Shanghai in 1950. The last of these arrests was headlined in the *Hongkong Standard*: "Prominent U. S. Businessman Jailed by Reds."

When this worthy finally was released and deported he gave a press interview on reaching Hongkong, gravely explaining how terrible he had found conditions in Red China.

A more normal type of American businessman I knew in Shanghai was the chief representative of an American firm engaged in large-scale and varied business operations. He and I were not close friends, but I knew he was unable to get permission to leave China because of the unsettled condition of his various businesses. He obviously thought he was being unfairly treated; whether he or the Shanghai municipal government was right about it I had no way of knowing.

Whatever the merits of his case, the life he led in Shanghai was far from a nightmare. He was driven to and from his office by a chauffeur, lived in Grosvenor House, one of Shanghai's best apartments, and was free to go about as he pleased. He regularly telephoned his mother in Washington; and his overseas calls, like those of other foreigners, were made without hindrance.

The last time I saw him was in the fall of 1953. He knew I was on the verge of leaving for home, and wished me well. In answer to my query about his prospects, he shook his head. The funds required to settle his affairs evidently were not going to reach China. He was sure his New York office wanted to send them, but there was the matter of United States government approval. "I'll probably be here till hell freezes over," he said glumly. "Or until Washington sees fit to unfreeze me." Finally it did, and his departure from China was noted in the American press in the spring of 1956.

There remain those Americans who were imprisoned on charges of having committed political or military offenses such as espionage, sabotage, working with Kuomintang underground agents, and so on. It is upon these people and the "torture" or "brainwashing" they are said to have suffered that the interest of Western intellectuals almost exclusively centers. Indeed any observer out of China who has failed to confirm such stories finds himself under a cloud of disapproval.

Thus, when the English journalist James Cameron wrote a book called *Mandarin Red* after a brief visit with the Attlee delegation in 1954, he was taken to task in *The Nation* by Edgar Snow, who used to be less gullible about such matters, for omitting "any detailed consideration of such items as brainwashing . . . slave labor, mass executions. . . ."

It is, of course, possible that the Chinese have made a practice of mistreating Americans in their prisons, but only in the sense that all things are possible. In view of the absence of conclusive proof and in view of the extreme lengths to which the State Department and the press have been known to go in order to elicit and stage-manage horror tales from returnees, I do not believe that the truth of these allegations has been established or that it can rationally be assumed. On the other hand, there is no way that allegations of this kind can be conclusively disproved except by statements from each and every one of the supposed victims. When some alleged victims have made statements denying mistreatment, like Mrs. Rickett and Dr. Bersohn, they have soon found themselves without an audience or under official disapproval.

The fact is that Americans in China of any variety have generally led a life more comfortable and easy than they would at home. Very few of them, or Westerners in general, would find it easy to live the day-to-day existence of an average Chinese. The diet of an ordinary Chinese family, their toilet facilities, their stone-like *kang* or bed—to mention a few particulars—would impose considerable hardship on Westerners and, in many cases, mental anguish. Consequently Americans would find it most difficult to accustom themselves to a Chinese prison where they would have to live at a Chinese level.

The idea of unprovoked jailings of Americans in China gets a jolt when facts come to light, as occasionally they do, about the nature of certain Washington-directed activities. Officials of the Central Intelligence Agency, an arm of the military answerable to no one but Allen Dulles and the President, have boasted in print of the millions they have spent on the smuggling of spies, saboteurs and trouble-makers into "Communist-dominated" countries, including China.

Newsweek Magazine, in a report on the Central Intelligence Agency in its issue of February 23, 1953, said: "The U. S. has been going in for . . . subversion and sabotage . . . in an important way against the Reds on the Chinese mainland." In March of the same year *Collier's* carried an eyewitness report by an American newspaperman, Peter Kalischer, headed, "I Raided Red China with the Guerillas." And the *Saturday Evening Post* gave the details in a semi-official account of C.I.A. operations, contained in a series of articles, in the issues of October 30, November 6 and 13, 1954. On this the syndicated columnist Dorothy Thompson commented:

> "They [the articles] confirm charges the Communists are perpetually making—that the U. S. is engaged in conspiracies to overthrow Communist or unsatisfactory governments by force, is spending 'hundreds of millions' on underground activities all over the globe; that 'about one out of three of the people arrested by Communist governments' actually is a spy; and that American agents are responsible for blowing up bridges, derailing trains and other acts of sabotage.
>
> "Since this publication, written and released with CIA collaboration and consent, thirteen Americans have been imprisoned in Red China as spies.
>
> "The U. S. has protested that the men, missing since the Korean struggle, are POWs, and their trial is an infringement of International Law, as it is if the Chinese charges are untrue. But are they untrue? After reading the *Post* articles nobody could be sure.
>
> "The articles reveal just about everything except names, addresses and codes: How agents are recruited and trained; how many buildings CIA occupies in Washington; how many employes it has—half as many as the State Department—and how few members of Congress know what 'black' expenditures they are voting for.
>
> "Even more serious is the published admission of engineering violent coups against governments. . . .
>
> "Enough has already been revealed to lend substance to every Communist charge, and justification to the arrest of any American or suspected native citizen anywhere."

We have also been treated to tales of horror from missionaries returning from China, although some who were imprisoned denied that they were abused. The idea that no missionary could possibly have done anything to elicit a charge of espionage in China may need some revision in the light of these frank statements by Father Harold W. Rigney, as quoted in the *New York Herald-Tribune*, September 18, 1955, on his arrival in Hongkong after four years of imprisonment in China:

"I fought them before I was arrested, and all I could do was admit that by their standards I was a spy."

The *Herald-Tribune* dispatch also said:

Father Rigney admitted that he had given verbally some "intelligence" to "some O.S.S. (Office of Strategic Services) people about the liberation army" before the Communists took over Peiping.

The missionary was sentenced to a ten-year prison term in 1951 on a charge of "bribing Chinese government personnel in collecting military, economic and political information." He was released in 1955. Like others released from prison in China, he gave a somewhat different account after returning home. The implications of his statements made publicly and voluntarily upon his release, however, seem reasonably clear.

What About Chinese Aggression?

China's present leadership in Asia, now universally if here and there grudgingly admitted, derives less from her physical size and strength than from the equanimity with which her neighbors view her future intentions. Hostile governments in the West have talked about China's "Red aggression"; but neighboring nations—India, Burma, Indonesia, Pakistan, Japan—have shown little anxiety and have cultivated cordial diplomatic or trade relations with the "menace." The SEATO nations of the East, banded together with the West in one of Mr. Dulles' "defense pacts," have evidenced a singular lack of fear or hostility in their practical day-to-day relations with China.

The reasons for this untroubled Asian view of China were well summed up as long ago as November 1, 1954, in an article written from Bombay for the *Christian Science Monitor* by Gordon Graham. He posed the question in conventional terms: "Why has the West failed to enlist the cooperation of the major Asian democracies in its defense against international communism?"

To this he offered three answers. The first: "considerable resentment that colonialism, which withdrew rapidly and widely in the post-World War II period, should now be staging a rearguard action on the 'pretext' of Communist aggression." What he was referring to here chiefly was the Southeast Asia Treaty Organization, or SEATO pact, embracing the United States, Britain, France, Australia, New Zealand, and just three Asian countries—Pakistan, the Philippines and Thailand.

As his second answer Mr. Graham cited "the fact that the initiative for collective action in Asia always seems to come from the West. 'How would the United States like it,' one Indian said to me, 'if a group of Asian nations sponsored a defense alliance among the countries of Central America?' "

"Item three," Mr. Graham continued, "is the American attitude toward Communist China. 'How can one claim democratic principles and at the same time deny the right of the Chinese to choose and maintain their own form of government? What is China supposed to do—invite Chiang Kai-shek back? The retort that Communist China is an aggressor nation does not impress the neutral thought here, which regards the American behavior in Asia as, to say the least, provocative."

China's efforts toward reuniting Formosa* with the mainland are often pointed to as evidence of "aggressiveness." This, however, is a comparatively recent view. Few Americans, including high government officials, dreamed of disputing China's claim to Formosa until the China Lobby, with Senator Joseph McCarthy as its loudest spokesman, launched a vociferous campaign of agitation early in 1950.

---

*The appellative attitudes of the American press toward Chinese place names represent one of the more antic aspects of the cold war. The Chinese name for the island which the English-speaking world has known by the name *Formosa* for more than a hundred years is Taiwan. American newspapers called it Formosa until January, 1956, when the State Department abruptly decided that it really was Taiwan and began so designating it in official papers. The press obediently adopted the change.

On the other hand, the city which the Chinese People's Republic made its capital in 1949 has been known as Peking (meaning Northern Capital) for centuries. During the Japanese invasion when the capital was moved to Nanking (Southern Capital), the name was changed to Peiping (Northern Peace). Since 1949, when it again became the national capital, it has again been known as Peking all over the world except in the newspapers of the United States, which religiously and unanimously persist in referring to it as Peiping, perhaps under the conviction that this somehow strikes a telling blow for the free world.

Prior to that, in March, 1949, General MacArthur had renounced any American military interest in Formosa. In an interview given to the United Press on March 2, 1949, he outlined what he called America's "defense perimeter." It included neither Formosa nor Korea. Secretary of State Acheson similarly defined our "defense perimeter" in a speech in January, 1950. On the fifth of that month both Acheson and President Truman strongly reaffirmed the American view of Formosa as an inseparable part of China.

"The traditional United States policy toward China," said Truman, "calls for international respect for the territorial integrity of China. . . . Formosa should be restored to the Republic of China."

This, of course, was at a time when hope was still entertained for the restoration of Chiang Kai-shek to the mainland, and Truman by his reference to "the Republic of China" meant the visible remnant of the Kuomintang. The principle of China's sovereignty over Formosa had been clearly confirmed, however, with no qualifications about the form or personnel of China's government. What caused Truman to alter his principle was the orchestrated hullabaloo that ensued, led by Chiang's friends in Washington. The drive was spearheaded by Senator McCarthy in his first major bid for his own peculiar kind of fame —the Senate speech in which he charged that China had been sold out to the Reds by "205 Communists in the State Department." (Later investigation proved his figure to be an overestimate of exactly 205.)

This high-powered application of Red smear accomplished its work. Truman backed down, and when fighting began in Korea the following June, he ordered the Seventh Fleet into position to "save" Formosa, although China was not at that time involved in the hostilities.

China ever since has been unmoving in her determination to win back Formosa as part of the national homeland. To call this "aggression," or a "threat" to other nations whose borders begin thousands of miles away, is to rob words of their meaning. For a parallel situation, according to the Chinese, one would have to imagine a deposed American political boss setting up his own "Republic of America" on Key West or Nantucket or Hawaii or Puerto Rico with the support of a foreign power, and inviting the said power to help him conquer the United States.

If the foreign nation sponsoring him then dispatched its navy to shield his maritime stronghold and oppose American claims to its possession on the ground that such claims were "aggressive," we would then have, in the Chinese view, a rough but not inaccurate counterpart of what has been going on in the Formosan Strait.

The cry of "Chinese aggression" always seems to wax loudest when international tension shows signs of letting down. An illuminating example occurred in the spring of 1955. Saner influences in the American government had just brought about a withdrawal from the brink of a "preventive" nuclear attack on China. As people everywhere leaned back to breathe freely again, reports and rumors began appearing in the press about a Chinese "air buildup." The stories continued, with maps and calculations, for several weeks during April and May; a Chinese air strike, one might gather, was imminent.

The "crisis" bubble was abruptly deflated, however, by two dispatches in the *New York Times*—one from Quemoy Island, headlined, "Quemoy Reports No Red Build-up"; the other from Formosa, headed, "Peiping Build-up in Air Discounted."

In the first dispatch, dated May 17, Mr. Tad Szulc, reflecting the *Times'* current dismay at "the logic of death," reported the opinion of Nationalist commanders on Quemoy Island that they were "not in imminent danger of a Communist invasion." He quoted a General Chow as saying that "there was no air base on the mainland that was as yet sufficiently operational to threaten Quemoy."

In the second dispatch, having proceeded to Taipei, Mr. Szulc cabled on May 20: "The Communist air build-up along the mainland coast opposite Formosa is still in a preliminary stage. As of today not one jet strip in that region is operational." He added that this estimate "represents the considered opinion of the highest United States military and civil authorities in Formosa and emphasizes the degree of exaggeration in recent press and other reports on the scope of the present build-up."

Such phenomena can be be better understood, I believe, if considered in relation to the peculiar status of the aircraft industry in the United States, which depends largely upon military orders. They are illuminated by such items as this New York *Daily News* headline of July 27, 1954: "China Sea Fight Story Booms Aircraft Stocks."

Perhaps even more striking were these sentences from a *New York Times* story on January 25, 1955, during the "Formosa crisis" of that period:

> The stock market reacted decisively yesterday to President Eisenhower's message asking Congress for permission to fight in

defense of Formosa. Industries that would benefit directly from increased military spending recorded notable gains.

Aircraft issues in particular shot ahead. Steels, metals, machines and machine tools moved up. Other segments of the market, however, had a generally dull day.

Heavy pressures are exerted on Congress, the Administration, and the organs of public opinion. As reported in a United Press dispatch on February 22, 1956, the president of a leading aircraft manufacturing concern testified before a Congressional committee that 99.7 percent of his business comes from the government. He denounced current efforts of the Government Renegotiation Board to cut down plane profits as "shocking . . . appalling . . . sickening."

The same inquiry brought forth testimony from the executive vice-president of another aircraft manufacturer, the Fairchild Airplane and Engine Corporation, that his concern had hired four retired Army Generals and two retired Admirals, including the same Robert B. Carney who not long before had been vociferous about the need to "combat the menace" of China.*

In the press generally, and in the columns of the more belligerent feature writers particularly, the drumming up of war scares has become a routinized occupation. The story, endlessly repeated, has one unchanging moral: War is the true reality, peace a dangerous illusion, and only a constant outpouring of billions into the pockets of the aircraft manufacturers can save us.

What About Korea?

China's role in the Korean conflict is sometimes cited as an example of her supposed "aggressiveness," and is apt to be used as an argument by those who seek excuses to delay the normalization of relations between China and the United States.

During the early months of the fighting—that is, in the summer of 1950—I was struck by what seemed to me a general lack of excitement on the part of the government and the people alike. Angry denunciations were issued at the intervention of the United States Seventh Fleet in the Formosa Strait; but the actual fighting still was removed from China's borders, and no thought of Chinese participation was

---

*New York Post, February 25, 1956. For a comprehensive roster of former military leaders now holding high corporate posts, see "The Power Elite," by C. Wright Mills (Oxford University Press, 1956), pp. 214-215.

evident. The prevalence of this atmosphere was remarked upon by K. N. Pannikar, India's Ambassador to China at the time, in his book, *In Two Chinas*. Mr. Pannikar voiced some outspoken criticism of the internal policies of the new Chinese government; but in his chapter on Korea he wrote as follows (page 103):

> U.N. intervention in Korea caused no particular reaction in China; in fact during the first three months of the Korean war there was hardly any noticeable military activity in China. But the intervention in Taiwan was considered to be a direct threat, though even in this matter the Chinese behaved with exemplary patience.

A little farther on in his account he tells of an official conversation he had with Premier Chou En-lai on October 2, 1950. American forces had landed at Inchon and were moving north toward the 38th Parallel. Washington was talking no longer about merely "repulsing aggression," but of "unifying" Korea militarily by driving clear north to the Chinese border. Chou informed the Indian Ambassador that, "If the Americans crossed the 38th Parallel China would be forced to intervene in Korea."

"I asked him if China intended to intervene," Mr. Pannikar writes, "if only the South Koreans crossed the parallel. He was emphatic: 'The South Koreans did not matter, but American intrusion into North Korea would encounter Chinese resistance.' "

Mr. Pannikar immediately communicated this information to the British Minister and the Burmese Ambassador in Peking.

"Nothing happened during the following two days," he relates. "There was no definite information that the Americans had crossed the parallel. But the U.N. with historical insousciance was discussing a resolution to authorize MacArthur to cross the parallel and bring about the unification of Korea. On the eighth of October at eight o'clock I heard on the radio that the United Nations had formally approved the resolution in the full knowledge (which had been communicated to the State Department) that the Chinese would intervene in force.

"I noted in my diary as follows:

" 'So, America has knowingly elected for war, with Britain following. It is indeed a tragic decision. . . .' "

The entire subject of the Korean conflict—its origins, its real objectives and its conduct by the forces of both sides—is obviously a question of huge proportions which cannot possibly be treated within the scope of this book. Historians only recently have begun delving into it on any scale; without doubt it will continue to be written about for many years to come. Regarding the truth about its origins and about how it was waged, historians around the world are by no means of a uniform opinion. All agree, however, that it was unsurpassed in bitterness and that it left grave scars on both sides.

At this particular moment, when the tragedy is three years past and a calmer atmosphere holds some promise of peaceful relations between the two sides in the future, I doubt very much whether any useful purpose would be served by reviving the bitterness and reopening the scars. Korea has bound up her wounds and is rebuilding her devastated land. The Chinese have held out the hand of friendship, and a growing inclination to grasp it is evident on the part of Western peoples, including the American. In the face of all this, to rehearse the details of the grim drama would seem to serve destructive rather than productive ends.

Yet this feeling, which I believe many sober-minded people share at present, does not diminish the necessity for an ultimate true assessment of the facts about Korea. The idea that has so far prevailed in the United States—namely, that the North Koreans were "instigated to attack" by the Russians, and that the Chinese joined in because of something "aggressive" in their nature—is not, as I have indicated, given credence by many qualified observers in other lands.

In this country, however, little has been heard that does not reflect this attitude. A book called *The Hidden History of the Korean War* by the well-known Washington journalist, I. F. Stone, which quotes the pronouncements of the U.N. and the United States government and their spokesmen to cast grave doubts on their own version of the origins of the conflict, was rejected by twenty-eight American publishing houses. It was finally published by *The Monthly Review*, an independent publication, and has been carefully ignored by the general press. Similarly, a book called *Cry Korea* by the distinguished British war correspondent, Reginald Thompson, has failed of publication in this country and is unavailable either at bookstores or to library borrowers. In it Mr. Thompson, while completely sympathetic to the American political and ideological viewpoint in Korea, bitterly criticized the way the fighting was conducted and what it did to both soldiers and civilians and to the country at large.

These are only two examples of a great deal that has been written by responsible observers and commentators tending to refute the official American account of why we fought in Korea and how.

Why is China So Anxious to Increase Her Trade With the United States?

China is anxious to increase her trade with everyone. Her vast industrial program requires capital goods which America could supply. The rapid rise in her standard of living and consumer purchasing power has created an unprecedented demand for consumer goods. On the other hand, the huge increase in her productivity has placed her in a position to export goods on a large scale, including scores of commodities which China never exported before.

Yeh Chi-chuang, Minister of Foreign trade, reported late in 1955 that China's total imports and exports in the previous year had "amounted to over nine million tons, worth 8,486,730,000 yuan (almost three and a half billion dollars)." He added that "there were some increases in the first half of this year compared with the corresponding period of 1954."

Summing up his report, Yeh said: "Our First Five-Year Plan lays a substantial foundation for expanding our foreign trade. China now trades with over sixty countries, and her foreign trade grows daily. We will establish trade relations on equally and mutually beneficial terms with any country in the world which wants them, irrespective of social systems. That has been our policy in the past. It will continue to be our policy in the future."

The sixty countries, as is well known, include our allies both East and West. Our State Department insistence on their withholding certain "strategic" goods has caused considerable strain in our relations with them. While our own China trade is held down to virtually nothing by the fear of Senatorial wrath, the "free world" nations—Britain, France, West Germany, Japan—not only profit by present trade but solidify their trade positions against the day when normal conditions return.

Even the Nationalist Chinese on Formosa, according to an admission by Under-Secretary of State Herbert Hoover, Jr. in March, 1956 before the Senate Permanent Investigations sub-committee, have been shipping "quite a number of million dollars worth of goods every year" to the mainland. Mr. Hoover hastily revised his testimony to meet the resulting howl from China-hating Senators, but the cat was out of the bag. The trading operations with China which Generalissimo Chiang enjoys, but which are barred to American businessmen, are of course financed with American funds contributed to by those same business-men through their taxes.

China is particularly interested in trade with the United States for two reasons. The first is that we can furnish many things she wishes to buy and can use many things she has to sell. The second is that trade makes for amity, and amity with the United States is the key-stone to peace with the West. The feeling as regards her commodity needs is that if she cannot get them from us she can obtain them elsewhere, produce them for herself, or if necessary do without. But there is no substitute for peace, and no peace without American participation.

It is quite true that trade with China has never in the past amount-ed to more than a small fraction of America's total foreign trade. This must be looked at, however, in relation to the almost constant condi-tion of war and civil strife that disrupted Chinese life during the twenty years before 1949. While at the present time China probably has more to gain than the United States, in the strict commercial sense, from an increase in mutual trade, this may not always be the case.

America's productivity has increased by the astounding figure of fifty percent since the end of World War II. It keeps on growing. Constantly increasing production means a normal state of health in any industrial nation, but the question sooner or later must arise: who is going to consume all these goods?

By March, 1956 the inventory of unsold automobiles was an-nounced as the highest in history. Dealers were complaining of high-pressuring by manufacturers to force them to get rid of cars faster in a contracting market. "Hard selling" had become the keynote throughout a large part of industry to induce the consumer to absorb the constantly growing volume of product.

In such a situation a new consumer area has to be found, or else something has to give. Complicating the problem is the evident fact that a decrease in consumer buying-power, such as might be caused by even a relatively mild slump in employment, would prevent industry from disposing of its high output at the necessary rate.

The obvious solution is a new market. The goods China could absorb from the United States could not stave off serious economic trouble should that arrive. But the amount she could buy, and wishes to buy, could make the difference between disaster and solvency for many American manufacturers and between unemployment and jobs for thousands of American workers.

There is a precedent in the depression days of the early Thirties. America and the Soviet Union then, like America and China today, were scarcely on speaking terms. And yet, without benefit of credits or of diplomatic recognition, the Russians purchased more machinery in the United States than any other nation. In 1930 they bought 74 percent of American exports of foundry equipment, 67 percent of agricultural machinery, and 65 percent of all machine tools. In 1931 nearly 40 percent of the entire output of the American tractor industry went to the Soviet Union.*

The *Wall Street Journal* has said editorially: "We suggest that the punitive use of trade in peacetime is as ill-advised as the deliberately proselytizing use . . . there is always the question of who in the end is punishing whom. . . . Those who believe trade should be used as a means of expressing annoyance with people and systems they don't happen to like must also ask how far it is proposed to carry this notion. Carried far enough there might soon be little trade of any kind anywhere."

What About Personal Freedom in China?

The first thing to be noted about the status of individual freedom in China is that, however one may view its condition today, it is in vastly better shape than it was before the establishment of the People's Republic.

Personal freedom *per se* is a new concept in China; it was scarcely thought of as a right or a possible condition under the Kuomintang. That, in fact, is what the revolution was largely about. It is also worth noting, I think, that few of the people now so gravely concerned about it ever gave it a thought while Chang Kai-shek ruled the country.

Very little has been heard on this side of the Pacific about the Constitution of the Chinese People's Republic, adopted by the First National People's Congress at Peking on September 20, 1954. It is

---

*The Parliamentary correspondent of the *Christian Science Monitor*, on March 21, 1956, reported the growing restiveness of the British regarding restrictions on trade with China. He also noted British reaction to the Chinese offer to purchase 1,000,000 tractors in the next twelve years.

By May, the first shipment to China of 60 160-horsepower tractors was reported in Britain.

doubtful whether more than a handful of Americans know that this document exists and functions as China's fundamental law.

The Constitution was adopted as a permanent charter to replace the Common Program, whose inauguration in 1949 as a temporary instrument I have described in Chapter Eight, and whose operation I had opportunity to observe. The two documents are substantially similar in their main provisions.

The Constitution, framed and adopted by a body of elected delegates—the First National People's Congress—after more than a year of public discussion, contains among its provisions a charter of individual liberties. Among its basic guarantees are two which, taken together, provide immunity from unlawful entry, search or seizure. Article 89 states:

> Freedom of the person of citizens of the People's Republic of China is inviolable. No citizen may be arrested except by decision of a people's court or with the sanction of a people's procurator's [i.e. public prosecutor's] office.

And Article 90 states:

> The homes of citizens of the People's Republic of China are inviolable, and privacy of correspondence is protected by law. Citizens of the People's Republic of China have freedom of residence and freedom to change their residence.

Chapter Two, Section Six of the Constitution sets up a national and local judiciary. Article 73 provides that:

> In the People's Republic of China judicial authority is exercised by the Supreme People's Court, local people's courts and special people's courts.

Article 76 states, "Cases in the people's courts are heard in public unless otherwise provided for by law. The accused has the right to defense."

No mention is made of rights such as trial by jury, confrontation of accusers, etc., that are traditional in Anglo-Saxon countries. These are not found in all democracies. French jurisprudence does not regard trial by jury as an inalienable right, or always desirable from the standpoint of an accused. Nevertheless, since I am comparing the Chinese Constitution with the American, I feel that the omission of these guarantees from the former is a serious defect. It may be argued that the guarantee against the abuse of power by officials (Article 97) protects citizens from injustice in court; but this can hardly cover all contingencies.

Other basic rights and freedoms are specified in Chapter Three of the Constitution. Article 85 proclaims the equality of citizens before the law. Article 86 guarantees to all citizens, "whatever their nationality, race, sex, occupation, social origin, religious belief, education, property status, or length of residence," the right "to vote and stand for election."

Article 96 specifically guarantees to women "equal rights with men in all spheres—political, economic, cultural, social and domestic." Article 97 is worth quoting in full:

> Citizens of the People's Republic of China have the right to bring complaints against any person working in organs of state for transgression of law or neglect of duty by making a written or verbal statement to any organ of state at any level. People suffering loss by reason of infringement by persons working in organs of state of their rights as citizens have the right to compensation.

The question will arise as to what extent these Constitutional guarantees are "paper" guarantees and to what extent they are put into practice. This may be asked about the constitutions of all countries. From what I have observed of procedures under the Common Program I can say that China's basic law appears to be as well implemented for the benefit of the people as ours.

Individual liberties in the political sphere are guaranteed to China's people in Article 87 of the Constitution, as follows:

> Citizens of the People's Republic of China have freedom of speech, freedom of the press, freedom of assembly, freedom of association, freedom of procession and freedom of demonstration. By providing the necessary material facilities, the state guarantees to citizens enjoyment of these freedoms.

These closely parallel the freedoms prescribed in the First Amendment to the Constitution of the United States. And, as in the case of that document, or any constitution in the world, these freedoms are not absolute and cannot be. In the United States they have been severely limited by legislation such as the Smith Act, court decisions, the pressures of Congressional investigating bodies, etc. In practice these freedoms are suspended or denied where the authorities decide their fulfillment would, or might, present a "clear and present danger" to the state.

Individual freedom that is absolute in degree—subject to no restriction of any kind—is an imaginary thing, without existence anywhere and advocated by no one except perhaps by anarchists.

Both the American and the Chinese Constitutions list freedom of speech among their people's guaranteed rights. This does not mean, either in China or in the United States, that a citizen may advocate revolution.

In China as I saw them under the Common Program, the freedoms of assembly, of demonstration and of procession meant—as they doubtless mean today under the 1954 Constitution—that citizens are free to engage in these activities for any purpose that is not held to be destructive of the common weal. And so it is in the United States, where real "freedom for the thought we hate" has not been encountered outside the history books these many years.

Must the Chinese resort to the cry of "You're another" to answer accusations of repression or dictatorship? Not in the least; but there would seem to be little sense in applying to one six-year-old nation a set of standards that have no real existence—not even in another nation, born in revolution 180 years ago, which accepts the mantle of world moral leadership.

The Chinese people have the kind of freedom they actively believe in: freedom to move forward in their own country toward their chosen goals. Jealous of their new rights, they know how to hold their own if need be against public officials who, they are constantly reminded, are their servants.

What, finally, about freedom of the press? What meaning can it have in a nation where, as in China, the press and radio are controlled largely although not wholly by the government?

The difference between the Chinese and the American concepts of press freedom does not lie in the question of whether one is free and the other restrained. Neither is wholly free nor wholly restrained. The crucial difference is in the respective sources of restraint, and in the kind of society from which the restraining pressures arise.

The editors and publishers of Chinese newspapers and periodicals reflect the social orientation of an elected government that has the overwhelming support of the people. The editors and publishers of American and other Western papers reflect the viewpoint of a "free enterprise" which, I am far from being the first to note, is not always free or always enterprising, and whose first concern must by definition be with its balance sheet rather than with the public weal.

American newspapers, frequently reminding us of their "freedom" and the fearlessness that supposedly flows from it, compare themselves favorably with the press of certain other lands. Yet it is in the United States, and not in China, that one looks in vain for a newspaper that will champion the cause of labor as against management, or advocate fewer privileges for the rich and more for the poor, or exhibit the connection between war scares and private profits, or plug for international amity when that is not the fashion, or expose wholesale corruption and bribery before the aroma has become too overpowering to ignore. The history of American journalism, in fact, is strewn with the bones of newspapers that dared to make such matters their major concern.

The question of press freedom in China or anywhere else is not a matter of yes or no. It is a matter of how much, what kind, and above all, what for. In that context I do not think freedom of the press, or freedom in general, in China fares badly in comparison with the West.

My answers to the foregoing questions, like my observations throughout most of this book, present largely a positive view of today's China. It is possible, of course, that this bespeaks nothing more than an emotional bias on my part. But the possibility must also be taken into account that my favorable report is grounded thoroughly on fact. That, having started from no ready-made viewpoint, and having had the good fortune to see the new Chinese nation with a thoroughness and intimacy shared by few Westerners, I have drawn conclusions more accurate and fair than the kind of hearsay stories that have become so familiar.

I remarked in my opening pages that it would be better from America's standpoint to know China as she really is, rather than as one might prefer to imagine her. Straw men of the imagination are easily overcome; but such victories leave nothing solved. In a time when men's patriotism is often judged by the loudness with which they assert it, anyone who wishes to spread counsels of fear, hate and bluster can find a ready audience. I believe such patriots serve their own little interests far better than they serve their country.

The United States is still the strongest and most resourceful nation in the world, strong enough to hold her own against all comers in peaceful rivalry—the only kind likely to leave survivors. For my part, I could wish that our policy makers and opinion makers had sufficient faith in that fact. The brightly packaged fantasies that so impress their authors in Washington and Times Square are apt to evoke only mirth or bewilderment in other lands and make our cause suspect in the eyes of nine-tenths of the world. And sooner or later they are bound to explode in our faces.

I believe it is this element of fantasy in our conduct of foreign relations, growing largely out of the basic unreality of our official attitude toward China, that has caused many of the frustrations met with by our diplomacy. This view has been gaining force even in conservative quarters as a result of the almost unbroken series of diplomatic disasters suffered in Asia during recent years.

My report on China doubtless is different from what many would expect. Yet I believe it to be not only a true but a reassuring one. True because it shows the China that really exists. Reassuring because that is a China from which the American people have nothing to fear.

INDEX

251